Unspoken Love

M. Georgene Roth

M.G. ROTH PUBLISHING COMPANY
MIDLOTHIAN, VA

©1999 M. Georgene Roth. All rights reserved.

Published by:
M.G. Roth Publishing Co.
3905 McTyre Cove Rd.
Midlothian, VA 23112
804-744-8770

Photographs in *Unspoken Love* were taken by family members and various commercial photographers.
Photograph on page 296 © 1998 Goins Photo Image. Used with permission.

PRINTED IN THE UNITED STATES OF AMERICA

Publisher's Cataloging-in-Publication
(Prepared by Quality Books, Inc.)

Roth, M. Georgene.
    Unspoken love / M. Georgene Roth. -- 1st ed.
    p. cm.
    Preassigned LCCN: 98-91706
    ISBN: 0-9666264-2-7

    1. Roth, M. Georgene. 2. Nurses--United States--Biography. I. Title.

RT37.R68A3 1998   610.73'092
                                 QBI98-989

For Dr. Roth

This verse was written after the death of Dr. Roth by one of the women who had worked with him. It expresses perfectly the totality of this humble man.

He was a man's man,
gentle to the ladies,
and hard to the core,
built on the model they threw out years ago.
Rugged, tireless, fierce and strong—
the kind of man from Homer's song.
Up early, down late,
in the field, if need be, at dawn.
He didn't smile at idle jokes,
except the ones made on himself,
and then his mouth turned up and down
as if to ask if God had meant
to let him blunder
or if his fault was just a fluke
that he would need to refine.
Introspective, tough, enduring to the end—
hit in the heart, he got up again.
Independent, fearless, diplomatic only
when diplomacy meant results—
a scientist with a mighty hand.
And day or night you knew he knew
what was going on in his house,
his job, and with the world
he called his friend.
He was a simple man,
and a brave man.

God bless,
Judith Mosby

Jack, Dr. Albert John Roth, at his desk.

Table of Contents

Acknowledgments vi
Foreword vii
ONE: Da Shares His Visions 1
TWO: Mom 13
THREE: Family Tragedies 23
FOUR: Family Reunions 37
FIVE: Jack and Gene Meet 53
SIX: Forest, Ohio 65
SEVEN: Springfield, Ohio 73
EIGHT: Frankfurt, Kentucky 83
NINE: New Life in Virginia 89
TEN: Richmond, 1962 99
ELEVEN: Achievements 125
TWELVE: Values and Pets 135
THIRTEEN: Creative projects 143
FOURTEEN: The Phone Rings 161
FIFTEEN: Family Performances 171
SIXTEEN: Life after Retirement 183
SEVENTEEN: Birding 193
EIGHTEEN: Celebrating 205
NINETEEN: Relative Influence 209
TWENTY: Happenings 219
TWENTY-ONE: Knee Deep in Pain 235
TWENTY-TWO: Reflections by Author 243
APPENDIX A: Computer Written Letters 257
APPENDIX B: About the Author 281
APPENDIX C: Third Place Family Reunion, 1998 ... 287
APPENDIX D: Tally of 50 Years 290

Acknowledgments

I thank my many family members and friends who assisted me in the writing of this book: David Roth, my son, advised me to purchase, and accompanied me in the selection of, a computer. He taught me how to use it and remained positive toward book-writing efforts. Elizabeth Yeamans kept me on track of my goal by frequently inquiring as to how my book was coming along. Rosalie Grace Heacock, of Heacock Literary Agency, Inc., was the first agent who requested, then reviewed, a portion of my manuscript and conveyed to me the encouragement to pursue my publishing efforts. Chiara Gentilini, a previous working colleague and friend, helped me to name my book, as she and I spent time over coffee while discussing our writing projects.

To my family and associates who served as resources in detailing various events, I am very grateful. The many photographs accrued over the years prove my stories to be valid. To my working associates in Springfield for their collective poetic composite comes my big thanks again and again. To Judith Mosby, who describes my husband in a totally dignified poem, I am humbled.

To my parents, I owe everything for giving me the free-spirited belief that I could achieve anything I chose to tackle, no matter how little or how significant.

Foreword

Growing up in this family of nine children, with two very capable parents, prompts the telling of this story. Stanley, better known as "Da" to his children, reveals to his daughter Gene how he feels his children will turn out as their lives unfold. Lela, the silent leader and mother of these strong-willed children, implants solid and dignified values, which guide her offspring throughout their lives.

But one has to wonder why they failed to verbally express their love to each other, although they related openly to the animal world. Was it due to the place and time of their lives, or was it a trait inherited from these stern parents? Along with a stable atmosphere, fun-loving attitudes were also instilled. The ability to establish positive relationships with whomever they came in contact is evident in this family.

Gene's life unveils a progression which identifies her creative and rewarding achievements. Generations follow with behaviors apparently learned from Stanley and Lela's siblings. Values of lasting quality are practiced as this family reveals the unfolding of their father's predictions.

*Mom, Lela Idella Graessle Place
High School Graduation Picture*

*Da, Stanley Bryan Place
High School Graduation Picture*

Chapter One:

Da Shares His Vision

It was a lovely Spring morning on April 1, 1953, in northwestern Ohio on the family farm. Stanley, the father of nine children, was married to Lela, the mother of these nine children. They were married at the early ages of eighteen and seventeen in 1916. Being viewed as prosperous in this community implied some good managing and productivity as an effective farmer and farmer's wife. Furthermore, buying land in hard times while raising a large family meant just plain hard work.

Stanley was known as "Da" to his children. (Pronounced by his children as "da-ee".) Da was greasing one of his John Deere tractors when he felt an excruciating pain that hit him in his upper midline abdominal chest area. He struggled to the farmhouse presenting profuse perspiring and other symptoms of shock. For a second, one could have wondered if this fun man could have been acting out one of April fools' jokes. But here was a man presenting some life-threatening symptoms, and it became vividly apparent that this was not one of his good humor stunts.

Emergency action was immediate and Da was admitted to the hospital fifteen miles from the family farm. What was causing his sudden pain and life-threatening situation?

By the time each of the nine children were notified and arrived at the hospital, the attending physicians had tentatively diagnosed his condition as acute pancreatitis. This —until then — healthy family was about to hear news they would refuse to accept as being true.

"Your husband and father will not live through the night," said the attending physician and surgeon. "There is nothing we can do. Operating at this time is out of the question."

What was happening to Da? He had never been ill and was the leader of this family. This fifty-five year old seemingly healthy, 220-pound, six-feet two-inch tall man was fighting for his life. A few hours before this crisis he appeared in the best of health, displayed an excellent physique, and obviously was a very handsome man.

Of course this family would not accept the possibility that their father was going to die. Who could they get to see their father and save his life? Ohio State University was contacted in order to reach the physician who was considered the best in the field for treating pancreatitis. He quickly joined the medical team by phone from Columbus, some one hundred miles from Lima. A test to monitor the potassium level was done by some equipment at OSU which was not available in Lima. The potassium level was an indicator of pancreatic functions.

Moving Da to OSU was ruled out as any movement was believed at that time to cause sudden death. This was also the reason for not transferring Da to the Mayo Clinic. Da's wealthy brother, Virgil, felt Stanley should be sent there for the top treatment and care in the country. Uncle Virgil lived in South Bend, Indiana. His son had graduated in medicine from the Mayo Clinic and this certainly was another resource this family clung to in their frantic efforts to find the best physician to save Da's life.

Da lived through the night of the admission day. He was in shock with a racing pulse, delirious as he ranted and raved all night. The medication ordered never touched his devastating pain. The next day passed and so went the days. Wrenching nausea and the stress of the pain took its toll. Weight was lost, and intermittent periods of orientation became apparent. Few answers could be given to this man who was once always in charge of his own destiny.

Days moved on to weeks, and Da continued living in severe pain, coping with gross physical destruction. How was this once healthy and handsome farmer managing to live? April had passed and it was the first of May. Da weighed 165 pounds and showed every sign of his impending death.

"Lela, we have to talk," begged Stanley.

She related that Da had stated this request to her on several occasions. And she would tell him they would do so soon. She too was suspicious of his wanting to discuss the possibility of his impending death. She did not want to accept this fact and so believed that if they avoided discussing it, it would not happen.

Surgery was contraindicated in the initial stages of his illness. Surgery could at one time have been his only hope for survival. Finally, surgery was attempted after many weeks when there seemed to be no other management avenue. The abdominal surgery revealed that the pancreas had been destroyed by the enzymes produced by this essential organ. The duct that permitted these enzymes to escape into the digestive tract through a tiny duct had been blocked by a gallstone. Susan and Gene witnessed the surgery at the urging of the surgeons whom they had known as student nurses. This was very unwise, as it was apparent from the moment the surgeon showed them the huge bag of fluid around what once was the pancreas indicated that death was imminent.

Gene visited her father every day by driving to Lima in her sister Kassy's car on loan to her. The distance of forty miles from Gene's home meant she had to plan to leave her two small sons in the care of their father and the lady who lived in their upstairs apartment. Gene's husband, Jack, was a practicing veterinarian in the small town of Forest. Da had requested that Gene come and care for him daily. She came every evening as his nurse. The capable assistance of her immediate family made this possible.

"Would you sit down and stop being a nurse?" Gene's father said in his commanding manner.

She constantly was trying everything she knew to keep him as comfortable as possible, while maintaining a cheerful approach. She did not fool him, as time would tell.

"Gene, do you know how I believe all of you kids will turn out?" Why was he wanting to talk with Gene about how his children were going to turn out? Caring for Da every evening for seven weeks meant that Gene was given the opportunity to be with her father more than at any previous time in her adult life. Did he want to tell her that he knew he was dying and that she did not have to hide this fact any more? The thought of their discussing his death was unthinkable even after she had witnessed his surgery and knew that his pancreas was destroyed. The medical team openly conveyed that they knew of no one living without a functioning pancreas.

What are the rights of a person who believes they are dying? He begged his wife Lela to take him home. He was so close to his youngest child Karin, who was eight years old. Both parents were forty-seven years old when Karin was born by a cesarean section. This method of birth was indicated as the initial time of the pregnancy was estimated. (Lela thought she was experiencing menopause symptoms in the early period of this pregnancy.)

Obviously Karin became her Dad's pride and joy. He had time to spend with her and enjoy her. She was a beautiful child and slept in his arms every evening before going to bed. Since Karin was only eight years old when Da became ill, her brothers and sisters felt for her and tried to substitute parental skills in order to make up for the loss she was feeling.

During these evening hours in Da's hospital room, a close relationship developed between Gene and Da. This was a change. The family never discussed how one another was feeling and had been taught to not show affection or their feelings. So when Da started discussing with Gene how he believed each of his children would "turn out", she did not know at that time that he really was telling her he knew he was going to die. Discussing death and dying was not something this family was capable of doing. They were a family with few failures. Experiencing the death of their leader seemed incomprehensible. This was not possible and each one tried to dismiss the thought every time it seemed to be mentioned by one of the physicians.

Lela never could bring herself to comply with Stanley's request of "we have to talk." She told Gene later that she kept stalling this encounter and soon it was too late and she regretted it forever. What would he have told her to do with her life and how did he want her to raise Karin? The rest of the eight children were grown adults and most all had established their lives once they married during this crisis. Karin was the only child living at home.

On June 1, in the early evening, just two months after the onset of Da's devastating illness, death became so evident to Gene for the first time. She and Kassy grabbed each other and cried together. Showing these feelings could not be held at bay any longer. Yes, Da died without any of the family telling him they loved him. They never gave him a chance to tell them good-bye. They have learned now that feelings and thoughts should be discussed in order to help each other accept death between family members.

◆ ◆ ◆

Ned, the eldest of the three sons, quickly surfaced as the male leader of this strong-willed family. When Ned visited Da in the hospital, he would just look at Gene for some word of encouragement. He often conveyed to us the stress Uncle Virgil felt thinking we had let Stanley die. You see, Uncle Virgil controlled all business situations and his family and just could not see why he did not have the power to keep his younger brother, Stanley, living.

Kassy, the eldest of the six girls and next to Ned, at times avoided the reality of the situation by not discussing the seriousness of Da's condition. She often listened to the views of her husband, Bob. Bob was a very successful practicing veterinarian. Kassy often related what Bob thought should be done. This method of coping prevented her from having to say what she thought and truly believed.

Betty lived in Lima and worked for the prominent doctor who managed Da's illness. She was always very supportive to anyone who needed her assistance. She looked after Karin while Mom visited Da in the hospital. Her support to Mom and the rest of the family during Da's illness was apparent as she lived close to the hospital.

Susan also lived in Lima not far from the hospital. She often followed the wishes of her husband before her own desires. She displayed a definite need to keep peace and never make waves. (She operates on this premise today.) Susan cared for her father until substitute nurses were found. There was no close bonding between Da and this daughter. She seemed out-of-step with some of the views in this family of dominant personalities. Susan was unlike the others; she had learned as an adult to measure her values and actions materialistically. Many of Stanley and Lela's children had definite opinions and prided themselves on expressing them. This was not Susan's case. She reluctantly took stands. It seemed to make her too uncomfortable.

Julia seemed to be Da's pride and joy while growing up. She was a beautiful child and demonstrated understanding this role when she was an adult. When she tried to twist Da too far, he rose to the occasion to say, "No, that is enough." Julia usually was for having a good time, and Da had this fun streak in his personality. This commonality may have contributed to their bonding.

Gene became a nurse even though Da expressed a desire that she not enter this profession. "Carry a pot all of your life?" summed his views of what he did not want her to become. But limited resources and then becoming engaged to a veterinarian student limited her educational goals at that time.

Stanley, Jr., known as S.B., was destined to remain the farmer with Da since Ned and Bill went into the military service. During World War II a third son was classified to remain at home to farm. This was not S.B's choice, but made by the draft board. Farming was important to feed the world population and the U.S. was viewed as primary in this endeavor. S. B. became very close to Karin by living on the family farm and having children near her age. His influence as a father figure to Karin became very important.

Bill was in the Air Force and stationed in Puerto Rico when Da became ill. Bill's one month's leave while his wife stayed in Puerto Rico turned out to not be long enough. Bill had to return to his base while Da remained critical. With Bill's kind and tender nature, this took its toll on Bill. He related many times later to us that when he saw the chaplain come to meet him, he knew he was to hear of the sad death of his dad.

And so the conversation between Da and Gene regarding how his children would turn out promised interesting responses and achievements. How will the nine children of Stanley and Lela turn out? Will Stanley's predictions come to pass?

Upon leaving the hospital the evening of Da's death, all of the family drove to the farm some fourteen miles away. The family dog Duchess, a two-hundred pound St. Bernard, stood guard at the door of the family farmhouse. Prior to this night she would meet them and never attempt to stop them as they came and went to the farm during Da's illness. It wasn't until Mom arrived and talked to her telling her it was okay. She then seemed to join this grieving family as she pulled her huge body to the side and let them pass.

When Da strolled the farm on Sunday mornings in a leisurely manner, Duchess walked beside him carrying his hand in her mouth. There was a special arrangement between this man and his dog. Duchess joined this family at the age of one year when Da found her locked in a chicken house not far from the farm. She was starved for food and love. Upon seeing her for the first time when Stanley brought her to the farm, Lela pointedly announced, "If that dog stays, I am going!" Time proved they both stayed and joined forces.

In Duchess' passing years, she broke multiple storm doors at the sound of thunder in order to get inside to hide in the basement. She totally destroyed flowerbeds near her cool resting-places. When it was announced that someone was going to the pond on the farm to fish, she positioned herself in the back of the pickup truck. Of course she was the first to plunge into the water. Guess where the fish went when you were about to begin fishing? Soon, you were showered from her shakes and the volume of water held on a two hundred pound St. Bernard.

Gene recalls vividly seeing her son David riding this small pony named Duchess at the early age of four or five years. Grandpa Stanley walked the dog as the grandchildren rode this friendly pal. Riding Duchess was one of the favorite things to do by all of the many grandchildren when they came to visit these grandparents.

Unspoken Love ♦9♦

*Top: Ned, Barbara and relatives at the hitchrack on the farm
Above: The farm home place*

Family Photograph, 1939: Da, Bill, Susan, Gene, Ned, Julia, Kassy, Stanley, Jr., Betty and Mom

Duchess was almost as popular as playing on the hitchrack. This heavy round piece of metal pipe was placed at the edge of the driveway in the yard by Da's parents when they were young and horses were the mode of travel. This once served as a place to tie the horses many years ago. Walking the hitchrack, swinging on it and of course falling off of it were a few of the creative maneuvers each child performed. All nine of Stanley and Lela's children grew up with this acrobatic device. Now, their children were performing and enjoying it as much a generation later.

Mom in her splendor.

CHAPTER TWO:

Mom

Mom loved to travel. Fortunately, Da and Mom traveled to Arizona for the winter for several years when Da spent some time assisting Uncle Virgil to build homes in Tucson. This traveling started when Karin was three years old. As Mom became older, she often flew to Virginia to visit Gene and to North Carolina to visit S.B. and family. She spent several winter months visiting Julia and Betty in Florida.

Mom made it quite clear that she preferred to travel with her kids. In fact, except while in church, she usually didn't identify in many situations with those of her own age. She and her children and grandchildren had some fun trips as she attended the graduations and weddings of her grandchildren.

We often laughed about her visiting Gene and Jack in Minneapolis in 1948, where Jack was stationed in the service. Da stayed home while Betty drove Mom and Karin there for a long weekend. The weekend was a hot one. Mom was always too warm. So one night while in Minneapolis, she went to the screened porch to sleep. As the story was told, she was suddenly awakened by the milkman early one morning. Jack had fun billing Da for Mom's sleeping with the milkman. A sense of humor was always apparent.

This is another memory of the great sense of humor this family revealed. Much of the fun experienced by their children and in-laws was initially perpetuated by Da's great sense of humor. Mom was more reserved as result of her upbringing in a very strict German Methodist family environment. It was hard to realize that Mom was not permitted to play cards or display fun enjoyment in her home as she grew up. No one enjoyed laughing any more than Mom. She must have stored up all of her laughs during her childhood. As a kid, Julia would try to get my mother's brothers to laugh. But they would only snicker as laughing out loud was not permitted in their home.

Card games were one of the major recreations in the home of Stanley and Lela. They played many different card games with their children, neighbors and friends. The son-in-laws looked forward to this entertainment. Of course the games were never the same without Da playing. But the playing of cards seemed to be another way of showing closeness and caring without expressing it openly. Card playing helped all of them deal with stress.

While staying with Julia in Florida at the time of Ford's (Betty's husband) death, card playing was the primary activity. The whole family learned to play "99." Ford never wanted anyone to be sad. Betty announced to all in attendance that he would be remembered with happiness and fun. Mom had a problem with the playing of cards and telling of jokes and laughter. She reservedly joined in as she was never the one to change the game plan.

Many of her trips included some fishing. She loved to fish and was a good fisherwoman. She was always ready to go if it meant a trip, fishing or something of enjoyment. She fished while visiting S.B. in North Carolina. They fished off of the Eastern Shore, not far from S.B.'s home. Some really big fishing stories have been told about all the fish caught in North Carolina by the whole family.

"How did S.B. get to North Carolina?... Why did he leave the family farm in Ohio?... Was Mom living on the farm when he left Ohio?" Yes, but she too accepted the fact that he needed to go where he felt he could better succeed in purchasing land.

S.B. answered an ad in a farm magazine. A large dismal swamp area owner wanted a farmer/cattleman to manage his huge ranch. S. B. was hired, so he and Bernice moved with their three children to begin a totally new lifestyle. This area had roving black bears and rattlesnakes near their front door. This ranch was in the middle of the Great Dismal Swamp.

This courageous venture was admirable and required social isolation from their families in Ohio. They were very lonely initially. But they stayed. They raised their three children and eventually bought some of this land. S.B. took his bulldozer from the farm in Ohio and cleared this new land. This virgin soil produced well the crops without any of the East Coast hurricanes. With hard work and good management by both Bernice and S.B., they became successful and are now, apparently, permanently settled in North Carolina.

Ned assumed the farming responsibilities on the family farm for Mom. He devoted weekends at the farm as he managed his own farms and his full-time federal job while traveling from his home in Tiffin. Ned and Barbara raised their five children to adulthood after moving to Tiffin. All of these five children graduated from college. Barbara also graduated with a master's degree while teaching school. Their children studied at Bowling Green and Ohio State Universities. Teaching was their main choice.

Mom enjoyed Ned's weekend retreats to the farm. She cooked and visited with him, as living alone for her was never really acceptable. She coped with hypertension and angina. She stressed herself greatly by worrying that someone might break into her home on the farm. This worry was related to the fact that the stone quarry across the road from the farm housed a cheap group of weekend dwellers. This manmade resort attracted a less than desirable group of people. However, they never ventured to Mom's home.

Mom developed chest pain one night when Susan was temporarily living at the farm. Susan grabbed Ned's partial bridges rather than Mom's dentures. They both had a habit of leaving them near the sink in the kitchen. When Mom was admitted to the Intensive Care unit in Lima that night, Ned's dentures went with her.

The next morning, Ned concluded what had happened once he was told of Mom's admission to the hospital. He had an important meeting scheduled in Columbus that morning. So, he presented himself at the entrance of the ICU early that morning.

"You have my teeth in there with my mother," he related to the nurse who tried to respond to his inquiry.

When the nurse conveyed some doubt, he responded, "Step aside nurse, I need my teeth."

This had to crack-up these nurses once the scene played out. Needless to say, Mom was given her own teeth. And she recovered rather rapidly from this admission. Once she had the feeling of security that she was okay and not dying, she calmed down and this helped her heart and blood pressure problems.

Soon she relinquished the mowing of the lawns to a neighbor boy. Of course he did not take care of the yards like she wanted. She was a very detailed person. She had worked hard all of her life in the home raising these nine children and this began to take its toll. When traveling, she finally accepted some assistance at the airports. Her exercise was limited as she reduced her workload and so her cardiac strength diminished.

◆ ◆ ◆

Chest pain appeared again after several years of manageable health problems. She was admitted to the Catholic hospital in Lima. Her condition worsened and she was coded. She stroked during this code. Her greatest fear was a stroke since this was a condition in her family's health history.

Gene was notified in Virginia of Mom's condition. Within hours, Jack and Gene were driving to Ohio. This was immediately after Thanksgiving in 1976. Gene went directly to see Mom after this twelve hours of travel. Mom mumbled, "Geanne is here." She seemed to lapse into a coma from that time. She lived three more days. She was seventy-eight when she died on November 29th. Since her death was imminent, her children were with her.

Knowing that Mom was so aware of how she looked and what she was wearing, her funeral was planned well by her daughters. Betty picked out a pink satin blouse with a full-length brocade skirt. Gene had given her this pink blouse that previous Christmas. She had worn this outfit that very Christmas. Six tiny pink roses were pinned into the backdrop near her body representative of her six great-grandchildren. Her grandsons were her pallbearers. Her grandchildren loved this lady just as much as her children and friends. The community came in droves to the funeral home. The weather was bad in Northern Ohio and ice and snow had blanketed the ground. Even so, these people, some of them over ninety years of age, came to express their feelings. They wanted also to see Mom's children and their grand children. Many of her children were now living out-of-state in Florida, North Carolina, Pennsylvania, Texas, and Virginia. This community wanted to see this popular family again. All nine of these children had grown up on this family farm. It was the largest family having graduated from the local school. They were viewed as smart students and were expected to be high achievers.

Before all of the children had returned to their homes, they all met at the farm to conduct a serious discussion regarding the estate. The main goal was to keep the family farm in the family as inferred by their parents. It should be kept in the Place name and that meant that one of the three sons should be offered the opportunity of buying the farm. Ned expressed more of a desire to buy the farm than did S.B. or Bill.

Ned and Kassy were designated in Mom's will to be co-executors. After many years of negotiating, Ned and Barbara finally have all parcels of the family farm in their name. It was not an easy task, but it was accomplished. All household goods and personal items were divided among interested family members. The piano was delivered to Karin's home by the men the next day. Karin did take piano lessons and it was felt that she should have this treasure. Most of the older children recalled when the piano was delivered to the small house where they all lived while Pa and Ma lived in the big house. They recalled Da having paid $100 for this new piano. This was long before Karin was born and somewhere around 1933. This family learned to love music from their parents. Mom and some of the girls played the piano by ear.

Ned and Barbara moved to the farm from Tiffin after Ned retired from his federal position. Ned loved the farm and soon was spending a lot of money on building repairs. New windows in the house, barn and schoolhouse were a start. The schoolhouse across the road was practically rebuilt with bricks. Air conditioning was added to the old farm home. Their children were grown and established in their own homes by the time they had moved to the home farm.

Mom maintained a conservative lifestyle on the farm while raising Karin to become a bright and successful adult. She was the valedictorian of her high school class, beating her classmate whom she later married. Karin's attempt at college did not succeed primarily due to her attachment to Mom and Terry.

Karin and Terry married and lived in Cridersville, some six miles from the farm. There they became the parents of two bright children, Chris and Lorraine. Lorrie graduated from college in journalism and has a very note-worthy position as top-notch reporter for the Lima News. Chris remains a bachelor and has recently purchased a home in Buckland near his paternal grandmother. Karin continues to master various positions in the working world.

Lela, known affectionately as Grandma, remained on this farm and continued to manage her finances quite well. Their will at the time of Da's death gave the land to the children. The benefits from the land were Mom's for as long as she lived. There was not extra money for maintaining the buildings, purchasing a new auto, travel and extra pleasures. But she managed well as she had done while raising these nine children.

Mom was one of the best managers of money ever known. She surpassed all of her children. She remade her own clothing in order to have something new for the many graduations, weddings and gatherings she attended. She too, just as Da, spent much thought and effort on grooming. She was a classy lady with a very keen mind. Her memory was superb. She grasped everything on the first go-round. It does take bright parents to have bright kids. Both Da and Mom had some good genes that are reflected in their children and grandchildren.

Da and Mom graduated from their two-year high schools. Mom was always interested in furthering her education, but her father thought education was only for males. Some stories that have been told about Da were relating to his only sister bribing him to go to school His sister, Aunt Bina (named Blanche) harnessed his horse and did everything to see that her Stanley boy went to school. Of course, Da denied these stories whenever they surfaced. With being parents of so many children then, they really had only one choice. They had to work and work hard to make a living and try to get ahead. Additional formal education for them could not even be considered at that time. They evidently reaped rewards through their own children's achievements.

Mom was truly a scholar. When there was a problem in math or Latin, it was Mom who had the answers and helped her children as they prepared their school homework. She was the reference library.

This lady never had an enemy. Her neighbors and community respected her to the highest degree. She was the stabilizing person of this large and strong-willed family. Often times, Stanley had ideas of grandeur as he speculated how to make a million over night. It was at times like this that Mom put her foot down and said, "enough is enough" and brought him to reality. The good part about Da's get rich quick ideas was that he never became overwhelmed by the vast responsibility of raising nine children, buying farmland and trying to achieve for their latter years.

Facing Page: Grandma Place ushered by grandson, David Roth, at another grandson's wedding.

Julia with her sisters (Susan, Julia, Karin, Kassy, and Betty)

Julia, Jack, Gene and Bill

Chapter Three:

Family Tragedies

While Jack and Gene were vacationing in Florida in 1985, they received a call from their son, David, in Virginia. He had just learned from Kassy's call that Julia had been murdered in her home in Florida. David had sounded quite ill and was short of breath. They advised him to go to the hospital immediately where he was admitted. He had an active bleeding gastric ulcer that depleted his blood to a critical level.

Both Jack and Gene were doubly stressed. After calling Bob, Julia's husband, they concluded they needed to rush back to Virginia to look after David and his family. Their hurried drive straight to Virginia from Florida with some icy roads in February only stressed them further. Gene always worried about Jack's health since his open heart surgery in 1978.

Details regarding Julia's death were sketchy. Julia was 62 and active in sports since her retirement from teaching. They lived in a comfortable neighborhood where most residents owned their own homes. A neighbor had rented his home to a large family. It was the oldest son, age 19, of this neighbor who admitted to stabbing Julia. The cause was never determined.

Bob had gone to his routine weekend trap shooting retreat. Julia usually went with him. But she had stayed home this weekend. She had just returned to her home on Saturday night after having eaten dinner out with a close girlfriend. This young man was believed to have been in the house and stabbed Julia before she could defend herself. After some eighteen stabs, with one considered the lethal one in her back, she got out of her house and went next door to the home of this young man. She informed the parents of their son's attack and died at their door. The young man had thrown the knife on the roof of his parents' house and left only to return on Sunday.

Since he admitted to the killing, no trial was held. He was sentenced to prison for twenty-five years. Bob believed that this would keep the man in jail until he (Bob) died. This was a very selfish view. It also kept the details from Julia's family. They never knew the reasons for her murder. Bob had Julia's body cremated before her family arrived in Florida. This family was not ready for cremation. Julia had expressed a desire to be buried in the family plot near the family farm in Ohio.

"Stay with David and don't come here for any funeral. There is no body here since Bob had Julia cremated before we arrived in Florida," came S.B.'s stressed and saddened voice as he called Gene in Virginia from Florida.

Yes, they stayed in Virginia as David was quite ill. S.B.'s call did seem to reduce some of Gene's stress. Gene recalled hanging her bagged clothing, which she had selected to fly to Florida, in the closet in the foyer of her home. I think that I'll be going somewhere soon and will need these as they are. I'll leave them like this as they will be ready to go.

Bill, now living in Tennessee after leaving Texas, attended Julia's memorial service along with his new wife. He had related that he did not feel well while in Florida. The rest of the family felt badly too. They didn't understand that maybe he had a physical problem as well during this time of stress.

Soon all of the family who had gathered in Florida were arriving in their own homes in Ohio, Tennessee, North Carolina and Pennsylvania. Upon arriving at his home in Nashville, Bill told his wife that he wanted to rest in his lounge chair before going to bed as she went on to bed.

The following morning, Bill was found dead by his wife in his lounge chair. Bill was fifty-four with no known cardiac problems. Still in shock from Julia's death, this family had difficulty comprehending Bill's sudden death. What was happening to this strong family who seemed always to be in control?

This family seemed to be reaping a bitter harvest. The weather in Ohio was the reason for the governor pronouncing all airports closed and restricted travel, as Ohio experienced a devastating winter storm. This meant that Kassy, Susan, and Karin could not get to Nashville for Bill's funeral. Ned was in a Toledo hospital awaiting open heart surgery.

Jack and Gene had tracked this big storm by TV as it moved through the midwest. This meant that it would soon hit Virginia and Pennsylvania. So they left Virginia by plane before they became stalled in Virginia. David was then doing better. Gene was already packed as something had told her of this impending trip.

Betty could fly out of Pittsburgh and she did. It has been said of Betty, "Nothing ever kept her from doing anything she wanted or needed to do." She always flew to the family weddings, graduations and special events under adverse conditions often leaving an ill husband.

David had told Betty when she flew to his wedding with some travel problems, "Our wedding could not have gone on as planned if you could not have gotten here."

Stanley, Jr. and his son-in-law, Randy, drove his new truck from the east coast of North Carolina across the mountains to Nashville. They had a heroic trip with impassable roads due to deep snow, unless they could follow a big truck. It required them to carry gasoline to their truck, rather than hang up in four feet of snow if they had attempted to drive off the highway. This stressful trip showed on S.B.'s face along with the realization that his close brother had died unexpectantly. He and Bill had just been together in Florida the week before. Bill was the youngest of the eight children prior to Karin's birth when Bill was fifteen. S.B. was next to Bill and they had a close relationship since they were the youngest of the eight children. They were the two younger boys spoiled by the five older girls.

As Jack and Gene flew into Nashville, thick ice was everywhere. Only one runway was partially cleared for their plane to land. They made connections with Betty and all roomed at the same motel. They reserved a room near them for S.B. and Randy.

Of course, they all wanted to know why Bill had died. What had caused his death? A local doctor had diagnosed the cause to have been a coronary without having a post. Gene did not accept that fact and wanted it investigated more thoroughly. This was the nurse in her. In the end, blood tests did not reveal anything significant. Information gleaned with the medical procedure of a post may have been revealing. This could have been helpful for Bill's five children as well as his brothers and sisters.

Soon the family gathered at a motel as they arrived from various distant places with harrowing details of their travels. Bill's children soon joined them as they arrived from many different states. Kay had flown from Maryland, Brenda and family had driven from Virginia, Jim from California and Mike who lived near Bill in Nashville. Bill had developed a very close relationship with his grandson, Jason, Mike's son.

For the first time, this family was in a minority. Along with Bill's children and a total of his three brothers and sisters, they managed to keep their composure during the funeral.

Bill's new wife and her children seemed to separate themselves from Bill's immediate family. Bill's son, Mike, and his wife, Bernice, supplied vast amounts of food that had been prepared by their friends and neighbors. Bill's kin grouped together in their motel and tried to deal with Bill's death through discussions and finally card playing. Cards raised the spirits of the group. It seemed acceptable as it had gotten them through so many crises before. They communicated by phone to the family members in Ohio to try to allay their stress during the waiting period before the funeral.

To add to the stress at this time, Ned was awaiting open heart surgery in a hospital in Toledo. His surgery was scheduled for February 15th, the day after Bill's funeral. Gene had talked to Ned by phone from Virginia while he was a patient when she told him of Julia's death.

"Gene," he said, "she won't bother us anymore." You see, they never communicated well for various reasons that had their origin in prior years.

(February is a month that haunts Gene. She recalls it as the month Jack had a serious coronary in 1971 at the age of 47. They had just built a new home and worked very hard trying to establish a lawn. Gene had just graduated that January from the Medical College of Virginia with a BSN. She had started classes for her long-term goal of becoming a hospital administrator. With two sons in college, she changed her goals and helped Jack to adjust to a new life style and working schedule. He did well.)

At one time, when Bill lived in Texas, Gene was able to arrange for Bill to see four of his kids again as they lived fairly close to Gene in Virginia. It had been eight years since Bill had seen his kids. She kept in touch with Kay and Brenda since they lived in Virginia after their mother, Pat, remarried and moved to California.

"Gene, don't let those kids forget Bill and the rest of us," demanded Betty and other family members whenever they called her.

Pat and Bill divorced and she remained in Virginia before moving to California after remarrying a previous boyfriend. Four of

Bill's young children agreed to have their names changed from Bill's. Our family had fits to think that these kids no longer carried the Place name. Mike kept his Place name. But Bill hid his true feelings and always tried to play down how he felt about their name changes.

"It's okay Gene," Bill would try to reassure Gene.

But most of Bill's brothers and sisters wished Bill could have stood up and "kicked some rear." Fighting for his rights stressed him terribly. He tried to keep peace and often gave in to the other person to avoid conflict or confrontation. This was the way he was as a child and it caused him much stress in his adult life as he lost his kids and family.

When the family found out that Bill was dealing with a serious illness, a manic depressive condition, they understood better his behavior. He could not help himself. It took a crisis before the family was alerted to the seriousness of the battle Bill tried to wage alone for years as an adult and without telling his family. They weren't even sure he understood his own behavior or sought medical assistance once he recognized it before they became aware of the problem.

Gene received a call in Virginia from Bill's second wife, Jean, in Dallas. Bill referred to Jean as Cadillac Jean. She had met Gene when she and Bill had visited them in Virginia the year before. She volunteered that she had called Gene as she felt she was the only family member she could tell about what was happening to Bill. Gene listened before jumping and so Jean dropped a big one on Gene.

"I have called the paddy wagon and had Bill picked up as he was causing trouble with the neighbors," Bill's wife told Gene when she called her in Virginia.

Gene listened and sensed the seriousness of Bill's situation. Within a short time, Gene and Jack were flying into Dallas. Jean met them and briefed them from her limited reference. Jack and

Gene went directly to the hospital where Bill had been transferred to a psychiatric unit. Jean would not, or could not, go with them. She had no skills with which to deal with this total situation that had transpired over their ten years of marriage.

Upon seeing Bill, both Jack and Gene concluded immediately that Bill was deeply sedated. Soon his psychiatrist asked them to meet with him without Bill being present.

"How do you think your brother looks?" the Dr. asked.

"He is snowed and is not the Bill I remember," replied Gene.

Information about the family's medical history and how it related to Bill's symptoms was discussed. Bill seemed pleased that Jack and Gene were there but seemed incapable of handling a conversation. He withdrew to his room.

Jack and Gene left the hospital and went to Bill's home. While there Jean seemed eager to talk. The home was dark and dreary. Drapes were closed. Walls were painted dark colors. Bill's room was dark brown. Soon Jack and Gene were pulling the drapes and trying to get some light into this comfortable bungalow. Jean stood in amazement as they moved from room to room. This closed environment depressed both Jack and Gene prior to their drape pulling exercise.

The following morning, Jack and Gene visited Bill again. He was more alert and seemed to appreciate their coming in an effort to assist him. When the psychiatrist joined them that morning, he volunteered, "Yes, your brother had received excessive medications. Instead of the nursing staff giving him the either/or medication, they had given him both of the medications I ordered."

He thanked Gene for her good assessment of Bill's state of health. A good relationship developed between Bill, his doctor, Jack and Gene. Bill seemed on the road to recovery even though it would take a long time.

For the next couple of days, Jean never went to the hospital when Jack and Gene visited Bill. She always declined and used the excuse of not feeling well. Bill never asked about her when they visited him.

"Your brother can go home for a visit on Sunday," said the psychiatrist.

They were excited, yet still worried. How was Jean going to handle this? So much was left unsaid. Jack and Gene were quick to realize that the relationship of these two was less than ideal. This was not a quick-fix situation. Gene encouraged Jean to fill in some of the missing details. As she confided the terrible strain and fighting they had been experiencing for so long, Jack and Gene worried about Bill's coming home on Sunday. Gene explained in-depth how important it would be for Jean to be calm and restrained.

"Do not strike back verbally," was a command Gene stressed to Jean.

Jack and Gene picked up Bill at the hospital and agreed to have him back at the designated hour. Gene cooked him one of his favorite meals. Jean never came out of her room for hours after Bill arrived home. When she did, her makeup looked like she had ten layers on her face that must have taken her hours to do. This had been her daily pattern. She had consumed her usual vast amount of vodka that served as her crutch.

"How are you Patty Baby?" said Bill.

"You ——— so and so," shouted Jean.

Gene turned abruptly and rapidly assisted Jean to get out of the reach and sight of Bill. Jean stayed in her bedroom the rest of Bill's visit that day.

Bill knew how to get a rise out of Jean. By calling her his first wife's name, she reeled in anger as evidently he expected her to do. He seemed to get a kick out of seeing her go into a tantrum. He mumbled something about her deserving it since she had called the paddy wagon for him. Deep anger was apparent in Bill's voice and body stance. This was so out of character for this mild-mannered Bill. Gene had never seen him ruffled.

The behaviors witnessed by Jack and Gene had deep meaning. Just think, this marriage existed ten years under these stressing conditions. Jean had so little understanding of her own behavior. She didn't have the slightest insight as to what was causing Bill's behavior. She had been shifted from aunt to grandmother to others while growing up. There was no stability during her formative years. She had no positive role model. She lacked a good educational foundation. She lacked stability of a family and home, such as Bill had known. Bill's illness had been handled improperly over all of these years by both Bill and Jean. This illness may have affected his first marriage.

Succeeding visits with Bill on his trips home from the hospital were about whatever he wanted to discuss. He dwelled on discussing his brothers and sisters and their achievements as he recalled them in his eyes. He revealed that he was afraid of losing his brothers and sisters after the death of his mother and their home environment on the farm dismantled.

Upon getting a financial reimbursement from Ned for land he had sold to Ned, Bill concluded that the family was splitting. He had lost touch with his brothers and sisters since he rarely saw them. By living in Dallas, a good distance from Northern Ohio, his manic and depressive episodes were not observed by his family. His pompous calls to several of his brothers and sisters on the same day at which time often entailed some tall Texas jokes still were not recognized as illness. Instead, the family just thought Texas had rubbed off on Bill. Bill's manic-depressive behavior was never observed, since he was not near them during this phase. The mood swings associated with manic depressive disease need to be observed directly and without the patient disguising his behavior.

During one of these manic phases after he received some money from Ned, he purchased a red Cadillac for Jean. Bill drove an old pickup truck that he kept in excellent state of repair. He was a true mechanic and had displayed these skills at the early age of three. He had a great need to treat people and be generous in his gift-giving. He never saved anything for himself. His need was to please people. Bill's goal in life seemed to be one to keep peace and please the other person.

After his death, his coworkers told of him buying food and drinks for them and treating them on many occasions.

"Place was a wonderful guy; he never missed work, arrived well in advance of his scheduled hour, and was viewed as an excellent supervisor, so willing to show his men that he could do the work also," expressed one of Bill's fellow supervisors at Texas Instrument when viewing Bill at the funeral home.

◆ ◆ ◆

One evening before Jack and Gene took Bill back to the hospital, he said, "Jack, do you want to see where and how the flying saucer landed on my driveway?"

"Hell yes," Jack replied.

"How about you, Gene?"

"Of course, Bill, tell or show us," Gene responded to Bill.

"We have to turn the lights out here in the house," said Bill.

Jean remained in her room the whole evening.

Hearing their responses, Bill proceeded. "We have to get flashlights and lie on the floor. Will this scare you, Gene?"

"Not at all, Bill," she replied.

"When we hear the buzz, they will land on the driveway." Bill informed them.

Before they knew it, they were out in the driveway looking for burned marks where Bill said the flying saucers had landed.

All verified the burned marks on the driveway and returned to inside the house.

"One other thing, Jack and Gene. Do you know they program you with all the silver you have in your mouth?"

They answered that they could handle that. This little exercise Bill put them through reflected his thinking. He insisted that Jack and Gene take with them the silver from his home when they returned to Virginia.

"Of course," they assured Bill, "we could easily do that," Gene said.

When they boarded their plane, they had the silver they promised to take with them to Virginia from Dallas. They picked up the airline magazine on the plane after settling in for their flight back to Virginia. There was an article describing flying saucers and some of the suspected activity they were engaging in at that time. Time may reflect Bill's advanced thinking, known then as science fiction, to be realistically envisioned by his creative and inventive mind.

Bill had an excellent and creative mind. He elected to enlist in the air force for a four-year stint rather than go to college. His mechanical and engineering skills came to the front in his childhood and were seen at the end of his young life. He often created thrashing machines out of cereal boxes when he was a very young child. He would run them around home, while making the sound of a motor as he pushed these handmade toys. He did not have a television to watch. Therefore, he became creative and used his skills to invent toys and he reaped much enjoyment with these playthings. Children were able to entertain themselves well before the invention of television. Few toys were purchased for these nine children as money was not spent in this manner. Having to entertain oneself, when not actively playing with the family, certainly helped to bring out the creative skills in all nine children of Stanley and Lela.

As an adult, Bill worked as a machinist for several prominent companies. When he achieved supervisory status for Texas Instrument, he was very proud of his work. It was when this company was downsizing that Bill, along with many other supervisors, was demoted. Losing the supervisor status caused Bill personal trauma from which he never recovered. His confidence was destroyed. He never sought assistance in handling this personal trauma nor did the company provide any counseling. Unfortunately, Bill never shared his feelings with his brothers and sisters when this happened. However, most of them would have expected Bill to handle whatever came his way.

Having experienced a divorce from the mother of his five children, then the loss of his four children when their names were changed, were big tragedies with which Bill coped. The deaths of both parents, the loss of his supervisory position, and then the sudden death of Julia were events that compounded to Bill's state of health.

It was vividly clear to Bill's psychiatrist that he needed the assistance of his family. This doctor advised against Bill's returning to his marital setting in Dallas. He recommended that he stay with a family member as soon as possible. Quickly, a plan was developed to have Bill return to Ohio and stay on the farm with Ned. Ned was devoting the majority of his time to farming and staying at the home place while he completed the purchasing of the inheritances of the other brothers and sisters.

Kassy agreed overnight to fly into Dallas to accompany Bill to Ohio. Within hours of the plan being finalized, Kassy was in Dallas. Bill was adamant that he drive his truck to Ohio with his selected treasures. Kassy and Bill packed the truck and headed toward Ohio. Bill insisted and Kassy agreed that he drive the entire way to Ohio.

When he arrived in Ohio on the farm, Kassy and Ned helped Bill reestablish his life on the farm. He was to continue on the medical plan for manic-depressive disease. He was referred to another psychiatrist in Lima near the farm. Bill responded positively to the treatment and his familiar environment.

Before long, he moved to Nashville to be near his oldest son with whom he had always maintained a good relationship. This son was old enough at the time of the name changing that he refused. Mike and Bill developed a closeness. This father-son relationship was a first for Bill as he never learned to know his other four children. His former wife had moved his small children to California at an early age after the divorce. Mike introduced Bill to his third wife.

When Jack and Gene attended a national meeting in Nashville, they had an opportunity to meet Bill's new wife. This marriage did not seem to enhance Bill's self image. Bill's failure to achieve in the working world to please her caused some openly discussed concerns of hers. Bill was embarrassed and tried again to pass over this dissension. It seemed apparent to Gene during this visit that Bill was losing ground in his managing his manic depressive condition as this wife seemed to lack the knowledge and understanding Bill needed. He was in the process of inventing a heating stove about which he tried to convey his enthusiasm. However, this project did not seem to have a market. He did give excellent information to Gene and Jack about what points to look for in the purchase of their first fireplace insert. His recommendations proved very valuable. Bill was trying to cope with the losses that had previously devastated his life. This new marriage seemed only to stress Bill more. He had connected to another wife who had little understanding of his health problems or even what his needs were.

Mike's three-year-old son, Jason, became very fond of his grandfather. Bill loved children and had patience galore. He was never able to discuss how terrible he felt about losing his own children at their early ages. Mike and Bill became great pals.

They discussed Mike's building projects. They fished together. They laughed together and from this Bill seemed quite pleased with living near Mike in Nashville. Bill was very handsome, and women spotted him in a group. It becomes baffling as to why he settled with three women who did so little to build his ego for which he needed in order to survive. Could it be that he had too many domineering sisters and selected women in their image? This may be what some psychologists might say today as being a possible influential factor.

◆ ◆ ◆

Sadly enough it was at Bill's funeral in Nashville that Jack and Gene would see Jason again. He was bewildered at the age of three as to what had happened to his grandpa. Bill's sudden death left a huge void in little Jason's life. The short time Bill spent with Jason after moving to Nashville was one of the very positive rewards Bill experienced in his life.

Bill with his children

Chapter Four:

Family Reunions

*How do you get a reunion started for this family?
David and Barbara could speak to this question.*

David and Barbara arranged a visit to Ohio in 1990 whereby they would meet in person most all of the key persons in this family. With their living in Virginia and not coming to Ohio since Grandma Lela's funeral in 1976, they had to re-establish relationships again. So much time had passed. Few in Ohio knew this now adult family of Jack and Gene. David asked Gene to accompany them on this trip as they had forgotten how to get to the farm and other family members living nearby. This trip proved invaluable.

Being on the receiving end as this reunion took shape was exciting when the letters started coming from Barbara and David. One of the first questions was: "Would you be interested in attending a reunion for the descendants of Stanley and Lela, your parents or grandparents?" Most all of the family responded positively and in a timely manner. Questionnaires were prepared, sent, and completed with detailed responses and returned to David. This helped to define when, where, for how long, etc. Barbara and David handled all of this. Soon the family members were making

1992, First Place family reunion

Unspoken Love ♦39♦

1995 Second reunion group

reservations a year in advance for July 4th weekend in 1992 at Salt Fork State Park in eastern Ohio.

What a wonderful thing had happened! This family had made a commitment to hold their first reunion since the deaths of their parents. This family was finally meeting in a planned first reunion for a weekend in Ohio. There would be the meeting of grandchildren, their spouses, and their children for the first time. Recreation for all ages was available. Food was prepared by the lodge, so more time could be spent getting to know the relatives. Past events would be discussed. A special program with talent from all ages was presented at the dinner banquet.

The camcorders were rolling during the dinner and special program. These videos are priceless. Ned gave a dissertation of events when he used five of his nine lives. Betty's Bill did a rendition of George Burns that was really great. David presided with the fullest confidence and dedication. Gene was quite proud of him. He displays so many physical traits and behaviors of his grandfather Stanley. Ned's granddaughter, Stephie's daughter, performed a piano recital. Betty, Susan and Gene pantomimed a lip sync of the Andrew Sisters of the 1940s.

The Second Place Family Reunion, held at the Salt Fork State Park in Ohio on the July 4th weekend in 1995, was very successful. Much of the credit was directed to David and Barbara's leadership. A trophy was presented to them for an outstanding job. Sonnie, Ned and Barbara's eldest daughter, had done her thing with her committee. This reunion brought out family members we had not seen in a long time.

The following pages contain David's reflections and Sonnie's letter to the family.

As Barbara and I and our two sons (who originally were not sure what a family reunion would have to offer a couple of teenagers) left Salt Fork Park, we all felt that the weekend had offered opportunities for fun and a meaningful renewal of family ties. The success of the reunion can be attributed to the efforts of everyone who took time away from their busy family routine on a holiday weekend to attend. Special thanks goes out to those who assisted with the final planning and preparations for the program on Sunday evening.

Those of you who were not able to attend were not forgotten. Even though you were not among the sixty-six of us who were present, you were recognized as part of the introduction, and you were in our thoughts and the subject of many of our discussions. It is hoped that the next reunion will afford the opportunity for even more of us to attend. That's all right, there are plans being made for the next Place Family Reunion! It was decided that the next reunion would be held in 1995. A committee chaired by Sonnie Kattman was appointed to start organizing this event. Your continued support and valuable input will be needed as the planning progresses.

In closing, Barbara and I would like to thank you for all of the support we received the past two years in the form of your responses to our letters and for the enthusiasm which was shown for the reunion. Your acknowledgment of our role in helping to establish what we hope will be an ongoing tradition is very much appreciated. The award you presented to us will be kept in a special place in our home.

Thanks again.

Sincerely,
Barbara and David Roth

Dear Family,

When I returned home from the reunion, I wrote a press release and zipped it off to the *Wapakoneta Daily News*. I thought I would send it to all of you with this letter. However, this week I was tired of watching for it to appear and contacted their society editor. She said that it would possibly be reworded and run later. What a disappointment as the family has many relatives and friends in the area. I have included what I sent to the Daily News on the back of this letter.

I would like to take this opportunity to thank each and every one of you for attending the recent family reunion. We were sixty-eight strong. It was my pleasure to head it up this time. However, my success was only made possible by all of you. You made the job easy by responding to my correspondence so arrangements could be made.

It was so good to see everyone again! Aunt Gene's minutes, which we received shortly thereafter, were a welcome commentary of activities. It was wonderful to sit and listen as our grandparents who were so poignantly remembered. These ancestors would be proud of their descendants and the people they have chosen to share their lives. We represent a good cross-section of stable Americans of whom we are justifiably proud.

For all of you who were unable to attend, you were in our hearts and discussions. We missed you and look forward to seeing you the next time. I am turning my reins over to Ellen Baker, Kassy's eldest daughter, and other family members all of whom so graciously volunteered to serve as organizers of the next event. We voted overwhelmingly to have the next reunion in three years and at a location nearer the folks on the east coast.

I have enclosed an updated address list as of July, 1995, and photography information for your convenience.

Sincerely,
Sonnie

Unspoken Love ♦43♦

*Card playing dominates reunion activities.
These photographs capture card games played the night before the banquet in 1995.*

♦44♦   M. Georgene Roth

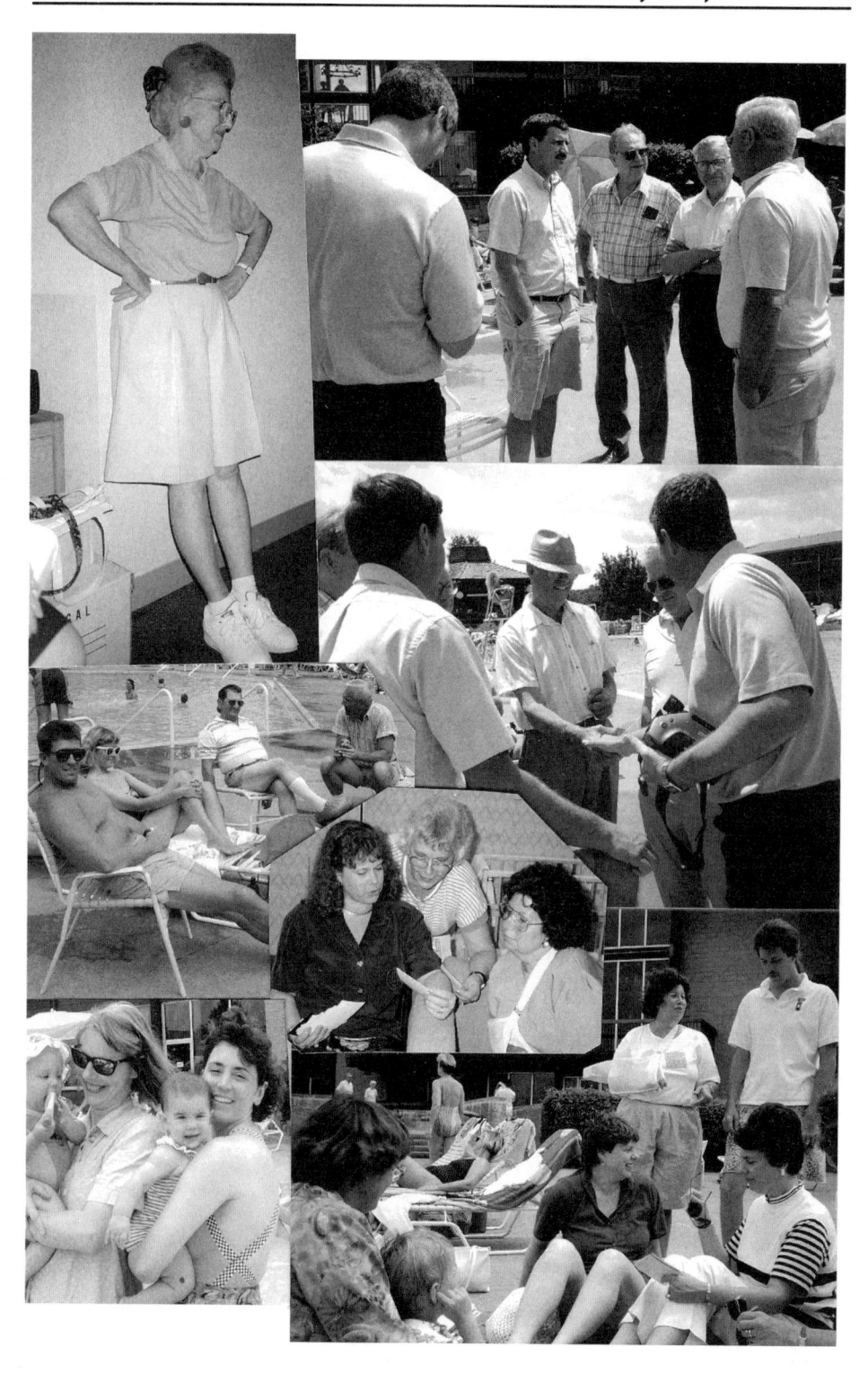

THE SECOND PLACE REUNION

DESCENDANTS OF STANLEY AND LELA
SALT FORK RESORT IN OHIO
JULY 1-3, 1995

    Upon arriving home here in Virginia, I stumbled upon the movie —*The Grapes of Wrath* playing on my TV. The many parallels in that family and ours certainly made me watch this old movie again with wonderment and amazement. Recalling the scene vividly conveyed by Betty as she told of our family living in a tent in Florida and coping with this transient environment, my mind seemed possessed in documenting various discussions and visits with family members which occurred at this reunion. Of course, all of us had various conversations with the 59 relatives during this weekend retreat. Some of the following experiences are still fresh in my mind. So I'll share with you some of my thoughts as I concluded that we are certainly a lucky bunch of descendants.

    As Tom found his way to the registration area after winding his way from the highway, with Allison and me recalling our visit of three years ago, he informed us that someone was following us and he thought it could be one of our relatives. Well, Neal and family pulled up behind us and jumped out to welcome us and we joyfully hugged them all. This happy start set the tone for the weekend. Soon we were to meet more of our young relatives now adults. And were to get to know his wife and two lovely girls much better.

1995 Reunion in action

We arrived before our rooms were ready; but at the registration desk we were informed to check back and our rooms should be available by 3:00 P.M. You see, we had driven from Virginia on Friday and stayed at Marietta, Ohio Friday night. Allison had flown into Richmond on Thursday morning from Charlotte and Tom had driven to my home on Thursday night from Apex, N.C.

Other members of his new family — Gray, Seth and Alison had elected to not join us this year.

The arrival of S.B. and Bernice at my home on Wednesday, June 28th, got us into the visiting mood. They started for Ohio on Thursday from my home, so they could meet Janet in Dayton on Friday where she was to arrive from California.

Our anticipated trip to Ohio caused us some concern since Virginia and West Virginia had just experienced serious flooding in areas that might affect our travel. However, travel went well, and it was good interstate all the way. Tom shared the driving of my car and Allison let us know she loved to drive as well. Trendy stayed in the kennels and we called it her vacation away from us.

Soon we were loading our belongings onto the carrier and locating our rooms. That was a real reunion! Upon finding our rooms, we soon learned that Betty, Susan, Kassy, Ned, David and others were on the third floor. Tom and Allison joined the others on the second floor as they could walk out to the pool from their sliding doors. We heard that Sandra had an animal get into her room during one night by way of the open sliding doors.

Betty and Bill set up a temporary bar in their room. And with glass in hand, some strolled across the hall to my room for another get-acquainted session. During this exchange of information someone would announce that others had arrived. Then we heard that many were to arrive on Sunday as their work schedule did not permit the freedom of joining us on Saturday.

I heard — where is Janet, Brenda, Kay, Milton, Sandra,

David, and Tom, Ann, Lorrie and Chris, Jill and Grant, Scott and family, Ellen, Bruce, Pam and family, and Pam and Randy and family, and so it went. Each time a new arrival appeared, there was a new grouping and their conversations took another turn.

Marty guided the play of Elizabeth and Sherry, both 4 years old, as did many husbands of family members while watching their young ones. This afforded free time for more sharing of stories.

Soon Sandra and Barbara (Roth) were taking a head count as to those wanting to eat at 6:00 P.M. or 7:00 P.M. in order to alert the restaurant to an increased number of hungry guests. Those eating at six did not have to wait. They also were the testers of the food. It was soon gleaned to stay away from the special Prime Rib as it was tough and not too fresh — so Eric attested. Barbara celebrated her birthday with a cream and ice cream covered brownie and candle.

The card room filled quickly Saturday night with this card playing family. Seeing Ned play cards with his brother-in-laws was a surprise to all of us. S.B. supervised the playing of his older brother. Many hidden talents came out over the weekend. Bill, Betty. David and I tried some bridge; Susan and Larry took on Jo and family in euchre. Their adjoining table of Karin, Barbara R., Tom and company played spades and other kinds of cards. Then in the corner with a big round table were Randy, Pam, Neal's family, Milton, Janet and Bernice plus others in a hot and heavy poker game. In addition, we understand that Allison had a poker game going on in her room with Eric and Jason. Betty wanted to play "99" before the night ended, but since it was late we tabled that idea for Sunday.

Plans were tentatively made for golf with tee times starting at 8:00 A.M. Sunday. Betty of course was as eager to begin as David. Eric seems to have lit his golf interest also. Hugh joined the three and they headed out on the morning dew. This course has many hidden greens and all the rains prevented driving off the cart paths.

That made hill climbing popular unless you kept your ball on the cart path. Betty's score of 57 was the only one made public.

When I looked for breakfast partners at 10:30 A.M. on Sunday, the large gathering in the lounge informed me that I was too late. Bernice was serving breakfast in her room. So Milton and I strolled up and were served a full breakfast that ran into lunch. When I joined Tom and Allison for lunch in the restaurant, I was not too hungry. The sociability in the dining room was great.

As others gathered for lunch, a group headed by Tom and Sandra collected other relatives for a hike into the open spaces. I guess they hiked some four miles. That is a good walk. Kay, Bob K. and others joined this nature hike. We never did get a report from this adventure into this wild country.

A reminder went out that picture-taking at the main entrance was to start at 5:00 P.M. We had been advised in Sandra's letters that it was semi-formal and so everyone looked dressed in their best finery. The picture taking took off and many individual family groups were taken. All seven of us remaining out of our nine had a grouping taken.

Oh, yes, the weather had turned perfect on Saturday. It was a change for some of us having experienced rain for days. This provided an opportunity for the 59 to select what they wanted to do. I remember seeing Karin and Barbara R. trying to determine if they should swim outside in the cold pool water or go inside to the heated pool. Decisions! Decisions!

The banquet and evening program brought laughter and tears.

Food was good and followed by a program presented by the four eldest children of our parents, Stanley and Lela Graessle Place. Ned spoke as if he were Grandpa Dorsey Place and this was listened to intently by the younger set. Then came Kassy dressed as Maw (Maid) Mary Place. Kassy recounted Maw's life like she may have told it had she been present. Betty, dressed as Grandma Lorrena Graessle, revealed more history and family connections. Susan discussed details she recalled about Grandpa Phillip Graessle. The republican and democrats came to life as she revealed that Grandpa was a staunch republican and our Dad a staunch democrat. This program triggered many thoughts of others in the audience and they added to the positive memories of all four grandparents. This program provided history and related the good and the strengths of our ancestors. The 30- to 40-year olds were spell bound and I'm sure experienced some of the pride they had heard about and witnessed from their parents. A real pride was felt as Uncle Lowell joined in the validating of details — especially when he met the train when Mom arrived home from Florida with the five children and one on the way (me) in 1926. Uncle Lowell always adds so much to the group whenever he can join us in these gatherings.

Christmas came in July again this year. Kassy did it up big. She wrapped packages for each and everyone. This caused a lot of excitement and interest. How did she get all these packages there? I do believe that I saw Bruce carrying huge bunches of packages from his truck — there was no nap sack! How can we top this the next time? Gene took second seat to Kassy when Mary Kay hand care kits were handed out to the hard working individuals screened by Ann, Lorrie and Gene .

Chris and Lorrie Whetstone drove back to their homes following this delightful visit. We all shared together on this special Sunday.

Sandra and Bob K. were given much praise and all of us expressed our gratitude for their production. Sandra volunteered to assist Ellen and Pam Baker plan and execute our third reunion on the last weekend in July, 1998.

Each family member present was introduced starting with

Ned and Barbara's family. Barbara was hospitalized prior the reunion and could not attend. We all send our wishes for recovery and that she will join us in 1998.

As those present were introduced, it was noticeable that others were not present. In fact, Bill's girls asked that some of us try to get the men members of their family to attend. So we will work on Mike, David and Jimmy. It is always great to see Bill's family and their husbands and children. John Baker and family have not attended the first two reunions. It was good to see Neal and family, Tom, Janet, Lorrie, Greg and precious young children, rising teen girls and boys and some teens attend this second reunion. Hopefully, Bryan will join us at the next reunion. Scott and family were unable to fly from California this time. Cindy was joined by her son Greg, and Aaron was missed when Ned's family gave an accounting of those in attendance. Milton came alone and we are still waiting to meet his grown teenagers who we understand are very busy in their music endeavors. Dan stayed in Wisconsin to work on plans for his upcoming wedding on July 29th. Pam reported that Renè had other plans, but she needs to know that we missed her and have not had the pleasure of knowing her as a young 23-year-old adult. In total, all descendants of Julia and Karin were in attendance. Let's make it 100 percent at the next reunion in 1998 for the rest of our families.

The pictures of the ancestors were displayed for all to review. I am amazed at the work that Betty and Kassy go through to bring and assemble these precious memories. Thanks for this class act.

Ellen remembered to bring and display the family flag made by Gene for the reunions. Thanks Ellen for being the keeper of the flag. It is always a pleasure to have Roger, John's brother, join us all the way from Chicago.

We stepped back into history as we watched video of our parents, brothers and sisters with their spouses, their children, friends and others at the home farm. Our now grown children saw themselves playing as small youngsters in the straw and on the hitch-rack.

Seeing the little red wagon getting pulled by Mom, Bill, and others as various small riders enjoyed an ever lasting memory of ancestors. Sadness hit us as we viewed family members strolling through these video and who are not living presently. However, we all know that life ends here on earth and memories sustain us throughout the remainder of our lives. The message is to live everyday to the fullest and share your love with those who mean the most to you. Thanks to Betty these recordings will always remain a valuable connection to our once living family members.

Randy and Pam provided great entertainment by showing their videos from their viewpoint as divers and photographers.

Upcoming events that need recognition and support are:
- The wedding of Dan.
- The birth of Scott and Donna's infant in January, 1996.
- The surgery of Jim Kinstle.
- The recovery of Barbara Place.
- Allison's entry into the college setting.
- Neal and Patty's new home now being built.
- Pressure applied to family members needing to attend thereunion.

Keep in touch and soon we will be gathering somewhere for another PLACE reunion. Good luck to the new planning committee. Thanks Ellen and Pam Baker for volunteering. We all promise to assist in any way we can. Just ask us!

Share your pictures with all of us. We failed to record our events in motion this year. Sandra, we are awaiting the editing of your video from 1992. Maybe after the wedding you will find the time to do this. Just let us know the cost of getting a video from you. These are priceless recordings. Thanks for everything you have done to make the 1995 reunion a big success.

Thanks to David R. for his leadership in starting the whole process and making it a reality in 1992. It is apparent that we oldsters have nothing to worry about in having so many capable young-to-middle agers at the leadership helm. Thanks to all of you for coming and participating. What each of experienced can never be taken away.

Recorded by Georgene Roth July 6, 1995

David and Betty at the 1992 reunion.

CHAPTER FIVE:

Jack and Gene Meet

Destiny figured into Gene meeting Jack. She was fifteen years old and had gone to Kassy and Bob's home in Spencerville to make the turkey dressing for the family Thanksgiving dinner. The year was 1941. Bob had a thriving veterinary practice after graduating from Ohio State. While Bob was completing his veterinary education and traveling back and forth from Columbus, he met a young veterinary student who lived near Bob on a dairy farm. This student was Jack.

Jack rode with Bob as they came home from Ohio State on several weekends. This young handsome college student struck up a conversation with Gene's sister, Kassy. She mentioned that she had this sister, Julia, also a college student and that she would try to introduce them. Julia was a student at Ohio Northern University, which was not far from the farm home. But Julia had not come home that weekend. So Gene was introduced to Jack. Jack asked Gene for a date over this Thanksgiving holiday. When Gene accepted this invitation, she had to convince her Mother to let her go. Gene, of course, told her mother that it was okay with Kassy and that should make it okay for Gene to have a date with Jack, since Kassy had checked him out. Kassy was the oldest of the five girls before Karin's late birth. Gene was the youngest of the five older girls. Kassy's influence helped to

Gene from fifteen to when she married Jack at age twenty.

get a positive response from their mother.

Jack and Gene's first date was a wonderful experience. Jack had not dated in high school and had very few dates in college since he devoted much time to working and studying. Gene had a crush on a drum major of the band at Wapakoneta, but dropped this friend after she met Jack. Soon Jack's parent's maroon Dodge was coming up the road to Gene's home every chance he got to come home from Columbus through hitch-hiking.

◆ ◆ ◆

Jack's father was a dairy manager on a farm three miles North of Gene's home. In fact, their farms were on the same road. But since Jack was in another county, he went to another school and the reason for never having met Gene earlier.

Jack's veterinary education required five years of college. Five years were condensed into four by going year-round for four years. Jack was a good student and studied hard. Gene recalled that he would often tell her he was flunking out as he lacked self-confidence. Instead, he achieved well in this difficult program and schedule. His parents rarely praised him for his accomplishments. Instead, his father would express concerns of his succeeding. Gene's parents rarely praised, but established an atmosphere that "of course you can do it and you can be the best at doing it." They did not destroy self-confidence. And they had no formal education in growth and development of children. Gene's parents were proud of their children wanting to go to college even though they could not afford to send them.

Jack's parents did not want him to go to college. They tried to convince him to stay on the farm with them. The encouragement came from the local veterinarian who came to their farm and his high school superintendent.

Jack enrolled at Ohio State, which was one hundred miles from the farm. This meant some loneliness while at OSU. He was an only child in this closeknit family. Jack often mentioned the terrible lonely feelings he had when the bell rang every evening. His mother washed his clothes and mailed them back and forth to Columbus. Mail was cheap then and it saved money to launder his clothing in this way. His participation in the ROTC military program helped to finance his education. (World War II was ending when Jack graduated in 1945.)

By the time Jack graduated from OSU, Gene and he were going steady. They became engaged when Gene was a senior in high school. She entered a nursing diploma program, which was only a three-year program versus a college four-year program. Also, the college program was quite expensive as compared to a diploma program. They were married in 1946 with Gene having one more year to finish her training. Students were just beginning to be given permission to marry while in training. Gene was the first one married in her class of eighteen. When she entered nursing training in 1944 her class had forty-four students. Attractive paying jobs enticed some from the class, but most students left due to poor grades or disciplinary actions. It was tough to get through nursing training at that time.

Jack and Gene were married on Gene's twentieth birthday on April 10, 1946. Her Dad had not wanted her to get married so young. He thought she would not finish her training. She assured him that she would as she was a very determined young individual.

They were married in the Methodist Church at Wapakoneta on this Wednesday morning at 10:30 A.M. They kept their wedding simple, as they had no money for anything else. Gene had to be back in school at 10:00 A.M. the next morning, so they spent their one night honeymoon in Columbus.

Jack and Gene established their new home in a small

farmer's town, Columbus Grove, thirty miles from the hospital where Gene was in training. Often she spent twelve hours at the hospital. She had split hours and had no way to get home for the three-hour intervals. She studied at this time as well as when Jack was driving her to and from the hospital. While home with Jack or helping in his office, she gave anesthesia for his surgical procedures.

One evening, while Jack was out on a farm checking a laboring cow, a big burley farmer came in to see the Vet. He questioned his whereabouts as he moved toward Gene. Gene was suspicious of this man and maneuvered toward the front door. This took some skill, as the office was spread out in one long row. When she got this man outside, she dashed back into the office and locked the door. Jack returned to the office. When Gene alerted him of this man's behavior, Jack left suddenly to go beat up this big man. He drove to the farm. Fortunately, when Jack engaged him in a discussion, he was in the presence of the farmer's wife. He was informed by Jack to never enter his office again. Also, he would need to seek the services of another veterinarian. The farmer complied with Jack's command.

Gene was alerted to the need to protect herself. She was given some classes as a student nurse for self-defense. Many patients try to make advancements to their nurses. It can't all be credited with illness. The true behaviors seem accentuated many times with illness. Self-defense was not openly discussed in 1946 as it is today in 1997. Behaviors at that time were more subtle and rarely discussed in the open

They rented an apartment above a store in this little farmers' town. It was drab and dreary. In fact, it was unsafe with little consideration for how one would escape in case of fire. The floors were poorly finished with heavy oil. It was heated by open gas flames. There was only one door at the front of the apartment. Soon they looked for a safer residence. They purchased a small

Jack and Gene's wedding picture.

cheap home not far from Jack's rented office.

Plans changed abruptly. Jack heard from the draft board that he could be drafted unless he enlisted immediately for active duty. In order to get his commission as a second lieutenant, he enlisted into the army. This meant that he would repay his ROTC obligation. His classmates waited out the threat and were never drafted.

(Life brings to all of us some bittersweet harvests. It is how we deal with the bitter that helps to enjoy the sweet experiences. Focusing on others and not dwelling on one's personal losses seemed to be what Gene was capable of doing. To put it simply, she demonstrated the ability to pick up the pieces and go on when the going got heavy. The family views her as a very strong family figure. Just maybe she would prove her father's predictions.)

They had to sell this house within months of buying it. Gene made plans to rent a room near the hospital where she could finish training within walking distance. Jack had their one auto. At first, he was stationed in Chicago and came to be with Gene on weekends. Within months, he was sent to Ft. Riley, Kansas where the cavalry once was maintained. Soon he was detailed to Springfield, Missouri where he traveled to the various states to purchase food for the army. Jack was in Springfield for their first anniversary. Gene was in Akron for her three-month pediatric affiliation at that time. She went with classmates to watch a movie *The Anniversary Song* with Al Jolson singing. Having one of the young doctors at the children's hospital reassuring Gene that Jack would get there prepared her for a big let down. With this false encouragement and seeing this tear-jerker of a movie, Gene let the tears flow. An encouraging phone call and red roses that evening helped her to get her emotions in control.

Jack spent his free time at a veterinary hospital where he met three life-long veterinary friends who ran the hospital. Jack purchased a trained two-year old registered fawn boxer dog named Wrinkles while helping at the hospital. The previous owner was in show business and needed money in a hurry. He also loved this dog and tried to buy her back as soon as he recovered financially. Wrinkles traveled with Jack back and forth the six hundred miles to Ohio to visit Gene on weekends. She was a beautiful dog and became fond of Jack and Gene also. Jack was encouraged to have Wrinkles bred with another registered boxer. They showed Wrinkles in Oklahoma where she won ribbons in a large dog show. Now, Wrinkles was pregnant and due to have a litter of puppies in February 1948.

When Gene graduated in nursing in 1947, she joined Jack and Wrinkles in Missouri. They drove to Ohio for Gene to take state nursing boards in November. Gene now had time to travel to the various states with Jack, since he drove his personal auto for those trips. With Gene expecting their first child, she kept busy making little things. She had a thing for tangerines. New friends had a fruit market where she bought them by the peck. Everywhere she worked in their tiny apartment in Springfield were little piles of tangerine peelings. To this day, their son, David, eats tangerines almost as abundantly as his mother did during this pregnancy.

David was due in February when Jack received a sudden notice for his transfer to Fort Snelling, Minnesota. This required that Gene wait in Ohio until their child was born. Gene stayed with Susan and her first husband. Her parents were in Arizona for the winter. David was born on March 4th after a very quick delivery. David was three weeks late, which seemed like an eternity for all concerned. Finally, when David was ten days old Jack got to see his son. He had saved his leave so Gene and David could travel with him to their new home as they drove to Minnesota.

Wrinkles delivered seven puppies a few days before Jack and Gene said good-bye to friends in Springfield, Missouri, and packed to move on to Ohio, and then to Minnesota. The puppies were cared for at the veterinary hospital. Since Jack and Gene could not move Wrinkles as they had no place to care for her, they sold her back to her original owner. He agreed to pay for the care of the puppies and to sell them. But he then left town with Wrinkles without paying for the puppies' care or finding them homes. The Veterinarians handled this problem and found them homes since Jack and Gene had to move on so Jack could report for service in Minnesota.

As they drove out of Springfield, Gene cried for miles at the thought of never getting to see Wrinkles again. The attachment both Jack and Gene had with Wrinkles was tremendous. Reality had to set in as they could not move her at this time. In time, they lived with her memories and adjusted as expected. They were sure the owner loved her too and believed she would be well cared for and have a nice home.

Jack was a captain in the army and so could live off the base. Money was allocated for housing. So they rented a nice apartment within walking distance of a grocery. Gene had the use of a laundry facility and vacuum sweeper once a week. Jack was gone during the week while David and Gene spent the week alone in their apartment. David was a good baby and never cried. Gene really enjoyed taking care of him and the weekdays went fast.

When Jack returned from his week's journey for the army, Gene was teary-eyed and sobbed at not being able to wash or use the sweeper but one time per week. Jack wanted to correct this problem for his "Geanne" right then. He opened their apartment door only to find Mrs. Olson, the apartment manager, listening at their door. This triggered Jack's Scottish temper. Mrs. Olson accused Jack of pulling rank since he was a captain. Jack then announced to Mrs. Olson that he and his family would be moving.

Locating and moving into a suitable quarters was not easily done. Jack had his name on a list for this apartment as soon as he learned of his transfer to Minnesota, but moving was now something that they both agreed they should do. How were they going to find a suitable place and do it within days?

Gene suggested she write an advertisement stating their needs. She wrote a poem which cost $5.00 to place in the Sunday paper. This productive ad went like this:

> It's true we came from Missouri
> And landed here in a hurry.
> If we'd had time to look around,
> A suitable place we might have found.
> So, if you're from Minnesota,
> You'll help us fill our quota.
> A doctor, a nurse and David three months,
> For information, contact at once.

Gene's ad brought many responses. Some wanted Gene to give "Dad" his insulin for the rent of their home. But one special family met their needs. When they went for an interview, David was snatched from Gene's arms by the matronly wife. She was a nursing supervisor of the nearby Shriner's Children's Hospital. This friendly couple had grown children going to nearby University of Minnesota. Within minutes they had accepted Jack and Gene upon sight. They rented their lovely home to them for the duration of their army assignment in November. This meant that the owners would have to stay longer than usual at their cottage in the northern forests of Minnesota.

This beautiful well-kept home was located on the campus of the University of Minnesota. It had lovely furniture. There was a washer, sweeper and lots of linens and silverware. It rented for $75.00 per month. Jack had paid $100.00 a month, his allotment, for the apartment. The beautifully cared-for garden of flowers and trimmed lawn had a fence that set it apart as well as added security. With the three bedrooms, screened porch, and other comforts, Gene and Jack welcomed family visitors from Ohio.

Living in Minneapolis was lonely at first, but turned out to be a very positive experience for them. Jack spent the weekdays out of town for a week at a time. When they were together, they had a lot of pleasure enjoying this clean city. They enjoyed picnics at the various lakes. Gene walked to the grocery with David in his buggy and cared for their lovely flowers, yard and comfortable home, while Jack was on week long special trips for the army.

On Election Day in November 1948, Jack and Gene voted and left Minneapolis. As they had all their belongings packed into a new Pontiac station wagon, they headed for Chicago. This was the destination where Jack was discharged from the army. They stayed in Madison, Wisconsin, the first night out on the road, which was election day. Since they had no radio in their motel room and certainly no TV in 1948, Jack kept checking reports from the auto radio to hear about the election results. When he returned to bed at 4:00 A.M., Jack announced that Truman had won over Dewey. These election results surprised everyone. Dewey had made earlier headlines as having won.

Jack and Gene as the years progress.

Chapter Six:

Forest, Ohio

Upon coming out of the service in 1948, Jack and Gene purchased a home in Forest, Ohio. Jack resumed an established a veterinary practice from a retiring veterinarian. This was a farming area with Forest having a population of one thousand. Their newly purchased home cost $6,500.00 at that time. It was nearly sixty years old. It had a converted heating system from coal to oil for the heating of hot water radiators. With twelve-foot ceilings, no insulation and multiple long windows and many doors, the cost of heating this home raised to $50.00 per month. This cost covered the whole downstairs. The downstairs included a big office area for Jack's practice. On the second floor was an apartment which was rented for $30.00 per month. This income did help to defray the heating costs. However, expensive heat was not really the major problem at that time.

Jack and Gene's bedroom was in a large room with bay windows at the front of the house. At one time, it may have served as the front living room when the house was newly built. David shared this room with them since he was only nine months old.

On the very first night that Jack, Gene, and David stayed in their new home, something frightened them so badly in the middle of the night. It was late in November in Ohio. Suddenly, they

Home in Forest, Ohio

were awakened by a loud noise that sounded like someone trying to get into their bedroom. The noise seemed to be coming from one of the three doors that opened onto the big circular porch. They both sat up in bed and wondered what they would do if someone came through the door. This was a small retired farmers' town that appeared to be a safe place in which to live. It was cold outside with a light dusting of snow. So why was someone outside their door apparently trying to get into their house?

The noise continued for another minute. Jack and Gene jumped to their feet. How would they protect David? Jack went over and pounded on the door from where the noise came.

"Get away from our door!" Jack yelled.

Silence for a moment and then the noise resumed.

"Who is out there?" shouted Jack.

He turned on the porch light which dimly lit the area. No one could be seen outside their doors or on the porch. Back in bed, Jack and Gene had pounding hearts as they tried to reason with what had caused the noise. They vowed to look for footprints in the snow in the morning in the daylight. They had no weapons and had no way to defend themselves if an intruder had come in. Frightened as they were, it took some time until they drifted off to sleep again.

When dawn came, Jack was outside looking for footprints in the snow, but there were no footprints to the porch. The porch roof covered the entire area above the three doors. Who or what had caused the noise remained a big mystery. Just maybe the culprit or culprits could be four-legged creatures?

While opening the garage door the following day as Jack was assembling kennels, a huge rat ran across the floor in daylight. Soon they discovered the property was infested with these huge old gray rats. This was a horrible revelation. This dictated an all-out effort to kill these dangerous pests. It meant great fear for the safety of David and both Jack and Gene. Immediately rat poisoning was accessible everywhere for the rats. They ate and ate. Soon dead rats were carried out in buckets. Supposedly, the poison used meant that the rats would come out of the hiding to die. That seemed to happen. But the fear of these hungry pests eating their way into their home and attacking them never left their minds.

Could they ever get rid of these rats? From where did they all come? Soon they did find the connection to a vacant home and lot next door. Behind that home was a huge vacated building that once served as a small machine shop. Somehow, these rats had infested many of the adjacent areas and no one had done anything about it prior to Jack and Gene's all out attack.

Meanwhile, one morning Gene reached for her bathrobe which was hanging in their bathroom at the end of a large oval tub with legs on it. She tugged to get it from the wall. Down behind the bath tub was a hole in the wall. Gene's bathrobe had been chewed off on one side and it was pulled into this hole. The wall was made of thin fiber board and spray painted. This was cheap partitioning construction in this old house.

Finding Gene's robe having been chewed by rats that could conceivably get into the house, was a chilling reality. They then knew that their actions to rid their property of these rats had to be stepped up and spread beyond their property. The owners of the vacant properties provided help. Concentrated efforts finally overtook these dangerous predators.

Fear continued for a long time. The horror of seeing and destroying these inhabitants never left them. They determined that they could safely live in this house and prevent the rats from returning. They loved the home and this positive overtook the fear of the rats. Decorating this challenging home was begun with minimal financial resources.

Jack's veterinary practice needed attention in order to build it up for adequate financial income. With time, Jack soon proved the area did not have the quantity of livestock for a frugal practice. Most of the farmers had learned to treat many of their cattle by purchasing medicine from the local drug store. Some drug companies even taught the farmers how to administer the medications. This had a big impact on Jack's potential income in veterinary medicine. These were small farmers that did not have expensive registered livestock. This financial concern meant facing the facts. If there were not enough livestock to support a veterinarian there; they were in the wrong place. This meant that they might need to change living locations.

◆ ◆ ◆

In the two-year period before their second son, Tom's birth on July 31, 1950, they had learned to love the people in this friendly town. If the livestock per acre was not there, how were they to increase their income? This veterinary practice required the work of both Jack and Gene. Gene answered the phone and handled the office when Jack was on calls. She helped with his small animal practice while he did surgery or treated them. Gene did not practice her nursing after graduating and joining Jack with David in the army. So the one income was scarce at first and looked it as though that would not change.

The thought of a possible move from Forest was entertained privately by Jack and Gene. How could they leave the friends who meant so much to them? They had learned to play bridge and were members of this elite club. The M. D., undertaker, pharmacist, and other processionals made up the three-table club. Jack and Gene loved to tell how they learned to play bridge.

◆ ◆ ◆

A week after moving to Forest on a Wednesday, the local doctor's wife (also a nurse) came to welcome Jack and Gene. She invited them to come to the bridge party which they were having the next Sunday evening. When Gene disclosed that they played many card games, but never had played bridge, Eileen Clinger, the doctor's wife, volunteered to come over Saturday afternoon and teach them.

Eileen came and taught them how to play bridge on this one Saturday afternoon. They went to the bridge party at the Clinger's home on Sunday evening. Dr. Ed took both of them under his wing. He was brilliant and a good teacher. They made it through the evening. In time, they were asked to join the club which they accepted. Jack refused to submit to the strict bidding rules and guidelines. He ignored the pressures from the women who were going to make him comply, so he never did enjoy playing bridge.

Soon they enjoyed the penochle club with some of the same friends. They had played this card game many years. In fact, Gene believed that she played penochle before she walked. Her family played it when they had to skate on the icy roads to the neighbors for this game.

The area around their home became beautiful and they spent much time devoted to the growing of flowers. A small fenced area was prepared as a play area that was safe from all the cars and trucks coming to and going form Jack's office and joined to the house. Gene labored to plant flowers outside the fenced play area. But one day she was suddenly surprised. David, age three, reached through the fence and pulled up all of the newly set out flowers. This quickly told Gene that David was telling her that the flowers were getting more attention than she was devoting to David.

◆ ◆ ◆

When Tom was a year old, a local artist offered classes for adults of various ages for $1.00 for one evening per week. Gene went weekly if Jack could be home with their sons. On occasion, she had to go home if Jack had an emergency. He needed their one auto and they didn't hire baby sitters if at all possible. These art lessons provided an outlet for Gene's artistic potential. She painted an oriental scene mural with the assistance of her teacher. Jack and Gene papered the other walls with gold paper that had been in a fire sale. It was expensive paper bought cheaply because it had been damaged by a fire. Gene made ruffled curtains out of sheeting. She starched them so stiff that it took hours to iron these bed sheet size panels. These large off-white, ruffled curtains were majestic at these long windows in the living room with twelve-foot ceilings. They filled the large cracks between the wide flooring and then finished the floors. Fluffy green and white throw rugs were attractive and fairly inexpensive. The room was set off with a bright red sofa and chairs. This decorating effort was a hit.

The more love they poured into this home, the harder it was when they concluded that they needed to relocate elsewhere in order to improve their income. So, sadly, they sold this practice to a young veterinarian. Jack launched his career into regulatory veterinary medicine, which proved to be his niche.

Jack was a teacher, researcher and not a salesman. In order to succeed in practice, one must be able to tell the cost of the service to the farmer. It seemed that Jack's early years of growing up on a dairy farm hampered his ability to try to earn money for his valuable services. He just could not charge the farmer the worth of his services or call. Jack had earned and saved nearly $1,000.00 while milking daily in the middle of the night, this was to help pay for his college education during his high school years. His father managed a large Holstein dairy farm and milked three times daily for records which made the cattle more valuable.

Jack's father was a good dairyman, but, he was not a businessman. When he came to America from Switzerland as a young man of twenty-five, he had a herd of cattle that tested positive for brucelosis. These had to be slaughtered. This put him deep in debt. This indebtedness prevented him from ever venturing into owning his own cattle again. Jack's mother's Scottish heritage influenced their actions. He seemed content to manage excellent herds for wealthy owners. He worked for meager salaries until he retired. This parental influence had a great impact on how Jack viewed venturing into any enterprising efforts for him and Gene.

When Jack wanted to become a veterinarian, his parents did not want him to leave the farm. It was the encouragement of their local veterinarian and Jack's high school principle that supported Jack and assisted him to become enrolled in Ohio State University in 1941. Jack borrowed money from his parents for his education. He also enrolled in the ROTC program. His clothing was mailed home for washing and mending. He hitchhiked home the one hundred miles when he had a special date with his Geanne. Hitchhiking was considered a safe way to travel in the 1940s. Jack roomed above the animal clinic with the barking dogs and other noises. This made studying somewhat difficult. In his free time, he worked at the university hospital kitchen doing dishes and waiting tables for his meals. He was a definite example proving if there is a will, there is a way.

Chapter Seven:

Springfield, Ohio

Home number three was purchased by Jack and Gene in Springfield, Ohio. This was in central Ohio, and seventy miles south of Forest. Jack was now responsible for the central counties in veterinary regulatory medicine for the Ohio Department of Agriculture. With this new position he embarked upon a new field as a teacher, enforcement of animal disease control, and some researching activities. Since Jack was definitely not a salesman, this new position promised a more enjoyable and productive working experience.

Locating their third house took only one ride by to have Jack and Gene find the house of their dreams. This lovely two-story cottage was located on three acres in suburban Springfield. It had close proximity to a good school where David began the first grade and Tom started in kindergarten. This was a progressive school and provided an excellent start for Jack and Gene's two sons. David never had the opportunity to attend kindergarten in Forest as this was before one was available.

Along with this comfortable home with a basement, garage and beautiful landscaping, went a pet cat named Hallie. This calico long-hair cat quickly became a member of the new owners' family. Also, with this comfortable home went a small building Jack used to raise chickens. Raising these five hundred chickens

Springfield memories, Tom and David

was quite an experiment. Gene often kidded Jack that the chickens had so much medicine that they were not permitted to eat them. She speculated that they might have even gotten polio shots. Only a veterinarian would know of all the possible illnesses a chicken could get. Prevention was Jack's philosophy. A coughing chicken could have brought them whooping cough shots.

Next to this property was a fairly large turkey farm. These turkeys strolled up on Jack and Gene's property whenever they got out of their poorly fenced fields. Even a turkey was treasured by this family. It fell into the category of "a bird and something to love." Well, one day Julia and her daughter, JoAnn, Mom, and Karin visited Gene and family. After a discussion of the turkeys being such a nuisance, in jest Gene told Jo that if she could catch a turkey, she would cook it.

Soon, this screeching and shouting could be heard.

"Aunt Gene, Aunt Gene, come here! come here!" "Here is a turkey for you to cook, Aunt Gene!" shouted Jo. There was this eight-year-old girl dancing around while holding the feet of this flapping huge turkey.

"Let that turkey lose, " shouted Gene feeling the neighbors might have seen Jo taking one of their turkeys.

"But, Aunt Gene, you promised us that you would cook a turkey if we caught one," Jo insisted. Jo took most everything literally and so she did just what Aunt Gene had said they should do. Of course, Gene's own sons knew that their Mom was only kidding, and so they got a kick out of Jo not understanding her or recognizing her sense of humor.

David and Tom were now old enough to have a dog. Jack did not want his sons to have a dog until they were old enough to prevent a dog from licking them in the face. Soon their dog, Cindy, was going to have puppies. They prepared a corner in the basement where Cindy could have her puppies and keep them safe and dry.

Both boys were in their bathrobes that Gene had made for them at this early time of the morning.

The puppies grew and took on their personalities. These boys became enterprising after their parents told them they could sell them for $2.00 per pup. These math-prone boys soon figured out that if they had 1,000 pups to sell for $2.00 each, they would be rich. It didn't take long for them to change their minds once they became attached to these six pups. They decided that they would not want to subject Cindy to this project and neither did they want to make money this way.

Before long, a Cub Scout group was formed with Gene as the den mother. There were ten young boys in the area at the age of ten. David was eight and Tom six. Tom joined this group anyway and was an eager and capable participant. Most of these ten-year-olds were neglected and eager for the attention Gene channeled their way. These small boys lacked discipline and took much of the meeting time disrupting the programs.

"Mom," said David, "You have to discipline these kids all the time. Why don't you just give up this group?"

David was right. But dissolving this closely-knit group was not easy. Each boy had started to enjoy the attention they needed so badly. They enjoyed the crafts which they could take home and give to their parents. But the energy and efforts Gene could devote were limited.

Tom joined the group even though younger and not in uniform.

The respect demonstrated by Gene's sons to her were evident. They were taught respect and what behavior was expected of them. Fortunately, Jack and Gene had the same disciplinary values and never were in conflict. These values learned by both Jack and Gene from their parents while they were in their formative years were paying great dividends as witnessed in their two sons. Both of these parents were excellent role models for their children. The respectful and calm discipline they learned was a very important reason why these young boys, and now grown adults, are liked by co-workers, friends, and neighbors. They can easily establish and maintain relationships in their lives.

When it came to Halloween, this always meant having Jack or Gene take their boys by auto as the homes were not close together in the country. On one occasion, Gene was dressed as big pumpkin which she had made out of orange broad cloth. She had a hula-hoop inside with a flashlight inside of this big round bunch of orange material wrapped around her. She crouched down when someone answered their door and the boys shouted, "Trick or Treat!"

"I bet you didn't know that my mother is inside that pumpkin?" said Tom.

He was five- or six-years-old and enjoyed these family outings. Gene always made orange popcorn balls as the treat which Jack passed out while they were out ringing other doorbells.

Christmas as well in Springfield continued to get a discussion. Jack and Tom had the mumps which they had gotten after David exposed them. During their illness, David had meningitis from the mumps. He was quite ill with a severe headache. The doctor saw no need for him to be hospitalized as he could be kept quite at home while recuperating. And, since Gene was an RN, she could nurse all three at the same time.

It had snowed a great deal, requiring the stoking of their coal furnace. Of course, Gene knew how and knew that Jack should not go up and down the stairs to the basement. A pharmacist friend owned a drug store nearby and Jack made arrangements for "Santa Louie" to deliver Christmas gifts for the boys and Gene.

Another Christmas brought the arrival of real cowboy outfits with cowboy hats that made stunning outfits. Jack and Gene had talked to Santa in Fort Wayne, Indiana when they visited friends that fall.

It was this Christmas that Gene remembers well for other reasons. She sat down in the big red chair in their living room.

"I bet you didn't know your gift is hidden under that chair, Mom?" said Tom.

Including Tom in on the secrets only added fun to the occasion. Gene's hidden gift turned out to be a Gruen self-winding watch. This beautiful watch worked for Gene for forty years. She guarded it with her life. In the nursing profession, someone always wanted to borrow her watch. This watch did not get off her arm.

Jack and his flying pharmacist friend, Santa Louie, had some great times flying around Ohio. Louie had his own single engine plane. Often he called Jack to fly with him to Columbus or Cleveland for a cup of coffee — and Jack didn't drink coffee.

Louie flew to Virginia to get Jack and Gene when Jack's father became quite ill in Ohio. They left the Culpeper airport before dark as there were no lights. The airport was adjacent to Jack and Gene's home in Culpeper. So they crawled over the wooden fence on a Sunday at 6:00 P.M. and headed west in this single engine plane.

"How do you know Louie that no other plane is flying toward us?" asked Gene.

"Intuition, Intuition!" replied Louie.

It was with these friends, Louie and Rita, that Jack and Gene began their bowling skills. Soon they joined bowling leagues. This was a sport in which the whole family could participate. Participate they did. They had lots of fun.

Teams were made up of a pharmacist, physician, veterinarian and dentist. This provided an opportunity for the various professions in the community to become better acquainted. Professionally, they worked on common problems in the community which involved the various professions.

Louie soon switched to helicopters much to the discouragement of Rita. She often expressed her dislike for his flying these noisy air machines.

◆ ◆ ◆

Years passed. Jack and Gene had moved on to Virginia when they learned of some very sad news. Louie and a local photographer were flying over Springfield one Sunday morning when the 'copter was described as suddenly lunging to the earth. They crashed and both were killed. What a stressful way to lose a friend and to witness the devastation to Louie's wife, Rita, and their three small sons. The good memories of the fun and joy that came into their lives by having known Louie and Rita outweighed the sorrow.

There were many memories during these five years for Gene as she developed lifetime relationships with co-workers in the operating room. It was in Springfield that Gene started back into nursing. She had worked with Jack in Forest as his assistant. This provided an opportunity for her to be at home with her two young sons, so nursing was put on hold from 1947 upon graduation until 1954. After the move to Springfield in 1953, Gene did some private duty for short surgical cases. This afforded an opportunity to regain her skills by working two to three evenings a week. Soon she was pressured by the director of nursing to increase her working days. Of course, they could use the money, as Jack's practice did not have the potential he at first thought when considering a practice in Forest. All earned money could be easily used.

This operating room gang recruited Gene for the operating room staff. This opportunity opened many new avenues. There she met some of the best surgeons in the nation. She worked with these eleven registered nurses on a full-time basis. Gene was the only RN with children, so many of the girls wanted to relieve her of the necessary on call duties.

The husbands joined the wives in card playing evenings, picnics, and fun and frolic outings. It was a fun-loving bunch. Gene had an excellent relationship with this operating room gang. They collectively wrote a poem for Gene when they learned of Jack's transfer to Frankfurt.

Farewell to Gene

Farewell ol' chap, it's really been great.
We know you'll miss this sweet darling place.
No more Watson, Jane, Betty or Katie,
Or even the extras, we send to Haiti.
Kentucky's all right, if you walk with a limp,
But, Geanne ol' gal, you'll look like a simp.
H. B.'s already been looking for others.
But, all he can find are becoming mothers.
Schanher's really been grieving a lot,
But, already La Donna's filling your spot!
Remember a few long years back,
You decided to join the OR pack,
A million times since, we've all wondered why.
But, now we found out you were Watson's spy!
But don't worry Gene, it's all in the past.
But since the words out, you better move out fast.
Imagine how it will seem, no splits, calls or scrubs
Especially when the phone rings, while in the tub.
Now dear Gene, won't you admit
You will miss us, just a little bit?
Ernie's so friendly, George's sarcasm,
Turner's hemorrhoids, say, we hear that you have 'em.
H. B. and his arterial grafts,

Menino and his hearty laugh,
Wild Bill and his monotonous screams,
And DEAR PAUL, JR. so supreme;
McLemore, since his gall bladder's out,
Has really turned out to be quite the scout.
Then dear Minor Surgery, many a day
You've spent pulling teeth, with such little pay.
Rinehart and his usual jokes,
Dear Potter, before his stroke.
We're glad for you Gene, really sincere,
We'll try and visit you; however, we fear
If any of us should happen to stop down,
Your maid would probably open the door with a frown.
And tell us the R——'s are not around.
They're spending the day at their country place.
So we would leave without a trace.
But, sincerely Gene, we'll miss you so much.
We hope you and your family Good Luck!
Make Tommy and David walk the white line.
Perhaps they'll grow up another Einstein.
Don't be cruel to dear OLD JACK.
We'd hate for you, by yourself, to move back.
The past three years you'll soon forget.
But, all your friends will remember yet
Your nice manner, sweet ways and smile
Which will certainly last for a long, long while.

(Collectively written by operating room 1959 gang)

David, Jack, Tom and Gene leave Ohio for Kentucky, 1959.

The Roths finish their new home in Kentucky, 1960

Chapter Eight:

Frankfurt, Kentucky

After nearly five enjoyable years of living at Springfield, Jack accepted an advancement in his field of regulatory veterinary medicine. He was appointed Assistant State Veterinarian for Kentucky. In 1959, Jack and Gene and two young sons moved to Frankfurt, the capital of Kentucky. It was not easy to give up their lovely home on Bird Rd. in Springfield, but they located a new home being finished on Mockingbird Drive in the Cardinal Hills Subdivision. They were really into birds again.

Jack's immediate boss, the State Veterinarian of Kentucky, was a dynamic person. He was a worker and doer. He and Jack worked well together with the needed mutual respect. Being very supportive of each other and both insisting upon the highest standards in the regulations, resulted in both of them resigning suddenly. In fact, they resigned on the same day due to their being forced to ignore principles of their work responsibilities. This all happened within the very short first year that they had worked together in Kentucky. Politics came into play in Kentucky. This was the primary reason for Jack accepting a similar position in Virginia and resigning in Kentucky.

When one is taught as a child important values and principles and learns to uphold them, it does not always make working situations enjoyable or even acceptable. Once Jack had settled into his position in Virginia while residing at Culpeper, he tried to live with the strong influence of politics in everything he did. Why did both Jack and Gene not know more about the influence of politics? Probably, they had not reached this level at which politics is such a strong influence in both their working and social worlds.

One of Gene's first encounters in Kentucky with politics occurred in her first week of living in Frankfurt. She went into town to get a Kentucky driver's license. When she failed to pass the eye exam because her glasses needed upgrading, the local police who handled the licensing process held her Ohio license. She was told to get new glasses and come back. Since she had driven there, she asked how she was expected to get home to her small children who were with an unfamiliar baby sitter. They said that they had no idea and just maybe they would not see her drive away.

Slightly upset, Gene collected her thoughts as with whom she might speak in this city since she knew no one and Jack was out of the office in the western part of the state.

Of course, she thought! I'll call a director of nursing. I am a nurse and I am sure she would want to help this out of state nurse.

So Gene called the director of nursing at the only small hospital in town from this police station where her license was being held. She was seeking the name of an opthamologist.

"Call Dr. J. and he will assist you promptly," advised this jolly and personable director of nursing." She freely filled Gene in on some details. This DON immediately interviewed Gene over the phone and learned that she had just left an operating room nurse position of three years in Springfield, Ohio.

"Oh, Honey, I do want you to come to see me about working here with us. Your experience is really great and you will have to come to work with us when you get settled," voiced this friendly DON to Gene sight unseen.

Gene called Dr. J. from the police department as just advised by this friendly DON. Soon Dr. J. was talking to the Chief of Police.

"What in the hell are you doing to a sweet nurse from Ohio?"

Within minutes Gene was at Dr. J's office. Needless to say, she surveyed every aspect of it since she was alerted by the DON. This tall, handsome, middle-aged and charming man with graying hair, greeted her and immediately, then proceeded with an eye exam. His office walls were decorated with many educational credentials. The DON had related that Dr. J. was an excellent eye surgeon. She warned of his dingy office with unkept floors and outdated furnishings. The eccentric influence was everywhere. No office nurse was present. In fact, no one but Dr. J. and Gene were in the office at the time of the examination. A large navy blue Cadillac was parked practically on the front door step of his so-called office.

With the eye exam finished, Dr. J. was calling to have the glasses made in Lexington.

"Can't you make these glasses and have them here tomorrow?" spoke Dr. J. in his authoritative manner while not taking his eyes off of Gene's whole body. He looked, but did not touch.

"Watch his hands!" warned the DON.

"Your glasses will be ready the day after tomorrow. Come to this office at 4:00 P.M. and I'll fit the glasses before I release them to you," smiled this flirtatious eye surgeon.

"If you'll wait a few minutes, I will take you home," spoke this helpful Dr. J.

Since the police chief had promised Dr. J. to treat Gene better, she was advised she could drive to her home where a new neighbor was sitting with her young sons. She thanked Dr. J. for his timely thoughtfulness and was relieved to get into her own car and head for home.

A day passed and it was time for Gene to get her new glasses. She arrived at Dr. J.'s office at four as previously advised. Dr. J. smiled and greeted Gene and walked straight toward her. As he peered down at her while holding the new glasses in his left hand, his right hand reached down toward Gene's left breast. She was wearing a Kelly green sweater, quite attractive at the age of thirty-three, with a good figure.

Watch his hands! Watch his hands! As his right hand moved toward Gene's left breast, her hands flew up into the air. Calmly and confidently Dr. J. pulled a piece of lint off of Gene's green sweater. Gene's face flushed. His eyes met hers. There was some understanding between them.

Gene traveled to her home and joined her two children. She tried to put this opthamologist out of her mind. She knew that she could not tell Jack of her encounter with Dr. J. Gene knew that if she accepted the nursing position offered her by the DON, she would be seeing Dr. J. again. He was reported to have a thriving surgical practice at this hospital. She vowed then to herself that she would forget the feelings she had experienced when her eyes met his in his office as he fitted her glasses. She knew that she was happily married. She was not looking for any relationship which could go no where. Gene also knew that the nursing profession made her vulnerable to meeting persons for whom she may experience some attraction.

Thinking about her encounter with Dr. J. reminded Gene of the time when she was a student nurse and working alone one evening in the operating room area. She was assigned to this area as she was reacting with a rash on her hands believed to have been caused by her exposure to penicillin. She gave many penicillin injections every three hours at that time.

"Oh Miss Place, I want to tell you that the paper you wrote on the obstetric exam I gave you was the best I have ever read," came this melodious voice from Dr. F.

Dr. F., fifty-five, six-feet two-inches tall, and just absolutely charming with all of the graces so needed by the most popular surgeon on the staff, was now standing next to Gene and touching her shoulders with both hands.

"You are very kind, Dr. F.," replied Gene as she slipped out of this potentially dangerous one-on-one stance.

"I need to clarify your surgical schedule with you for tomorrow," and Gene glided to the area where the secretary could become involved and provide a third person to this party.

Was Gene imagining the flutters with Dr. F.? Well, Dr. F. had five known old maid nurses who did private duty for him just to see him daily. Of course, he had a wife. Of course, his patients had the flutters for him too. Gene even recalled the days following this operating room episode that she would make sure that her hair looked good, her makeup perfect and her complete uniform exact when she knew it was time for his evening rounds at 9 P.M. She knew that he would invite her to accompany him on rounds. Student nurses were in a charge position on the evening shift during the war, because the RNs were in the service. Dr. F. would touch her arm in a manner that sent thrills through her. It was believed that the older, unmarried, private duty nurses were thrilled as well. Dr. F. passed his charm around to all.

Within a few weeks upon starting to work in the operating room in Frankfurt, Gene was scheduled to scrub with Dr. J. This eye surgeon had hands that flew. Gene had come with good experience with having scrubbed for eye surgeons at Springfield. Soon she became one of his favorite scrub nurses. He asked the supervisor to have her scrub for him on all of his cases.

Before long, Gene's management skills were recognized. The DON asked her to accept the obstetrical supervisor position. It was the plan of the DON to move out all of the staff in OB and start over with a whole new crew. OB had a very big problem. Gene did not like to work in obstetrics. Having been given charge functions early as a student nurse left her with a great fear for this stressful area. The chief of obstetrics and the DON both agreed to help her relearn the current obstetric knowledge. They pleaded with Gene to just try it for awhile.

Since Gene truly believed that one should avail themselves of all new learning opportunities, she agreed to reorganize the obstetrical department with the promised assistance. Dr. J. tried everything to block Gene's transfer from the operating room. This astute DON suspected possible motives being somewhat selfish on Dr. J.'s part, but Gene's short new obstetrical experience proved valuable. It gave Gene the opportunity to prepare herself for a position about to unfold in her future. It also impressed upon Gene's thinking that it was a good idea to try new nursing areas when the opportunity presented itself. This philosophy followed Gene everywhere in her forty years of nursing. Gene's short year at this hospital in Frankfurt ended abruptly. Jack accepted a regulatory veterinary position in Virginia after a political encounter in Frankfurt.

Left: Tom takes pictures of Tears, who joined the family in Culpepper, Virginia. Right: David holds her.

Chapter Nine:

New Life In Virginia

Jack and Gene moved to Culpeper, Virginia in 1960. Jack had gone ahead of Gene and the boys as they were to remain in Kentucky until the school year finished. Jack landed in the emergency room at Culpeper with a kidney stone. This new fifty-bed hospital would soon have a big influence on this whole family after they moved to Culpeper. Now, Jack seemed to need his family since he was feeling so much pain. So, arrangements were made to have the neighbors in Kentucky load Jack and Gene's furniture and along with other details. Gene was excused from finishing out her work notice at the hospital. Soon Gene, David, Tom, and momma cat with her kittens were riding toward Virginia.

Gene had never seen mountains, alone drive in them. She had grown up in flat northern Ohio, and in their two years in the service they had been stationed primarily in the midwest. With Gene at the helm of her old Oldsmobile and David the co-pilot, along with Tom, they were encountering their first mountains.

A severe storm accompanied them into central Virginia where they were to meet Jack. Lightening was striking all over the place as they chugged up and down one mountain after another, but they soon met Jack in the middle of the night as planned and verified that he was on the mend from his first kid-

FRANK DAWSON

Just as it is apparent that one possesses a sound body, so it is that this man possesses an exciting mind. It continues to be clear to those around him, those with whom he is working currently, that his obvious actions depict his views. His views are simply this, "I, as a person, am only as effective as the people surrounding me. People whom I teach, people whom I lead, people from whom I learn, but people whom I never push, people whom I never subjugate, whom I never treat like things."

This man can be harsh, he can be unreasonable, he can even be wrong, and is of course, the first to admit it. But he demonstrates in his day-by-day activity that man is in fact, a social animal, a failure as an island alone. He is a success in so far as he works with, cultivates, develops, but never uses the minds and hearts of others.

What is it about Frank's early environment that reflects in his actions? Why does he practice beliefs that have such tremendous impact on the nursing profession? If we all agree with Wordsworth's views that the child is the father of the man, then we must recognize that we are all products of the society which conditions us in our youth. This is so evident in my own personal life and the lives of our children. So it is with Frank. The parental care he received as a small boy in the Missouri cotton-gin-town of Deering, where his father was superintendent of a switch railroad, is part of his basic pillars. Likewise, his mother was a dispenser of loving help and healing to all displaying these needs. His growth and development were strengthened with these bright parents.

Frank was educated and grew up as a Catholic under the influence of the dynamic masculine experience while attending a Christian Brothers High School in Chicago. There the Brothers were famous for both the rigidity of their discipline and the warmth of their manly affection for the boys they were trying to prepare to become men. Because he anticipated the retirement of his parents and their moving to Florida, Frank enrolled in the University of Florida. He had time for one year of college prior World War II. As a young man, he volunteered for service in the Air Force.

After the close of the war, he returned to the University of Florida — this time with his beautiful wife, Jackie. He had met and married Jackie in New Mexico. They both majored in accounting. He graduated cum laude with a degree in business administration.

His business career after college began with an executive position with the Burroughs Corporation in Jacksonville. A critical factor in his life was his decision to leave the office machine business to take any savings that he had been able to amass and take a young family, his wife, and two children and return to college, this time in Virginia. Here he earned a Masters Degree in Hospital Administration from the Medical College of Virginia. This was followed by a one-year residency at the University of Virginia. He functioned as an administrative assistant for one and one-half years. Soon he became an assistant director of the University Hospitals. As an Assistant Director, he was involved in a five hundred bed expansion program. This preparation certainly readied him for the administrator position at Culpeper Memorial Hospital. There he directed the building and opening of this new and popular hospital. It was in Culpeper that his life began another era.

It was in Culpeper that I got in step with his band, but I am ahead of my story. Let us reflect upon the source of Frank's love for his fellowman. The close family relationship he shared with his parents as well as observing the love between his parents is repeated in his own personal life. He often displayed deep affection for his wife and children. He was envied by those without secure relationships in their lives. These assets and forces add additional fuel to this man's drive and ultimate happiness. Experiencing love makes it easier for him to transmit love to those with whom he contacts. This rich parental devotion gleaned as a child is a marvelous and priceless inheritance, for which no price in dollars can be matched.

The effectiveness of our being is the expression of our sense of values. This man is worth as much as the things with which he busies himself. Frank's deep conviction that the important meaning in life is to be able to do something so well for needy people gives him the zest to excel in leadership abilities. He is at the head of the class. He is out front in everything he tackles, but how does all this relate to Gene?

Let us start with the first hospital he developed and managed. This hospital was at Culpeper, Virginia. Here Gene witnessed his philosophy in operation. He believed that true management is concerned with the development of people. The better each of his department heads or employees produces, the better and bigger man he becomes. In order to make a business move, power and or money must be provided. An organization moves because its people move. Things get done through people and through the leadership of people. As a nurse on his team, Gene soon realized what he expected from the nursing staff. All of the employees soon realized their roles as they desperately tried to gain his approval.

Seeking a father's (or father figure's) approval was Gene's primary force in achievement. Not only did Gene's dad have the same skills as Frank, but he also implanted in his children the need to perform these skills. So when Gene and Frank functioned together, they understood where the other was coming from. This was not always the case for some of the team members who failed to follow Frank or get in step with him.

At the same time while trying to gain his approval, some employees were just a bit afraid of Frank as it was with Gene's Dad. If one didn't get in step soon (and were not trying to improve academically or performance wise), he would lose interest in you. Frank was very direct. You knew at all times just where you stood with him. He never left you with a vague moment. If you didn't care to improve yourself, enjoy the people around you, make a few sacrifices, and forget being so darn self-important, then you were going to be looking for a new job soon. Not that he came up with "You're fired!" You would find yourself out-of-step. Your drum would be playing to a different beat, and you would go marching off to another place.

He displays a keen sense for quality care. This includes the medical care as well as the nursing care. Likewise, the rigid code of this administrator demands absolute cleanliness in all areas at all times. His belief that a cluttered desk indicates a cluttered mind stayed with Gene. So at day's end, Gene's desk drawers opened and the desktop was cleared. Even today, she practices this skill. Out-of-sight for the sake of reducing the clutter in both the mind and the environment was required. His home, his person, and those with whom he socializes reflects his esthetic values.

It was Emerson who said, "What you are thunders so loud, I can't hear what you say."

Mixed with his esthetic sense is his sense of humor. (Realizing that an analogy between actual and factual is of essence here.) Consider the effect Cleopatra had on men. Pascal said in his Penises: "Cleopatra's nose, had it been shorter, the whole aspect of the world would have been altered."

But perhaps Pompeii, Caesar and Anthony would have found her undoubted intelligence, her personality and her appeal irresistible no matter what the length of her nose. Persons who knew Frank soon learned of his sensitivity to the shape of his nose. Actually, he is a handsome man with deep penetrating eyes regardless of what is parked between his eyes. With eyes like these, who looks at his nose?

His management style puts the focus on the development of

mankind. He displays a great understanding of human behavior. Meaningful work, mutual respect, honest communication and continuous learning opportunities are the ingredients stimulating the personnel around him.

◆ ◆ ◆

Frank and Gene were once seen outside this hospital near the front door. They were planting flowers and designing a lovely garden. Attention soon was on what they were doing. Gene's fairly advanced gardening skills surfaced. Frank always provides an opportunity for those around him to display their skills in knowledge other than their profession. Cultural skills surface everywhere in this hospital as the staff developed and presented a fundraising program, The Follies. The community became involved. All of Frank's projects were sponsored. Local artists continue to display their works in the hospital lobby.

As Frank moved on to bigger things and larger hospitals, Jack and Gene visited him in Florida. This seven hundred-bed hospital was managed similarly to the fifty-bed hospital in Culpeper. Gene was escorted with apparent pride and introduced as one of his previous Directors of Nursing. He continued to call the names of each employee as they walked forward. He recognized the work they were doing at the time. He was keenly into what was going on and it showed that he cared for the people doing the work. Frank walked Gene to her auto where he said good-bye after they had finished their visit.

This good-bye was forever. Having grown in stature in the public and the nation professionally did not prevent the tragedy Frank was to experience. Frank was on official business for the National Administrator's Committee as he flew out of a little town in an effort to get to Atlanta. He sensed that he should not fly on this stormy day. All efforts to seek other than air transportation failed. With reluctance, he boarded this plane. This plane soon crashed in a terrible storm. All aboard were killed in the 1977 crash.

Shock for Gene and all who knew him and loved him prevailed over the miles. The community of Boca Raton remained in denial for some time. Everyone soon recognized that Frank had lived life with zest and at a fast pace that seemed that he may have know that his early death would come to pass.

Is he missed? Of course. All who marched to his drum will never forget him. If you walked with him on the path to excellence, you had to go on and apply what he taught you. This is the way with life. Parents teach their children, so their values never die. So many lives were changed for the better because of their association with Frank. He left a legacy almost too large to fathom.

◆ ◆ ◆

But Culpeper will always be remembered for other sweet harvests. A true family treasure was given to Tom for his birthday while at Culpeper. Jack located a boxer puppy who became known as Tears because she cried several days when they were trying to name her. Tears became a real friend to all in this close knit family. The pictures reveal the pride and joy she brought to this family for many future years. Much love is expressed from all members of this family as they give Tears much attention for years.

Jack introduces Tom and David to Virginia Tech

Custom built home on Castlebridge Road, 1970

Chapter Ten:

Richmond, Virginia 1962

After Jack and Gene and their boys moved to Richmond in 1962, Jack continued his successful endeavors in the regulatory field. The Virginia Agriculture Department and the United States Animal Health Services were well aware of Jack's contributions and capabilities. Jack served as chairman of the National Brucelosis and Tuberculosis committees. These two appointments offered him an opportunity to travel to different areas in the United States. Jack traveled to Miami, Las Vegas, San Diego, Minneapolis, Buffalo, Denver, Dallas, Roanoke, Salt Lake City, Louisville and Nashville to name some of the interesting cities. Gene accompanied him whenever her working schedule permitted. While Jack was busy in meetings, Gene toured the cities with the one hundred and fifty women who accompanied their husbands at these large United States Animal Disease Conventions.

Jack and Gene had two houses for sale when they moved to Virginia. They held the one in Kentucky for four years before finding a good buyer. They also purchased an adjacent lot to this home to provide more room for their children to play. They lined their property with small maple trees which they had brought from Ohio. These trees were watched yearly whenever they drove to Frankfurt to check on this property on their way to visit family in Ohio. Finally they sold this home to the family who had initially rented it. On their last visit while attending a convention in Louisville, Jack and Gene had difficulty finding Cardinal Hills where their home was to be.

"Where is the Cardinal Hills subdivision?" Jack inquired of a man working in his garden.

"It's under Interstate 64 over there," replied the stranger as he pointed in another direction.

"They destroyed the last two streets of homes when they put the highway through here."

"That can't be," Gene cried out as if in agony and disbelief. "What did they do with our maple trees? Where did they put the rock garden that I engineered so carefully along the breezeway of our tri-level brick home?"

"Well, all of that had to go. You know when a highway department decides to take your property, they don't care that someone may have a real caring for the property. They believe that sufficient money for the property will take care of everything!" spoke this man as he moved away from their auto.

"How will we ever tell David and Tom about what has happened to 'our' Kentucky home?" (It is always your home even after you sell it.)

Upon recounting the events of their trip to their sons, they informed them of how their home in Kentucky was now under Interstate 64.

"What about our trees?" said David.

"How could anyone do that to trees?" chirped in Tom.

The routine in Richmond was resumed and their Kentucky house became a memory. Their new home in Richmond was welcomed since they had not lived in one of their own homes for the past two years while at Culpeper. Not living in their own home was deeply felt by this family.

◆ ◆ ◆

David and Tom grew into adulthood. They both graduated from the same high school, Huguenot, only a few miles from this home. It was considered an excellent school at that time. Later it became annexed into Richmond and lost its status and quality of education.

Both of their sons dated very little while in high school. When they were in college at Virginia Tech, two girls picked them off. Each of them were married after their graduation from college.

When Jack and Gene saw their two sons graduate and leave home, they learned to let them go. This is the way of life. This close family has remained a good example of a secure family even as their two sons are now parents with their children.

◆ ◆ ◆

Suddenly, Jack learned that his father was found dead in Ohio in a chair at their home in front of the television by his mother who had been out babysitting. This was on November 29, a few days after Thanksgiving. This necessitated moving Jack's mother to Richmond. Jack was an only child. His mother did not make friends well and isolated herself from everyone. She came from Scotland as a young adult. His dad came from Switzerland at the age of twenty-five, so there were no other family members close by during this crisis. His parents had met in Illinois when they had come to this country. Jack was born at Deerfield in 1922. His mother was very dependent on Jack's Dad. She did not drive. Had never worked away from their farm home, so the alternative was to get her settled near Jack and Gene in Richmond.

Eventually Jack and Gene decided to build a new home with an apartment for his mother. They were guided by David to a

♦102♦ *M. Georgene Roth*

Reflections of David's years

David's life and family

Tom's early years in progression

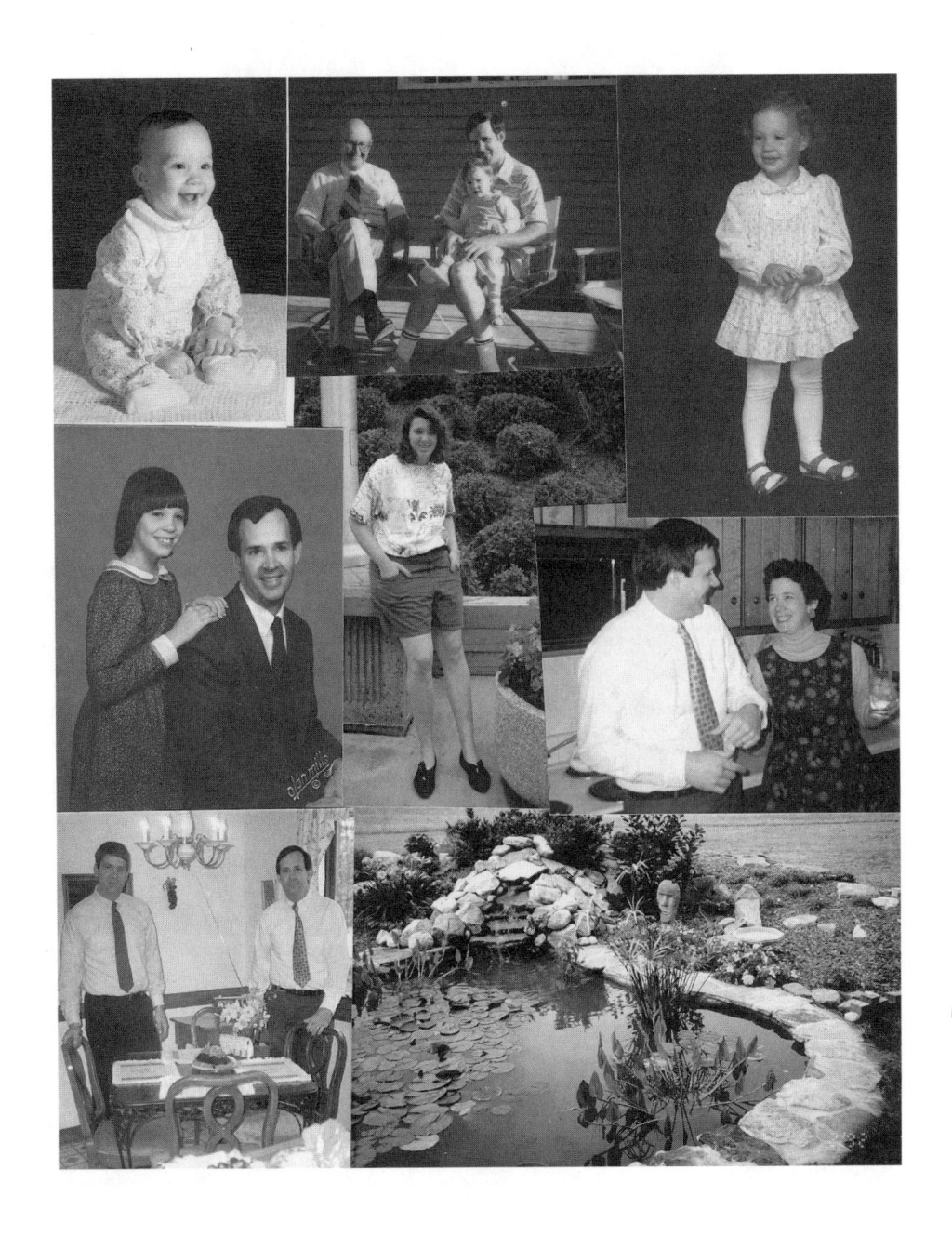

Tom moves on with his life.

Top photo: The backyard at Castlebridge
Bottom photo: Castlebridge aquarium, admired by Allison

new subdivision, Salisbury, through a friend he had met in college at Virginia Tech. A new golf course about to be built there was the primary influence. A lovely lot was selected on the top of a hill that backed up to the proposed fifteenth green. They paid $12,000 for this lot which seemed a terrific amount of money. One acre for this price seemed too much to these farm-oriented new owners. Next, they designed a colonial home and found an architect who worked for a builder starting out on his own and built a good home in 1970.

Since this home backed up to the fifteenth green, if Jack and Gene could find enough money to join the club, they would become charter members. Well, the money came along. From that point, the whole family became golfing enthusiasts. For the next eighteen years when Jack and Gene lived in their lovely home, they played golf and gardened every minute they could devote to these two loves.

David never really lived in this new house since he was in college at Virginia Tech. Tom started to college when the house was being built. However, he spent summers landscaping the backyard. There were always outside aquariums that had the cement poured when the foundation of the homes were formed. Each small pool had to be four-feet deep so the fish could hibernate during the winter.

Jack and Gene worked extremely hard trying to get the grass started. Their midwest background dictated that they have lots of grass. Early in February, 1971, Jack and Gene worked hard in the new yard to the point of them both having aching arms that evening. It was this big factor that seemed to contribute to Jack having a coronary, early on a Tuesday morning around 3:00 A.M. He had also had a tooth extraction on Monday.

It was a frightening time when Jack had this heart attack at the age of forty-seven. They had lived in their new home nearly one year. Jack made a remarkable recovery. Soon he was working his ten to twelve hour days. His co-workers had related that working with Dr. Roth could kill you. He seemed to love to work, expected to see all around him work as well as those under his supervision. His clients viewed him as a very effective professional. He was known to always follow through on everything he tackled.

Time passed. The grandchildren came to visit. They loved to accompany Grandpa as he golfed daily. He would undress from work and change clothing, grab his electric golf bag and set out for the golf course. The last of the golfers had cleared the course in the early evening hours, so no one was disturbed with this ritual. Many times Gene would take her golf bag and join him on the five holes they routinely played. Being one of the charter members who had battled many local children as they attempted to vandalize this prestigious course qualified him, at least he thought so, to play by starting from his back door.

His constant companion was Tears, their adorable boxer dog. Tom received this tiny puppy in 1960 for his birthday shortly after they had moved to Virginia. Tears made the transition to the new home with some difficulty. The first night had caused her great stress unknown to Jack and Gene until the following morning. Her new home was in the mudroom. Good insulation had prevented them hearing her stress, but during the night, she had chewed the frames of the doors in an effort to escape. This home was not a surprise to her.

From the initial stage of this house building project, Jack and Gene came everyday to see the progress being made. Tears always led them to the car the minute they got home from work. They drove the somewhat winding country roads with her eagerly watching for the sight of the new home. She would always jump out of the auto, walk the entire building, upstairs and down like a hired inspector. When this ritual was finished, she would go to their auto, bark impatiently, and expect them to leave for their old home when she barked demandingly. This went on for six months, but the first night she had expected to return to her old home. After that one terrible night she seemed content to dwell in her new home with Jack and Gene near her.

Gene has always loved to fish, so the ponds on the golf course had to be checked out by her. The pond behind their home was little, but deep. It was known to have bass and blue gills as well as copperhead snakes. Some of the golfers encountered the quiet copperheads and occasionally a dead one would be laid on the golf path to warn other golfers. She taught her three grandchildren how to put a worm on and catch the fish when they had a good bite. We understand the golf pro was unhappy with Gene's fishing there.

"You need to stop fishing here Gene," said the golf pro. "You have caught all of those fish five times!"

Buzz off Frank, I'll not get hit by a golfball, or concern any golfer who is trying to tee off above pond. Get lost Frank as I do plan to continue fishing here.

"Forget my fishing Frank. Look at the beautiful garden we have designed, planted and cared for so the golfers could enjoy as they pass near our backyard. Why don't you comment on the beauty we have created and forget my fishing?" she often told Frank whenever he brought up the subject of fishing. She knew how to distract, and it seemed to work over the years.

The bottom line or the underlying importance to Frank was that Jack and Gene didn't play up to Frank. They didn't play politics or feed his ego. They were not the social climbers to which Frank seemed so eager to cling. Whenever they did play golf with the mixed couples on Friday evenings, they were introduced repeatedly as newcomers since they didn't socialize at the club. They were not antisocial. They just loved to play

Jack, with his son and grandchildren amd Jack's golf ball collection

golf, garden and enjoy their home and family without the involvement of the club.

Jack's health seemed fine until 1978. He presented with chest pain which required open heart surgery. Jack accepted this surgery and expressed full confidence that he would make it as he was wheeled off to surgery at The Medical College of Virginia. He recovered quickly and soon was walking his miles every night after work. Day or night he walked the golf course. He soon learned to know where every rut or dip was as he walked these miles. He persevered and took the stress off his family.

Retirement became the topic of discussion. The need to get out of a bickering office situation with little evidence of colleague support, made Gene talk up retirement in a few years. They realized that a smaller home, less gardening on a flat lot was indicated and desirable. Gene drew plans for one whole year as they tried to convince themselves that they could leave this home they loved so much.

Soon, they had selected a flat lot in a nearby planned community. They both were fond of the golf pro at this location. They sought out the builder who had built this big colonial for them and discussed his building another custom home for them. Plans were finalized with some modern features, mostly traditional design inside with a one floor plan.

The building program began with many frustrating problems never anticipated nor witnessed in the previous building project. However, this builder was now building thirty homes instead of three as he was doing eighteen years earlier. He was now using acceptable supplies, but not the quality he used in their colonial house in Salisbury.

When a set of assembled rafters were left on the property after it was determined they were cut and assembled wrong, it was Gene who had to contact the lumber official and demand they be removed.

"What do you want me to do with them lady? Do you want me to chop up the wood rafters and destroy them?" this hostile man was yelling back at Gene on the phone while he represented top management of this lumber company.

"Why Mr. D., I can't believe that you would destroy property that could be cut down by someone trying to save money and utilize supplies effectively. You are yelling at me. Please stop your yelling and listen to me. You will have those rafters removed from this property by 5:00 P.M. today." Gene spoke calmly but firmly.

"Just how do you think I will get that done today?" responded this example of a southern gentleman not really willing or ready to deal with a female who holds people accountable.

"This is your problem. You should have the same resources that put the rafters here in the first place. I'll be checking our lot at 5:00 P.M. and I'm sure that you will have those rafters removed by that hour," and Gene said good-bye and ended the conversation.

Gene had heard her Dad speak in this manner when he directed a project. He expected his children to learn from him.

At 4:00 P.M. that day, the rafters were hauled away. When the builder came to the lot on his scheduled and prompt rounds, he never commented on the missing rafters. A previous discussion Gene had with him ended in the builder relating that he could do nothing to get the rafters removed. At that time, Gene told him she knew how and since he was not accepting his own responsibility she would intervene. This was the builders' reason for not giving the rafter discussion anymore attention. The missing rafters were never a topic of discussion again.

Gene had seen problems dealt with on the farm as a kid by her Dad in the very same manner. The problem was resolved and forgotten. No time was devoted to beating up anyone on already resolved problems. To never dwell on what was once a problem that had been resolved was a practice welcomed by all of us as we grew up.

Unspoken Love ♦113♦

The retirement home on McTyres Cove Road is built.

The retirement house becomes a home.

And so the building project moved on and the retirement home took shape with all of its trials and errors. Soon it would be their new home.

◆ ◆ ◆

After Jack and Gene moved into their retirement home in Brandermill in October, 1987, Jack made earnest plans to retire effective December, 1987. He kept busy trying to do some of the things he had on hold until February, 1988. On this gray, rainy Friday afternoon they were driving to their attorney to finish some transaction. Gene was following Jack in his car as Jack was driving their new Buick. Suddenly, without any warning or break lights, Jack veered off to the right, down a big ditch as the Buick bounced across an open field. This four-lane road was packed with traffic traveling at least forty miles per hour. Gene was trying to get stopped on the roadside where she could run to Jack and see what had happened.

Within seconds, Jack drove down this field, and up on the road, passing Gene who was parked on the right side in shock. He pointed ahead as she followed him while becoming more alarmed for his safety. He eventually pulled off into the parking area of a shopping center. When Gene reached him, he acknowledged that he did not feel well. His pulse was irregular and thready. He clarified his reasons for leaving the road.

"Suddenly I had the feeling of a vice holding my head. Everything turned black. I don't remember anything else. But, I don't feel well now."

Without hesitation, Gene was driving Jack to their physician's office which was closer than the emergency room. They left his car parked at the shopping center. His doctor was not in the office at the time, but his partner quickly assessed Jack's condition while hearing the details of what had just happened.

Immediately, plans were made to have Jack admitted to the cardiac unit where he could be monitored. It was concluded that the electrical system of his heart caused the blacking out episode. When would it happen again? Could it cause sudden death? As Gene recalled her nursing knowledge she did realize that sudden death was a real possibility.

◆ ◆ ◆

Jack was being treated for lymphoma which was diagnosed three years earlier. He had gone through chemotherapy without even one nauseating minute. He did not lose even a small amount of hair. It did not seem to affect his energy level. He had managed to work his regular schedule for the three years prior to his recent retirement. Gene had found all of the enlarged lymph nodes throughout Jack's body shortly after Jack had concluded an eight month stretch handling the Avian Influenza problem for Virginia. (He directed this project for the state of Virginia from their established headquarters in Harrisonburg.) During these months he had worked seven days per week and at least twelve hours per day. At that time, he showed no lack of energy and seemed to get recognition from the avian industry for his dedicated efforts.

Night sweats seemed to be the only symptom prior to the diagnosis of the lymphoma. The lymphoma was managed by the oncologist. This new cardiac problem was tackled with various new medicines in order to try to correct the electrical system of his heart. He reacted to the medicines with nausea, bloating, and a severely sore mouth. His blood count was erratic. He was given many units of blood in order to maintain body defenses. All of this medical management was done by various physicians in the medical group, depending upon who was on call. At times, it seemed that the left hand did not know what the right hand was doing. Both Gene and Jack let this physician group know they had some concerns in the management Jack's care.

Jack was discharged between the four admissions to the Cardiac step-down unit from February to May. He seemed alarmed for himself for the first time as he dealt with many serious health problems. He lost strength as his exercise program was curtailed. He didn't hear from his former office now that he was retired. They didn't even call or visit in order to give him some much-needed emotional support. It was while in one of those low ebbs that he expressed his regret of having retired. The support system long experienced from co-workers no longer existed. He felt like a man without a country. Work was so important in his life. His family was equally important, but he needed both during a crisis illness. Gene tried to boost his thinking by again reviewing why he had retired.

Jack's working world was always very stressful. Top management had changed and apparently was for the worse. It never was a serious supportive management. Everyone was suspicious of each other and especially if one were receiving more recognition than the other. This didn't hinder Jack from achieving, but when clients preferred having him to discuss various health care problems in animal health, the flag went up in his superiors' minds. Jack always saw the top appointments in his division as political rather than capable. Jack continued to believe that if you were honest, did not play politics, and worked hard, you would advance and that would give you satisfaction. Truly, this is what he believed and his actions reflected this philosophy. Gene concurred with him as these were exactly her views also. This commonality in their thinking was one very important factor in the solidarity of their marriage.

But he had retired. His sons devoted much attention to encouraging him to get well so they could play golf. So he sought out and agreed to have an angioplasty procedure to improve his

Recognitions for Jack of his achievements

vascular problem. This was designed to stretch his blood vessels and permit a better flow of blood to the heart muscle. Even though the original problem was identified as being electrical, the cardiologist started Jack thinking on this path.

The angioplasty procedure was agreed upon without it being discussed with Gene. Jack was to be moved to Henrico hospital from St. Mary's hospital for this procedure. The main reason was that a cardiac surgeon would be available if open heart surgery were indicated during the angioplasty procedure. Jack agreed to have the anterior of his heart done on the first day, and the posterior part the following day, Friday.

David and Tom were called by Jack from St. Mary's hospital the night before he was to have this procedure at Henrico hospital the next morning. The boys related to Gene that Jack had advised them that he thought they needed to come and be with their mother. Tom arrived early the next morning from Raleigh before Jack was transferred to Henrico hospital. Gene arrived early to follow Jack through the transfer. She had worked the night before at McGuire Veteran's Hospital as she adjusted her working schedule during Jack's recent multiple hospital admissions. She was very tired trying to be at the hospital, keeping their home and working a full-time schedule. She was very anxious about Jack having this procedure. You see the discussion regarding this procedure had taken place with Jack and his physician without Gene being present. This had never happened before in any of his hospital visits. She did not know why she had feelings of doom. Since the procedure was scheduled for later on that day, Jack encouraged both her and Tom to go rest and come back before he went for the procedure.

She drove to David's home who lived fairly close to Henrico. She could not locate their house key, and so tried to nap in the back seat of her car. She awakened suddenly with a sudden fright and sense of flight. She drove straight to the hospital. Jack was not there. Tom said that the doctors started earlier than planned. The doctor did not seem to care that Gene had not gotten to see Jack before taking him to the operating room. That the family was always to be with the patient before leaving for surgery was essential in Gene's views. Gene had not been there to say good-bye to Jack.

David arrived from his work and was disturbed also to learn that he too had not seen his Dad before he went to the cardiac surgical area. So, together David, Tom and Gene tried to cope in the waiting area with various surface talk. They heard a call for a code in the area in which they were working on Jack. With Gene's experience as a supervisor and in operating room, she revealed her concern to their sons. She alerted her sons that things might not be going well for Jack. They were all worried. They had not seen this fear from their mother as they waited together on numerous occasions while their Dad had experienced surgery.

Soon a nursing supervisor came to their waiting room to identify the Roth family. She advised them to stay where they were and she would be back. Her face revealed great stress. Gene's heart sank as she could read the face of this supervisor. Gene had been in a similar position many times when she had to be a part of delivering bad news to a family.

They were ushered into the doctor's lounge adjacent to the cardiac surgical area. The doctor came out to deliver the devastating news.

"Dr. R. died while I was doing the procedure. He was in excruciating pain. I gave him pain medicine and continued to the posterior portion of the heart in an effort to relieve his pain," stated this non-personable cardiologist.

"You didn't have the right to do the posterior procedure as my dad had not agreed upon this plan," quickly responded David as he looked the cardiologist straight in the eye. All three of Jack's family members wanted some answers.

"So, I made a mistake," the surely cardiologist stated abruptly.

"You agreed to divide this procedure because you had previously decided that doing the whole procedure in one day would be too much for my husband. Is that not right and the reason for this plan?" battled back Gene.

"Did you do the angioplasty?"

"Of course, I did." he replied.

Gene had seen one of the physician's partners scurry out of the operating room area just as they were going into the physician's lounge. It was made perfectly clear by both Gene and Jack that this doctor was to have been dismissed from the case days ago. They were suspicious that this doctor may have done the procedure against their instructions. The authorized cardiologist was dressed in a clean scrub suit when they saw him just as though he had just put it on.

"One of your partners, whom we had advised was not to take care of Dr. R. was leaving this area in a hurry as we came in here. What was he doing here? We had made it quite clear to you and stated the reasons we did not want him on this case," Gene stated in anger and sorrow. *They are not telling us the truth, she thought.*

When ushered in to view Jack's body, the three of them saw a distraught staff standing in disbelief. They tried to convey to Gene and her sons through their eyes since they were wearing masks that something went wrong. Gene was quick to pick up on the quietness of the staff. They knew something they were forbidden professionally to relate to this bereaved family. *What did they know that might have caused Jack's death? thought Gene.* It is understood that the physician is the one to tell the family details regarding the death. But, this staff wanted to tell Gene, David and Tom something that the doctor did not or would not tell them.

A funeral was planned. Gene's family came from Ohio and North Carolina. Jack had no close living relatives other than his wife, sons and three grandchildren. The funeral was small and held on Sunday of Memorial Day weekend. Jack's desire to be cremated was carried out. His business colleagues, and golfing buddies came to the funeral home and service. They sadly expressed regret at not having been more supportive to Jack from the onset of his recent life-threatening episodes up to his death. These regrets came a little too late for Jack to experience their feelings. Still, they were supportive to David, Tom and Gene after his death.

Gene and her two sons tried to deal with the questions surrounding Jack's death. Gene's family felt the cardiac specialist should be sued for malpractice. Gene felt that if she pursued this avenue, the whole medical profession would refuse to care for her should the need arise. This is how the system is believed to work, so no suit took place regarding delving into the unanswered questions surrounding the cause of Jack's death. The post did not reveal any rupture of vessels as the cardiologist had suspected. Jack's death came too soon. One is never sure of not being a part to someone's error. Man can make errors and that is what Gene, David and Tom have tried to conclude and accept. They know that Jack is gone. They all have many loving memories, and these beautiful memories will live on.

Jack knew he was loved. He was hugged and informed by his wife and two sons that they loved him. He had taught them how to express and show love. Love in this family was really known. Gene learned to express her love which her own family had never learned to do.

Next page: From Gene's Christmas card, 1988

AN ISLAND OF BEAUTY

No man is an island! But he can create one. Jack molded and nurtured an idea to add beauty for all of us to enjoy.

The flowing fountain enhance this Island with its stately and stylish design. In the aquarium below, fish glide freely as though life were so easy. Water lilies bloom in yellow, pink and white splendor —

But the blossoms fade as quickly as one's life.

Mounds of flowers keep blooming in spite of the heat and draught.

A large willow oak tree seems to command this Island, but at times bows to the style and grace of the smoke tree and lacy maple planted at its side.

At dusk, the Island is lighted; the fountain looks stately and confident.

This Island represents joy, beauty, love and privacy as was the man who wanted to care for it and see that others enjoyed his work of art.

His strength of mind, in the absence of health, propelled him to pursue a better quality of life. Sudden death during a cardiac procedure in May ended the many pursuits of this determined man. His loss to us will never be erased. But so many loving memories will always remain.

Yes, the Island is groomed and planted. The fountain will flow; the fish will flourish; the lights will glow; the trees will shelter and we, as his family, will be strong and proud of his thoughtfulness.

For what is life about if it isn't for the good we do and the love we share? This Island represents a true giving. Jack knew we loved him dearly as we shared our love and feelings so freely. Yes, we gave too.

Now, we share our Island with you and yours, Christmas time is the time to share with friends and loved ones.

Fondly, Georgene Roth, 1988

Memorial to Jack

Chapter Eleven:

Achievements

Gene's first working experience in Richmond offered her an opportunity to move into the area of teaching diploma student nurses. Having only her diploma in nursing was the topic of discussion of her other instructor peers. Some of these instructors had little to no experience in nursing application. The director of this school of nursing was quick to defend Gene's position. She had hired her for her clinical knowledge. This was the primary asset she was hired for as an instructor in this diploma-nursing program.

Gene constantly measured the skills of administration in every facility in which she worked. The director of the school was always put under pressure by the hospital administration to use students in a service situation for staffing the hospital. She would stand up for the fact that they were there for nursing education and not to supply nursing staff for service. Old-time schools of nursing used student nurses to provide free care while the hospital continued to charge the patients for the cost of care. These diploma students in Richmond paid tuition equal to college students studying in other fields. They had no obligations to supply free nursing service in exchange for their tuition. Susan and Gene paid a small fee for their three-year diploma-nursing education as they worked hard during these years by providing free nursing service during their nursing education in the 1940s in Ohio.

Gene began her formal education in an effort to get her Bachelor of Science in Nursing in 1967. She started evening classes at the local college, while continuing to teach at the school of nursing where she began in 1962. Starting with English 101 offered an opportunity for creative composition that she found to be a lot of fun and a chance for her known creative flair. Gene needed to work, as David was in college and with Tom soon to begin college.

She began her full time college pursuits, and was hired as a Director of Inservice Education for twenty hours a week. She started their first inservice endeavor. Before long, Gene and the administrator disagreed on important management principles and Gene resigned. She then accepted a position at the Medical College of Virginia, nationally known as MCV, where she was a senior getting her BSN. She taught licensed practical nurses to scrub for obstetrical cases. This combined her previous teaching, obstetrical and operating room experiences.

Graduating from MCV qualified Gene for a position that was new in this country. Being hired as an assistant director for planning the new hospital was a real challenge for Gene. This position offered her another new working situation in which she utilized much of her previous experiences and knowledge. She knew how to read plans by having seen her dad construct homes. She proceeded toward achieving a Masters' Degree in Hospital Administration part-time while working full-time as this planner. She was about to realize one of her goals. Having achieved her BSN and ultimately a master's, her goal seemed closer. Gene always believed that nursing was a victim of poor hospital administration. Hospital administration was a field that few females entered in the seventies. When she was accepted into the hospital administration program, she was told that she was the oldest and besides that she was a female. She started this program in January, 1971 after graduating with her BSN from the Medical College of University. She dropped these plans suddenly in February when Jack was hospitalized with critical health problems. Financial priorities changed her immediate goals. She did take graduate courses later at the University of Richmond in an effort to gain an MBA. But health problems arose for both of them and she put those plans on hold.

Gene's two sons reflect the values they were taught by their parents. Their parents were taught by their parents....and so it goes. David's two sons and Tom's daughter try to operate with these values. But today it seems much harder for teenagers to adhere to principles and values once thought essential. We could speculate as to the causes. It becomes apparent to some of us that few parents today learned these values as kids. It is very important for both the father and mother to have similar value systems in order to not cause conflict when raising their children. So how can one teach their children values they never learned? Peer pressure today seems to be the norm and sometimes bumps values of the parents unless learned well.

David and Tom each received a good education. Both graduated from Virginia Tech — two hundred miles west of Richmond. David received his Master's Degree in business administration after graduating in electrical engineering. Many additional classes in nuclear engineering makes him a well qualified Senior Engineer at Virginia Power.

David married Barbara after he graduated in engineering. Their two sons are adults now. Eric is a student in computer engineering at Virginia Tech. Bryan is still exploring vocational avenues. Formal education hasn't appealed to him as yet. As soon as he realizes that an education means more financial gain, he will collect his forces and possibly enroll in college.

Bryan is outgoing and friendly to everyone. He has a new girlfriend as soon as one tries to attach herself to him. His flirtatious eyes seem to attract the opposite sex. He is quite aware of losing his hair as a young adult. At the age of twenty three, he has a definite receding forehead. He tries to wear his baseball cap flipped back. Gene learned to love Jack even when he became bald on top. But even today people are non-accepting of balding. Bryan probably inherited bald genes from both grandfathers. Gene tries to make him feel that bald is beautiful. She believes this. So far, he does not buy her story. Gene tries to tell Bryan that Grandpa Jack's losing his hair only made him more handsome and distinguished. There was a time when Gene and Jack agreed to go separate ways whenever Jack became bald, and Gene lost her teeth. Well, they declared a truce when both happened at the same time. (Jack had beautiful teeth and Gene prided her lovely hair likely from her father's genes.)

Tom continues to display a marvelous sense of humor. He has a creative flair that is often reflected in his horticulture endeavors. Tom graduated from Ferrum Methodist College with an associate's degree. He started at Virginia Tech in architecture. Both Jack and Gene advised Tom of this field since it was predicted to pay well. But soon Tom was graduating in Horticulture. The advent of the fuel shortage at that time caused Tom to change his vocational field. He became proficient as a computer programmer.

Tom's marriage to Phyllis took place at Virginia Tech shortly after Tom graduated. Allison was born soon after Tom and Phyllis built a small, comfortable home a short distance from Richmond. Allison was a precious child and as an adult continues to be the apple of Tom's eye. This marriage did not last. Tom coped with his divorce for nearly ten years. He devoted his life toward spending weekends with Allison. He is firm with her in a quiet way. They seem to have mutual respect and enjoy each other's company.

Mutual friends introduced Tom to Gray — his present wife. She is a first grade school teacher and does special education for selected children. They have a lovely home with acreage that affords him a space for his creative landscaping pursuits. His outside aquarium with beautiful landscaping is in view of their kitchen and eating area. Elizabeth, Allison's dog, lives with Tom. She loves to eat the fish food as she reaches into the water. Her long hair covers her eyes and hangs from her chin drips with the water from his pond. She drags apples and pears around the yard after they have fallen off the trees. She is shut in her doghouse at night so she does not bark at the critters in the moonlight. Roaming deer are a challenge for her in the night hours.

Gray has two children from her first marriage. They have learned to love Tom and his caring ways. He gives a lot of himself to others. He has never made an enemy. David's boys are crazy about Tom. He always finds time to play with the young set. He rarely gives commands. He reminds Gene of her brother, Bill. Their response to the happenings around them is "It's okay."

In addition to Tom's degree in horticulture, Tom prepared himself to work as a computer programmer. He is very alert to his surroundings. Everything gets his attention. Nothing escapes his eyes. He and Allison find time to visit Gene on weekends. He treasures this time with Allison and she recognizes that he is a good father. Tom is always trying to get Gene to view the latest funny video. But when Gene goes to sleep, you can hear Tom saying, "Mom, wake up." There is the usual discussion as to deciding if it was Trendy or Gene who was snoring. When, in fact, it was likely that both were snoring.

Tom enjoys visiting museums when time permits. While visiting Gene one weekend they went searching for the old train station in Richmond that now houses the Science Museum. Locating this terminal brought memories to Tom of his train trip one Christmas when Jack, Gene, David, and he went to Ohio. They had planned well in advance to give these boys a train trip. When they boarded in Richmond to go to Washington, it became predictable of the crowded conditions they would soon be experiencing.

Heavy snows and severe cold weather had hit the Northeast. Suddenly travel by train was the popular choice. Tom and his family road in a modified cattle car even though they had their reservations for a long time. Cold air came from all directions as they tried to keep warm in this boxcar. But the novelty of traveling by train was the primary focus. This family had learned not to dwell on the negative since the negative was beyond getting changed at that time. They arrived in Lima, five hundred miles west of D.C. eager to visit with Julia, Gene's sister, who had met them and arranged for them to stay with her near in Lima.

Christmas in Ohio with Gene's family meant a fun time and visit with so many relatives seen once a year. Time was shared with Jack's parents who lived near the family farm. Christmas with Jack's parents was quiet and with fewer people. Having no relatives in the United States made Jack's family quite small. Most celebrations were solemn and quiet.

Visiting in Ohio renewed their close Buckeye bonds. It seems that people in and from Ohio are a proud lot. They take on a definite mid western behavior. Many writers have documented what this means. It means a lot to Gene's whole family. They believe that people from the mid-west are broad and long-range thinkers. Some speculate that this is due to their having flat land to see as far as the eye can take them. They have a calm and accepting attitude. This may take some time, but attitudes are reflected as positive. They display a trust in the other person. However, the other person must never give them any reason to mistrust them. Ambition is put to a good cause. Achievements by authors, astronauts, anchors on radio and television, comedians, actors, artists, musicians, and statesmen, and sportsmen also, are reasons for the midwesterner to display such a proud attitude. They have a right to feel proud.

Bob Greene wrote for Field Enterprises, Inc. "Quality never leaves them. When panic or despair takes over the thinking of travelers in the world, the midwesterner has a reserve that supplies him with a wholesome resource to remain calm."

None of us get to choose where we are born. And it isn't until we move away from the Midwest that we see the difference. There was not the emphasis on the class system that was experienced in Virginia by Gene and her family living there. Middle-class dominates the midwest and it is in this middle-class that values are more realistic and wholesome. She is a true Buckeye.

Just what is a Buckeye? Well, when Jack was introduced once as a speaker, he heard the following joke: "This man is like the state from which he comes, Ohio. He is like the true buckeye nut, bald and good for nothing."

The buckeye nut comes from a tree for which the state is named, and has no known purpose. In fact, they are poisonous to animals. They are brown and shiny like the chestnut. A true Ohio person carries one of these buckeyes as a good-luck piece. But if you don't believe in luck, and believe that each one makes their own luck, then that would apply to the native Buckeye even more. Stanley and Lela taught their children to work hard and gain in this manner. Never rely on luck when work was the avenue for fun and fortune. Work was also a means by which one learned to feel good about themselves. This value is quite evident in this family. It was generated in Ohio in their community with its rural influence. None of Gene's brothers and sisters have retired in the literal sense. They usually change their routines from one vocation to another. They simply have retired from one vocation or profession to assume responsibility in another position. Having something to do and being accountable for delivering a service or product gets them up and out among the living.

For instance, Kassy and Bob now do some delivery service for their son, Bruce. They set aside Thursdays for delivering eggs to businesses. Kassy packs a lunch that she says Bob eats all day long. They don't sit at home and grumble all day about how they ache or feel. They do not dwell on their own life. They are looking at who needs some food from having a death in the family. Kassy fixes her deviled eggs, a meat dish and one of her specialties from whatever may be a good buy at that time. Kassy gets the award for looking after the needy in her area at holiday time as well as all year long. Where does she get this energy at the age of seventy-nine? Is she fulfilling the prediction of her father? Does she have the gift of looking after others in her frugal manner just as she did as a young adult?

She is currently planning a big bash for Mom's brother, Lowell, who is having his ninetieth birthday in 1997. All relatives, far and wide, are to meet in Ohio on March 7th for this big event. Kassy will also be planning other events while detailing this big affair. Uncle Lowell is a favorite person of relatives and friends alike. He is a good listener, and this was a characteristic of Mom's whole family. They never tooted their horn. They never passed gossip. They practiced all of the principles of true German ancestors. Working, cleaning, cooking and eating well guided their routines.

Kassy and Bob take in every stray — man or animal. Bob was an active small animal veterinarian. They have worked and lived with dogs and cats their entire lives twenty-four hours per day. At one time they had five cats living with them like royal "cats." Nothing was off limit to these cats. But when they paraded on the table where the family ate, a few relatives and friends stopped coming to their home. The animals were put in line once the house was cleaned of the odor that goes with animals taking over.

Bob and Ned both graduated from Ohio State University in 1942. This same year, Susan graduated from her nursing school in Lima. Ned graduated in agriculture. He is still using that knowledge at the age of eighty today. He lives on the family farm with his wife Barbara. Their five children have all gone to college and have enhanced the educational fields.

Ned was drafted for World War II. He didn't get his commission as did Jack. But Jack enlisted so he could get the second lieutenant rank. A severe injury of Ned's elbow prevented him from going overseas for one of our bloodiest battles.

Ned enjoys cattle, primarily short-horn cattle. He and his children show cattle at the Ohio State fair. They win honors that make their cattle bring a higher price when it's time to sell them. Farm values are in this whole family. Ned loves the home farm and spends much money just in building upkeep. He has put new windows in the farmhouse and schoolhouse. The schoolhouse is across the road from the farm buildings. It has been rebuilt with brick work, a new foundation and roof. It is practically a new building. You can see the pride and the fact that taking care of something are values instilled in Ned too.

Farm buildings and school house maintained by Ned and Barbara

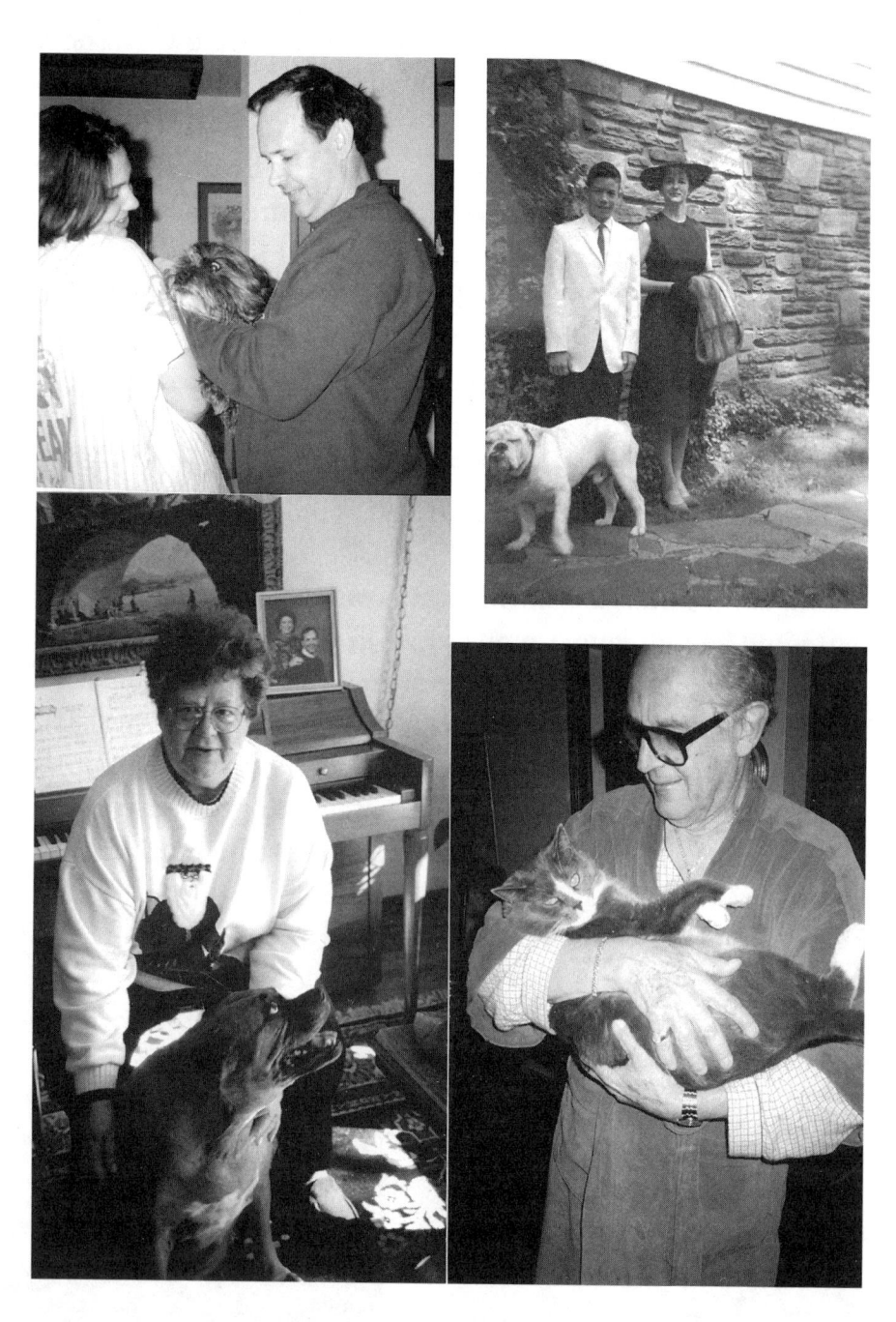

Pet pictures

Chapter Twelve:

Values and Pets

Quite often Gene reflected back to the hospital room where her father struggled to live. She could not forget how vividly clear Da had figured out each of his nine children. He believed in predestination as a basic religious view. It seemed to Gene at the time that Da predicted how his children would lead their lives, that each was predestined. And yet so many of his nine children have operated on the basic principles and values taught to them by both parents. Their teachings were done through role models more so than verbal expressions of values.

Da did extend himself by co-signing the mortgage for Jack and Gene when they purchased their house in Forest, Ohio. His assessment of the needs of this home were on target. His carpenter and contract skills quickly noted that a new chimney was needed. He didn't tell them to hire it done. Instead, he collected the needed brick and mortar and built a new chimney. There was no fuss or charge. He wanted only the safety of his kids and without the praise. By all means, Jack and Gene knew from experience that saying a "thank you" was sufficient — and say it only once. More than sufficient, continuing to express gratitude would not have been tolerated by Da. Saying thank you only once soon became a pattern all of the family practiced. They had learned to control feelings and held them within.

This family expressed many of their feelings through their pets. It was fine to hug the dog and show affection to your pets, but it was not considered appropriate to show affection to other members of the family. Nothing was really said as far as limits in this area. You just didn't see it done or encouraged.

We remember well, Little Ginger. Ginger was the pride and joy of this family. She was often dressed in baby clothing by Karin as she served as her playmate when Karin was three. Then Big Ginger had Little Ginger. This young puppy learned to be Karin's live playmate in place of the older Ginger who had done her duty. Big Ginger was set free then to work in the fields.

Big Ginger worked to kill the rats at the old schoolhouse on the farm. Corn was stored in this old building. These rats had tunneled many paths under this thick wooded plank floor. Stanley poured water into these holes seen at the foundation base. Big Ginger grabbed each rat at the neck, shook it and dropped it. She repeated this routine until the last rat coming out of the hole was dead. At times these rats seemed larger than Ginger, a rat terrier.

One evening after Ginger had spent the day roaming the fields, she failed to come to the house that night. This alarmed everyone. A search party began efforts to find Ginger. No one could believe that she had been stolen. She was cautious with strangers. In fact, she selected those she did not know to nip at their heals. She always barked when she wanted your attention. They could hear nothing when they listened for her bark. There was no barking. Finally, after many frustrating and nonproductive days of searching for Ginger, it was sadly reasoned that maybe Ginger had chased a rabbit or animal into one of the new tile drains. Da reasoned that she must have been caught, with no way to get turned around or out of the drain. The body of Ginger was never found. Everyone who ever knew Ginger suffered along with this family.

How did this family get so involved with pets and the love for animals? It was there before Kassy and Gene married veterinarians. There was always a connection to the animal world. Some of the spouse members alleged that the pets came ahead of them at times. This family had neighbors and relatives who didn't seem to be living for the pets. In this family, the pets and animals continue to take on such importance in their lives. Could the affection shown to animals have been the substitute for the forbidden actions of showing affection to one another?

Members of this family have had dogs, cats, goats, pigs, sheep, ducks, horses, chickens, fish, birds, etc. to name a few of their pets. Some of the names given to dogs were Oog, Jerko, Butch, Neuly, Cindy, Tears, Trendy and of course you have already been told about Dutchess. Many more pets have great importance in the lives of the many family members.

Two horses, Nick and Harry, were favorites until Nick died suddenly as S.B., Jr. was driving them in a field to meet his Dad. Harry was turned into the pastures along with the cattle to roam in the finest retirement. By this time, John Deere tractors had replaced Harry and a second team. But Harry lived ten more years and was cherished as much as the family members. Each time the family walked down the paths to round up the cattle for milking, Harry would come over for pats and scratching around the neck. Yes, he got real hugs before he went trotting off in the comforts he enjoyed.

Then there came a day when Harry couldn't get up or down. How could one think of parting with this beautiful family member? Our mother had the courage and fortitude to call and have the animal picked-up and sent on to his reward. S.B. had one of the closet relationships with these two horses. He was not at the farm when Harry left in the big truck. When he came home, he displayed the initial steps of acceptance once he was told of Harry's departure. First, the anger, denial, and then the sorrow and onto the acceptance of what was best for Harry. But he didn't get to say goodbye. That is a very important step even to the portrayed non-caring individual. These two horses needed each other just like people need other people. Harry had substituted the cows as his support when he found himself living without Nick. No one — animal or man — does well living without getting or giving love. Sharing love is one main reason for each of us having pets for whom we can care and show feelings of love and caring.

While living in Forest, Jack won a small gosling at a carnival while tossing pennies. This pet became a prized pet of David and Tom. This fuzzy little duck was named Peaches. Peaches never let these small boys out of her sight. She rode with them on their tricycles. When she squawked, Jack and Gene knew David and Tom needed to be checked.

When Jack and Gene made plans to move from Forest to Springfield, Peaches went to stay on the farm with Jack's parents until the move was completed. Peaches survived this temporary separation and was brought to the boys where they lived in a new subdivision. Within a few days as Peaches was playing in the yard near the boys, a stray dog following the walking mailman grabbed Peaches by the neck. Jack was to the rescue. But a duck with a broken neck couldn't survive. Jack rushed Peaches to the veterinary hospital where he and his colleagues hopelessly failed.

It has been said that children learn to handle the deaths of parents and siblings by experiencing the loss of their pets. In the following years, as each of the nine children dealt with their feelings at the time of the deaths of their parents, brother, sister, and spouse, they utilitized coping skills so necessary when faced with the loss of someone so close.

Have you noticed the non-caring attitudes of children around pets and animals when they have not shared the love of a pet? Whether these pets are goldfish, dogs, cats, birds, ducks, squirrels, pigs, horses, sheep, cattle, goats, snakes, aquarium creatures, skunks and or rabbits to name a few have been enjoyable pets to someone in this family. Can you imagine the stories that each one of these critters hallowed?

Gene's boys started with aquariums when they were quite young. Tom seemed to be fascinated by any creature that would live in these separate worlds. Suddenly one day, Gene heard, "Mom come here! David threw the football that hit the fish tank."

Water gushed from the broken aquarium. Glass, water, fish, sand and shells were gushing onto the carpet from their bedroom door into the living room. Everyone scrambled quickly to save the fish and put them into safe water until another aquarium could be purchased and conditioned for the fish. Then the discussion began on how and why did this happen. Why did the football get passed in the house? David took the view that Tom should have caught the ball. It was quickly settled that the ball would not be thrown or tossed inside the house. Tom had repeatedly expressed the view that he did not want to catch the football inside or outside the house. David didn't accept the fact that Tom didn't like to catch or pass the football.

Well, the football was passed again. Tom failed to catch this throw also. Gene came home from work one day and Tom greeted her at the door. His mouth was twitching and he was fighting off the tears. She found out the football had been thrown again inside the house, and once again Tom missed it The football hit a beautiful Haviland China plate hanging above the new piano. Not only was the plate broken, but the plate struck the piano and took a chunk out of the piano top. This was their only Haviland China plate. It had been a gift from a special aunt.

Just looking at the faces of these young boys revealed that they were suffering enough just knowing they had disappointed their mother. This recognition by Gene seemed sufficient discipline. There was no shouting, yelling or hitting of children by Gene. They had let her down and that hurt them terribly. They believed her word. When she stated that she wanted something done or that she would do something with them, they counted on it. You see, Gene's disciplinary approach was learned as a child. Her parents didn't destroy her when discipline was necessary. Promises made to her one time by her parents were also kept. That was where she learned this special art.

Gene promised David that they would play golf after she came home from work one day. This stressful and hectic workday did not provide an out. David reminded her that she had promised when she tried to convey to him that she was too tired. So, Gene took a pillow and laid down on the bench at the end of the first several golf holes in an effort to get some rest. After five or six holes, the pillow was stuffed into the walking cart and tiredness was no longer experienced by Gene. This joy of playing a game of golf with her sons gave her new strength as she played the game as promised. She soon forgot her hectic working world.

This value of fulfilling one's promises tells a lot about a person. If it is instilled in your value system as a child, you will have learned its importance when you become an adult. A problem arises when one encounters an individual who never keeps promises and reflects lack of accountability. This value needs to be learned as a child. It is doubtful one will learn it as an adult if not learned as a child.

What helps us to learn and become enterprising individuals? What do we mean by enterprising? What opportunities exist in our childhood that can help us to become enterprising? Having an opportunity to be creative as a child, and act out make-believe vocations, can help teach one to become enterprising. Gene often recalls the fun she had when she set up a mud bakery in the empty corn storage area when she was quite young. Her father would stop and pretend to buy some of her newly baked mud cookies. She looked forward to his visit as he encouraged this enterprising world.

Even as an adult, she loves to bake cookies and makes sure they are pretty for her family and friends to enjoy and admire. A true creative spirit was cultivated when Gene was a child. Never did she get a put-down. This value of control without hurting the child seems to be a real treasure so vividly remembered by Gene.

Gene's paintings since 1988

Chapter Thirteen:

Creative Projects

The home Jack and Gene designed and had built as their retirement home has many fine features that make this a comfortable, attractive, safe and airy home with lots of light — a workable home. Rooms are arranged around a center dining room with a twenty-foot ceiling. This is a square-shaped home with twenty-two hundred square feet. It is situated so the light comes into rooms all day long. It gives one a lighthearted feeling. Vertical windows near the roof and at the top of the dining room open with electrically powered motors. These front windows have sensors that sense them to close when rain touches the opened windows.

The guest area is placed on the opposite side from the master area. Privacy for the guests and owners is preserved. Rooms are pleasantly sized. The bedrooms are on the corners of the house to utilize the cross ventilation. Three full baths with grabbars for safety are situated for accessible use. For instance, Jack's bath is beside the large utility room that opens to the side outside door. He always wanted the bathroom accessible when he worked outside and may have been muddy when he needed to come inside. Each bathroom has an outside window for light and air. Next to Jack's bathroom is Jack's walk-in closet. This closet is next to a row of closets in the hall leading to their master bedroom. Gene's bath is privately tucked off the master room. Her need for privacy is believed related to her having grown up with this family of nine children and parents in a large farmhouse that had little privacy because of few but large-sized rooms found in farmhouses at that time.

The den serves as the computer room as well as the third bedroom which is used for guest overflow. Closet space in this room is deep with light switches as in all bedrooms. The living room has a bay window where flowers grow and bloom abundantly. This room faces the south where the sun comes gleaming through this open and glorious room. Next to the living room is a favorite room known as the "Ohio" room. Jack had named this room rather than having a "Florida" room. It has two glassed sides that lookout on the landscaped lawn and driveway which embodies the treasured island and next to a fifteen-by-fifteen-foot deck. Porch furniture and an umbrella provide a space on which one can observe and appreciate the action of the birds, squirrels and creatures of nature. Beautiful young trees are landscaped into a grassed lawn and blooming shrubs and flowers so native to Virginia.

The functional kitchen has an island that makes for easy entertaining, as well as restricting guests visiting in the area from getting under the cook's feet. This island is perfect for the scaled-down entertaining one does in the retirement years. A pantry area provides the electrical pad for the electrified windows above this area in the dining room as well as needed supplies.

The large utility room has a closet for outside clothing since it is the place one stops from the garage and north side of the house. Lovely cabinets with a folding area provide storage and more than ample space to make it a very functional. The washer and dryer are next to a large utility sink that is often used for soaking of the grill from the adjacent electrical grill outside this room. This necessary utility room is accessible for laundry needs from the master room as well as other areas of the home.

Security is guaranteed with a panel in the master area and near the door leading to the garage.

The double garage and one-half sized space provide additional space for the tractor and garden equipment. The walls are finished with good insulation and drywall. This space could serve for entertaining a large group should they want to do some outdoor casual partying. A large sink in the garage as well as the utility room provides an easy access for hand washing or the cleaning of shoes or work cloths. The changing of oil in the tractor, feeding the dog or replanting of plants are easily taken care of in this light, yet privately spaced windows. The windows are up high where one cannot look inside from the outside. From the garage, permanent closed stairs lead straight up to a fifteen-by-fifteen-foot insulated storage area for lawn furniture and a private retreat for hobbies and a place in which one can get away.

Jack did get away in this private retreat upstairs in the short time he lived in their special retirement home. He decorated the walls, with memorabilia from his working years. The many recognitions he had received were posted on these walls as well as in the den where he place them. Jack's subtle sense of humor gets your attention before entering this upstairs chilling room even though he is no longer living. On the door before entering this upstairs storage room is a large picture of a wild and vicious-looking bear. The bear's mouth is open with large teeth showing and with his eyes focused on you.

It is in this private room the library of treasured books are appropriately placed on shelves on one side of the room. All of that family loves books, treasures them, and sees that they take care of them. In a corner was once a leather golf bag with printing from Ohio State University. Jack treasured the fact that he graduated from Ohio State University in 1945 with his Doctorate in veterinary medicine. He worked his way through college and paid back the money he had borrowed for his education. He lived above the university kennels and took care of the animals in exchange for room rent. One can imagine studying with the perpetual barking dogs.

Jack worked hard at being a good student. He knew how to study. It was evident by his ranking in class. He loved to show records of his grades and tuition to their two sons as they compared college costs with the 1970s. Now, David has the costs of Eric's education in the 1990s to compare to his own educational costs. The changes from the forties to the nineties are great.

The building of this home caused stress at the time of building and in the immediate years. Since the house is square, it presented ventilation problems due to three cross sections being closed off by utilities placed under the house. Gene had a multiple fan system on a timer installed to move stagnant air under the house. The moving of the air under this house has created a well-ventilated space under her house. This is essential to avoid moisture damage in any construction project.

One of the workmen who had helped build their first home in 1970 was inspecting above the living room when he suddenly slipped. His leg went through the living room ceiling. Gene quickly asked if he were injured. Once it was determined that he was not hurt, she had the camera and the proof of carelessness and humiliation at the same time.

"The Roths are so fussy. Why did I have to fall through the ceiling of their home?" (the workman was overheard saying while talking to the builder).

With the various workmen trying to finish some construction details after Jack's death, they soon recognized that Gene meant business in her dealings with them.

"That is not the usual 'Southern Lady' to deal with,"

remarked the engineer who was trying to ventilate under the house. "She talks to you like a man." What he didn't know was that Gene had been taught well by her father as she grew up and learned to stand up for what she believed.

Jack and Gene moved into their second custom-built house in October, 1987. They had sold their home of eighteen years and moved into an apartment for the six months while their new home was being built. Before selling their home, they had the plans developed from their rough drafts. They had located a flat lot in a subdivision they thought would be good as a retirement area. Neither Jack nor Gene wanted to retire with all elderly people. They wanted a community mix of all ages and this is what they found.

Leaving their lovely big colonial home was made easier by having a family they liked and felt would enjoy their old home as much as they had done. The new owners loved gardening, golfing and colonial designs. They continue to comment that they just didn't know how much they were receiving when they bought Jack and Gene's home. Yes, they loved the fish in the large outside aquarium. The landscaping was greatly appreciated. The many varieties of azaleas surprised them. The fireplace made of Virginia green stone was a handsome feature and one-of-its-kind.

But Jack and Gene knew they needed to down-size. Their new home would be half the size, on one floor, with a security system, central vacuum, and indirect lighting, and set on a flat lot. Snow and ice could melt in front of the double garage doors. Gardening was going to be reduced and the grass could be easily mowed.

Having the same builder for this home meant that they had already established a good relationship and understood each other before this project got under way. Sorry to say, this building project was not the same enjoyable experience as the one eighteen years earlier. However, Jack and Gene made it through the construction with some enjoyment. Jack supervised the project daily. He even had the construction crew putting trash in containers daily rather than just throwing it freely on the lot and having someone else pick up the trash or burying it under the topsoil.

The rains came as they usually do in the spring. This flat lot became a pool of mud and water. Plans were made to put steel beams in the foundation to assure a stable foundation. Many loads of topsoil had to be put in place to assure drainage away from the building. The ugly trees were bulldozed down requiring a plan for replacement once the building was completed. When the builder removed the trees in preparation for the building of the house, he violated the area code for this planned community.

New and young shade trees were put in place in the fall of 1987. $12,000 of trees and shrubs added some missing elements in the landscape. These trees would grow and eventually be more beautiful and safer than any of the trees now seen on adjacent lots. A circular driveway took shape as planned and provided a safe exit from the property. Within this circle was a planned island which included another outside aquarium for the fish and frogs as promised to granddaughter, Allison. The waterlilies, smoke trees, miniature maple trees and one large willow oak tree added more beauty to the total island landscape.

Drapes for the entire home were hung the day after the furniture was put in place. Gene had a very capable lady meet with her at the house for the proper selection of materials months prior to the hanging of the drapes. Everything turned out perfect and the drapes were designed to match the decor proving much flexibility for future decorating. These drapes would be taken down, cleaned and re-hung by the same company whenever Gene saw the need for cleaning — a real treat.

David and Tom made no comments regarding their parents' relocating into another home and community. They believed that their parents were giving up a beautiful home that really was too large. So they had little to say. They did not compound to the goal of dow-sizing for their parents. They may have thought that everyone has to do their thing. They always supported what their parents decided to do. Likewise, their parents afforded them the same independence.

After getting settled into this new home, Jack announced his retirement for December, 1987. He occupied his time from December into 1988 by filling photo albums, posting memorabilia in a private room upstairs not yet finished, and insulated his retreat. He was trying to cope with his retirement after working hard ten-to-twelve-hour days for years. Gene planned to retire in 1988 from her stressful nursing position.

Jack experienced sudden illness in February when he developed electrical problems with his heart. He was hospitalized four times in the cardiac step-down unit before his sudden death during an angioplasty procedure. He died suddenly on May 26, 1988. He never got to live one full year in their new retirement home. But he did seem to enjoy many aspects of building another home. Gene did not hold back when Jack wanted to relocate and build a smaller home. She had never denied Jack anything he really wanted to do. Knowing this fact was some solace to her as she learned to cope with his death.

Grasping the thrust of selling one's home, building a new one, moving, Jack's sudden death and handling her own retirement within one full year were all tremendous stresses. Gene's family kept saying, "She will do okay and not have any problems. She is a very strong person." She was expected to handle all of these high stress events, but the family lived five hundred miles away. Their assessment at the time of Jack's funeral was partly based upon the fact that they did feel some guilt by having to leave her alone. They truly believed that she would cope. They returned to their homes saddened while they resumed their busy lives. This was expected of these family members. Feelings were to be hidden and this they did well. They had been taught to not express their feelings. This unspoken sorrow and love seemed to be understood by this large family.

Gene did seem to get in-step as was expected she would do. Fortunately, she had two very supportive sons who would always be there for her if she would only let them know what they needed to do. David lived in nearby Richmond which took forty minutes to drive to the West end. Tom lived in Raleigh, North Carolina. This was only three hours away.

Both of their sons had learned well their supportive skills as they had seen their parents demonstrate in their lives. David served as good financial advisor. Tom's landscaping skills helped in finishing this challenging property. His horticulture degree from Virginia Tech was obvious as he checked the new trees and shrubs for bugs and growth patterns.

Tom planted waterlilies in pans and sunk them in the small pond in the circle. The lotus lily has been simply beautiful. Much previous planning had taken place when this pond was excavated and cement poured when the house was being built.

Since Gene had always made their Christmas cards from ideas that seemed to pop in her head, she used a picture of the lotus blossom for one of her Christmas cards. The design of her cards are reflective of her artistic skills and of her vast interests. Friends and family tell her that they have saved her cards over the years. This kind of encouragement keeps her trying to top the previous year. She agreed to share some of her favorite cards for this printing. They range from serious to humorous and with much about nature.

◆ ◆ ◆

Gene kept Jack's car for a while, as it was very difficult for her, like many others, to part with the belongings of a deceased spouse. Before she sold the car, she was coming home from David's after celebrating Eric's fourteenth birthday when she eased Jack's auto into the back of an old Cadillac. She thought the Cadillac was merging since the lane was open, but she was wrong. The minimal damage which she assessed on Jack's auto turned out to cost a small amount. There was no damage noted to the huge metal bumper of the Cadillac. Gene suffered personal trauma at having damaged the auto that was known as Jack's auto.

Gene copes well while living alone and making decisions without having a spouse with whom one discusses the problems that arise. She is comforted to know for sure that Jack did do what he wanted to do when he was living. His only weakness was for having a new auto. Gene would tell him to buy whatever he wanted and he would get her approval of the auto after he had selected a particular model.

Many would not have gone through a second building project prior to their retirement, but Jack and Gene seemed to enjoy tackling projects for the purpose of achieving something they wanted. In their forty-two years of marriage, they lived comfortably while working hard. They had the pleasure of raising two sons who brought them great joy and fun. Their sons never gave them concerns while growing up and met with achievement in their adult roles. They amassed many life-long friends whom they often visited and enjoyed reciprocal visits.

Their two sons have let Gene maintain her independence after Jack's death without any advice. They listen to her elaborating about having to do the many chores and errands which were once done by Jack. Jack loved to go to the grocery. Gene had to learn to do this essential chore.

Since they had located their new home near a golf course and had joined the golf club, Gene was faced with managing her finances, which included monthly payments for the golf course fees. Gene established relationships with the nine-hole women's group. This provided her an avenue into a social setting of the community. She met some enjoyable friends. Even though her average golf skills led her to win some golf honors, she states that she prefers to be working among her flowers and caring for her lawn and home. Dropping her golf club membership is a real possibility.

She believes that when one lives alone, they become rigid and are tempted to be antisocial. Gene became certified in geriatric nursing and shows great knowledge in the care of the elderly. She recognized these traits could evolve in her and so attempted to establish a Mary Kay business. Soon she knew that she was not a salesperson. She had worked all her life as a professional delivering a service as a registered nurse. No, she was not a salesperson. And so she quickly closed out the selling part. She continues to order the required amount to maintain her consultant status. She likes the products and shares them with a close friend and uses Mary Kay products for gifts.

After staying home for two years after her retirement in 1988, she sought out the local Health Care Center for the elderly. She was hired as an RN for working every other weekend on the evening shift. This was not a high paying position compared to what Gene had done in her varied nursing career, but it did get her out of her home. She conversed with the residents, families and staff. She took interest in how professional she looked. This was always important to her. She contributed to the level of care as she had good credentials and served as a good nursing consultant. She enjoyed the feeling of being needed. Being needed is essential for all of us as long as we live.

Soon Gene was offered an opportunity to teach. Teaching had been one of her favorite endeavors. She became the staff development coordinator for all of the staff for all departments. She had flexibility of hours, methods of teaching and freedom she so enjoyed. This freedom was wonderful for a person with creative skills who like to present information in new and interesting approaches to a staff receptive to her programs. She taught nursing practice skills for which she was known to possess and uphold. The staff seemed appreciative of her efforts and presentations. This provided another avenue for her latent nursing enterprises.

Gene's creativity is ever-present. The art lessons taken in 1951 helped her to illustrate handouts. Her known teaching skills always involved the preparation of extended printed knowledge of the topic she was teaching at that time. She demonstrated an understanding that any student at any age or at any level of learning, does not always grasp the content in a one hour presentation. The staff had no workbooks for referencing unless they had a copy of her handouts to a later use to more fully absorb content after the class hour. Gene devoted much time to this avenue of learning and found it quite helpful in the success of her teaching. Her new computer assisted her to prepare professional looking teaching handouts which she prepared at home.

Gene experienced great satisfaction as she used previous painting skills as she produced five paintings after Jack's death. Her goal is to do additional oil paintings of flowers to be hung in her dining room.

"Merry Christmas to You and Yours"

A Christmas tree is a symbol of joy;
    For that reason, I'm writing to you, A-Hoy!
This family tree will best a-trace,
    Telling you of a family named "Place."

To not exclude my Husband's too,
    Will want to tell you first, it's true;
He is an only child you see,
    And so I'm writing of our family tree.

Since our families are a-far,
    We simply cannot travel by car.
To best illustrate our pride and glee,
    Will explain TO YOU our family tree.

They are scattered around in many locations;
    Working hard each in their vocation.
All share some joys and some sorrow;
    Much to be changed by many tomorrows.

Jack's parents are happy and quite well;
    No finer story one could tell.
Live in Ohio and retired from work;
    Their duties, they will never shirk.

My Mother resides on our home estate;
    Without my father, much missed of late.
Has worked hard and stood the test;
    Looks quite young in spite of the quest.

Ohio is the birthplace of us all;
    Ned is first to answer the call.
Has five children and a pleasant wife;
    This all helps alleviate his strife.

Next comes well organized Kassy;
    A spry and energetic lassie.
Bob and she reside in Illinois;
    With five tots, are tolerant of noise.

M. Georgene Roth

Unspoken Love

Philadelphia is a lucky place,
> To share Betty's talent and her grace.

Ford and children are at her side;
> Life's fulfillment, they abide.

Nursing adds much to Susan's life;
> At times is burdened with its strife.

Needlecraft and music entice her most;
> At which time, she becomes their host.

Quick and mindful, athletic and sprite;
> With the sports, Julia is quite right.

Bob is good for her you see,
> At Lima, they do live in glee.

Then comes me, one of nine;
> Can't imagine life more sublime.

We're now at Frankfort near the horses;
> With Jack and boys still taking courses.

Now Farmer, Jr., quiet and stately,
> Has the yen to travel lately.

With three children and lovely wife,
> Wouldn't want a finer life.

In Dallas, Texas, so big and strong,
> Lives Wm. Dale with five in throng.

Desires so much in education;
> Has traveled far in life's station.

At home living with my Mother,
> There is no finer and no other,

Than Karin Lynn, busy in school and play;
> To end this tree of rhyme today.

Will top this tree with our two boys;
> Looking forward to Christmas and their toys.

With them we wish you the VERY BEST!
> Come see us any time and be our guest.

Jack, Georgene, David and Tommy Roth, 1959

Christmas Card, 1966

Unspoken Love ♦157♦

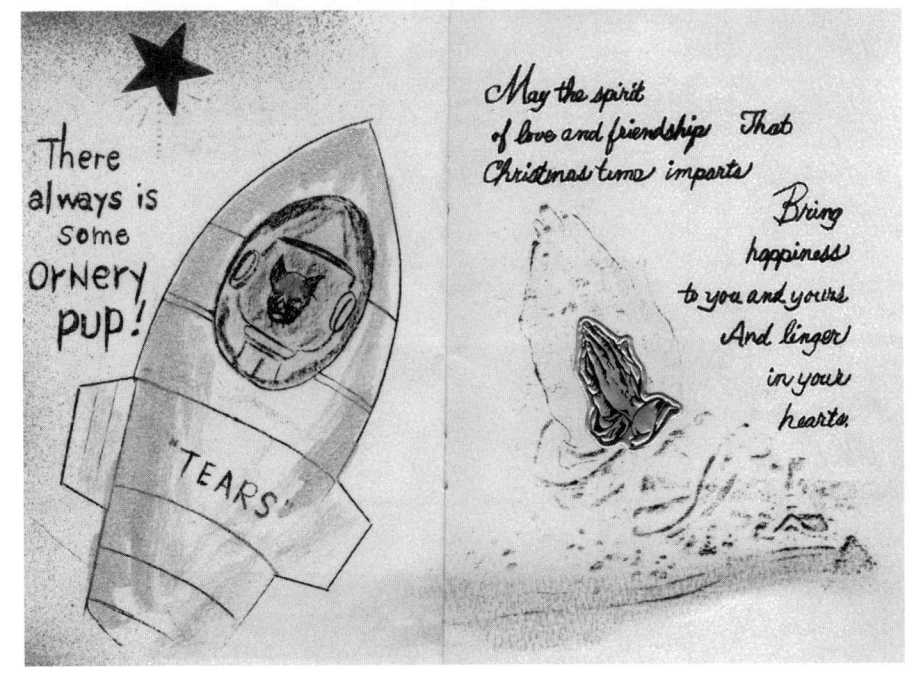

Lotus, water lily on the island

"Halo" to You and Yours,

Let me tell you the story of my prize lotus
    As you look at the picture of our pond.
This delicate pink blossom stands so tall
    With grace and beauty of which I'm so fond.

Having a waterlily with such heavenly stance
    Is another prize and treasured glee.
So, a Christmas gift to you we are sharing
    With you a picture that means much to me.

This treasure was started by son, Tom,
    From one of his special lotus sources.
Without his help and true horticulture guidance
    I would never have passed my lotus courses.

With the advent of winter about to show its face
    Our lotus, fish and frogs have gone to sleep.
They will spend the winter in quiet hibernation.
    Until Spring when they abound from the deep.

But for now, Trendy and I will enjoy winter
    And what it brings with a chance to rest and fare.
These extra hours give time to reflect and plan
    As we recall the Season's meaning is to care.

Oh yes, you noticed that I have a new computer
    With resources at fingertips toward education.
David has guided me thru steps toward my goal
    As he assembled and taught in all dedication.

I just need perseverance and strength to produce
    My book held in my head for many years.
Writing it will determine if I'm up to the task
    As the unknown perhaps raises some fears.

So, for now we're sending best wishes and cheers.

Georgene, Gene or Geanne and Trendy, December 1994

A fun loving family: Gene, playing pool at Tom's; Tom wrapped in a new X-mas gift; Bryan & Gene playing golf at Salt Fork; David dipping homemade ice cream; Allison at the beach; Eric playing pool at Tom's

Chapter Fourteen:

The Phone Rings

During a recent trick-or-treat night, a phone call interrupted Gene's train of thought as she greeted many children for treats upon answering her door.

"Hello Gene, this is your lucky night, this is your security man, Stan, and I am just a little bewildered," came this friendly voice over her phone.

You see, Gene has an outside security light that comes on when a warm body gets within the range of its sensor. For six weeks Gene had been trying to get Stan to come to her home and repair the non-working security light. It stopped working when the painter flushed the sensor while washing her house. But suddenly the night before the trick-or-treaters were to come, the light started working. Great, thought Gene, Stan had finally come and repaired her light. So, she called Stan to thank him.

"Thanks so much Stan for coming to my home and for fixing my security light!" was the message Gene left on Stan's recorder.

"That was a nice message you left for me Gene, but I have not been to your home as yet to repair your security light. It may have dried out and started working. But it will need to be repaired or it will not work when there is moisture in the air. I'll try to be by in a day or so and repair it, I promise."

For six more weeks Gene continued to try to get the light fixed. A friend's husband, an electronics engineer, tried for several weeks to match parts from a local store. His efforts proved fruitless. So, when Stan did not come by to repair the light as he promised, Gene left another message on Stan's recorder.

"Stan, please get this light fixed or refer me to someone who can do this job," was the message Gene left for Stan on Friday.

"Hello Gene, sorry to bother you on Sunday morning, but I got your message on Friday and concluded you meant business. I have been so busy. Our company is growing and everyone wants a security system," Stan rambled on in an effort to get a friendly dialogue going with Gene.

Gene soon warmed to Stan's humor and the conversation became pleasant and sometimes even funny. During this slaphappy conversation, Gene told Stan that she had referred to him in some of her writings that she had been doing on her computer. In fact, she had sent copies of a letter to selected friends and family members alerting them to why they had not heard from her.

"How did I get into your writings Gene? I am quite curious to know what you said about me."

"Well, Stan it is this way. When any repairman comes to fix something at my home, they bring their wives. The plumber brought his wife when he repaired some faucets. He brought her the second time when he had to make an adjustment on one of them. Others bring their wives and wait right with the husband while he does the work. Some make sure that they are between me and their husbands. However, I said that when my security man comes, he does not bring his wife. That is how you got in my writing Stan," Gene told him.

"Well, Gene, don't you know that you are so sexy?" responded Stan.

"Would you be interested in meeting one of my customers who's wife died two years ago?"

"That depends Stan. Tell me about him."

"He is around seventy, a dentist and lives in the west end which is the other side of town." *Gene knew that she was on the south side and that the west end was a forty minute drive.*

"If he is a dentist, he will want to look into my mouth."

"He may want to look into other orifices." Stan said with a laugh.

"This man may not even be available by now." Stan said as if he shouldn't have mentioned him in the first place.

"But if it's okay with you to have Dr. C.D. call; I'll give him your telephone number."

Gene thought for a moment and responded to Stan, "Well, I can handle that. I guess nothing ventured is nothing gained."

Gene gave much thought to having given permission to Stan to have Dr. C.D. call her. She was reluctant to answer her phone. Days went by to a full week. No one by that name called her. She thought that Stan was pulling a funny on her. This Stan is younger than Gene's sons and a happy and friendly character. He loves to shoot the breeze. Gene and Stan hit it off when he installed the security system when their retirement house was built and Jack was still living. Gene knew Stan's in-laws as they volunteered in Gene's working world before she retired in 1988 after Jack's death.

Why did she have guilt feelings? She had been real careful to not establish any relationships with the opposite sex.

Gene met Jack at the age of fifteen. She dated him for five years until she was twenty and they were married. She had forgotten how to flirt or respond to anyone but Jack. Now, she was feeling better since this Dr. C.D. had not called her. She had doubted that he would call her. Men do not stay single long and no doubt some widow had snatched him out of his lonely world by now.

Soon it was Friday again. Gene's phone was ringing.

"Hello, Mrs. R., I have been given your number by our mutual friend. Stan, my security man gave me your number and thought it would be nice if I called you. It is difficult for me to make a call like this. Since my wife died two years ago, I have not called anyone except the friends I have always known," said this soft and flowing voice.

"I am C.D. and I had some time this afternoon to call you."

Gene responded to his friendly voice. They talked for over one hour. They learned that they had a lot in common. Both had lost their spouse, with his wife having died two years ago and Jack having been dead six years. Both were health care professionals, she a nurse and he a dentist. His mother was from Lima, Ohio, where Gene went to nurses' training. This was near Gene's farm home. Each had a spoiled dog living with them in their own homes. Each had been happily married for forty-two years. They concluded that they both lived busy lives even now as both worked part-time. With their busy schedules as already planned, they tentatively agreed that they could meet sometime after December 16th.

The phone was ringing again.

"Gee, it was nice to get your letter today." C.D. responded by phone.

"I had thought about calling you on Monday," as he went on thanking Gene for the letter.

"You used words like commonalties which shows you are intelligent. I use simple words." he went on.

Gene had sent him a Thanksgiving greeting and thanked him for calling her. It seemed like a good icebreaker. This avenue provided another method of getting to know each other. Gene was thoughtful in sending a thank you note. She also thought that he just might write back and she could check out his writing since handwriting was so important to her.

This call came in at 12:59 P.M. as indicated on her telephone's caller ID They chatted until 1:35 P.M. when he suddenly remembered he had to get to his office for his 2:00 P.M. appointment. He had stated that he was trying to catch up as he was behind due to his trip to Florida.

As C.D. was quite a conversationalist, a lot of territory was covered during these two conversations. Gene heard about the happenings on Thanksgiving when he was preparing breakfast at his church for one hundred and fifty people with six other persons assisting him. It seemed that the beaters of his mix-master came out and splattered eggs around the church kitchen. He had gotten a lot of kidding since that time from his friends.

Then he told Gene about a drawer where he keeps linens for the table. A mouse had set up housekeeping there. This little pest had carried some of his dog's food to this drawer. This meant that he had all of these linens to clean as well as the drawer. He finished this big job last night.

In describing his trip to the Florida Keys, it seemed that he must have a lot of stamina. Gene had some concerns about his using good judgment. He had driven his van eleven hundred miles straight and packed it full of his granddaughter's belongings and driven straight back to Virginia. He kept in touch with the granddaughter by their CB's while enroute.

He is an early riser. His alarm goes off at 5:30 A.M. and then he does seventy leg exercises in his bed before he gets up. These exercises have reduced his waistline from forty inches to thirty-four to thirty-six inches. He was quite proud of this achievement. He uses his exercise equipment when he watches the news in the morning. This he credits with giving him more energy.

Occasionally, Gene could get in a question. These questions gave him continued reasons for telling her about himself. Soon she realized that he was mainly interested in himself. Rarely did he want to know about Gene's interests or her family. She related it when she could get a word into the one-way conversation. Every now and then, he apologized for talking about himself. As he related details of his education, marriage, building of their homes and or his in-laws, he did not seem to tell the details in a bragging way. He had found a listener for his stories that he loved to hear.

Gene concluded that this man was friendly, loved people, loved to travel and sounded like he was dependable. But what did this man look like? How tall was he? What was his age? Did he have hair? Was he a good dresser? These questions went unanswered as the various conversations took place. Even though Gene threw out questions in these areas, they were passed by as his achievements dominated. It didn't seem to be a case of avoidance but one of overly self-involvement.

But Gene continued to wonder what color his eyes were. Did he smile with his eyes? Was he a blond, gray, or was he once tall, dark and handsome? Does he have good-looking hands? She imagined that he did take care of his hands since he was a dentist. Therefore, she just knew that he had good-looking nails and took care of them as well. Does he dance and is he a good dancer? He does like music and plays an instrument.

On December 8, C.D. called Gene again.

"I am sorry that our conversation ended so abruptly yesterday when I announced that I had to be at my office at 2:00 P.M." C.D. said in a tender and kind voice.

This extended conversation revealed that his daughter was a dentist also. He would be retiring with her taking over his practice. He discussed his lawyer son and how he would be helping him move to his new farm near a little town in the mountains west of Richmond. C.D.'s wife had died of lymphoma. Jack also had lymphoma, but had died unexpectedly during an angioplasty procedure. Jack was taking oral chemotherapy for his lymphoma condition.

C.D. did not play golf or fish. He didn't really care about cards. He flew his own Cherokee plane. It seemed that he was on the move all of the time. But his interests were pretty self-centered. Gardening was something that he did because it needed to be done. He did not enjoy gardening like Gene did. He enjoyed eating out and often mentioned that this would be something they could do. He usually drove to a different special place to eat every Friday evening with a couple who had helped him through his wife's death. This conversation ended at 10:00 P.M. with tentative plans to go to see the Christmas decorations down town in Richmond on the coming Monday or Tuesday evening.

Surprise! C.D. called Gene on December 9th around 10:00 A.M.

"Hello!" sounded this chirpy voice so early in the morning.

It was early for Gene since she stays up late and is slow to get in gear in the mornings.

"This is a short notice, but my colleagues have encouraged me to bring a guest to our annual Christmas party dinner party tonight. It is being held at the Engineering Club in downtown Richmond. I had not planned to go. But some of my peers have called this morning urging me to go. They insisted that I invite a friend and attend this beautiful party tonight. Would you be interested in being my guest tonight?"

"That sounds exciting and I have nothing planned to do tonight. Yes, I would enjoy meeting you and your friends," replied Gene.

What was Gene thinking about? She had not even met this man. What did he look like? How would he dress? He had stated that the dinner was not formal but a fairly dressy occasion. Gene had the perfect outfit that she had just purchased.

She washed her hair, did her nails and took a leisurely bath for this special date. The cocktail hour and dinner was at 7:00 P.M. He acknowledged that he knew where Gene lived as he had been down her street when he visited a friend recently. This sounded a little strange to Gene. But at least she didn't have to give him directions to her home. He said that he would be driving his twelve-year-old Subaru. Gene wondered why he wasn't coming in his new Dodge Caravan. She had the house looking good before she got dressed. Trendy, Gene's five-year-old boxer did not like men she did not know. So she had her shut in their Ohio room. C.D. could see her without having her check him out.

At 5:45 P.M. a car turned into her driveway. Up the stairs came this medium sized man. When Gene met him and said hello, he did not give her any eye contact. He did not appear too comfortable. Gene was certainly uncomfortable at the thought of going into a new group as a guest of someone she was meeting for the first time. He was around five-feet eight-inches. Gene is five-feet-six and one-half-inches tall. He was definitely not the tall man Gene liked or had hoped he would be.

He was bald with white hair closely cropped around the side near his ears. He wore glasses with heavy lens. His complexion was pale and clear. He wore a conservative dark blue pin-stripped suit of fairly old vintage. His shoes were dull with a hard toe style.

With a short introduction and his not even acknowledging Gene's lovely home, they were entering his tiny antique auto. Soon they were putting down Midlothian turnpike toward downtown Richmond. This was the busy traffic hour and most everyone knew that this street was one of the busiest ones. When he seemed unclear how to reach downtown, Gene suggested the Powhite turnpike which she usually uses. He elected to try several routes in an unsafe area before they reached their destination. Luckily, they parked in front of the club. He opened Gene's door. Gene was not accustomed to riding in a small auto as she drives a Buick. She is not a little person, so this tiny auto made her feel like she was crammed into a small space.

They entered the party where they were welcomed by his life-long associates and their wives. It was a friendly group and everyone welcomed Gene into the evening's activities. C.D. talked to the daughter of one of his dentist friends who was sitting on the other side of him during the diner. This seemed peculiar to Gene since she thought he would have been more gracious in a social setting. But the dentist sitting beside Gene and his wife carried on a cheerful and continuous conversation during the evening. Gene was not left out by all the guests at their table. C.D. didn't have any hearing problems with the excessive noise in the room and that was a plus for his age.

Why did he not talk to her during this evening? She concluded that he was uncomfortable with taking a female friend to a dinner with his associates. This was new for him as well as for Gene. But Gene had social graces that would get her through any situation.

Maybe C.D. needed someone who would enjoy hearing him talk about himself she decided. Gene did not feel comfortable with short men. All of the men in her family were over six-feet tall. Jack was six-feet-one-inch tall. Shoes must be polished with a shine and of good style. Gene liked bald men as she had learned to accept when Jack lost his hair. Bald men looked handsome especially if they had beautiful eyes and smiled with good-looking teeth. Why did Gene even think she could find someone to match Jack's beautiful eyes and smile with such handsome teeth?

And where were the compliments? Jack had always told her how nice she looked. And that he liked her hair. He praised her for her good cooking and how nice the house looked. C.D. made no comment about how Gene looked, and she looked nice then as she always had before. He ignored her beautiful home. He didn't even seem grateful for her accepting his last minute invitation.

They said their goodbyes to his friends and toured downtown

Richmond to view the lovely Christmas decorations since their party was only a few blocks from the marvelous displays.

On the way to Gene's home, C.D. seemed to run out of energy. He had spent most of the day flying his plane and waited a long time to get some repairs done while at the airport. It had been a tiring day for him. He had not planned well to be rested for this outing. When he began to yawn and weave on the road, she tried to keep the conversation going in order to keep him awake. She would have preferred to be the driver.

Had this man run out of conversation about himself? No, she believed he was tired and this happened suddenly.

Gene invited C.D. to come in when they reached her home. All the while she did mention how tired he seemed to be and that it had been a long day. He did get out of his auto as she departed and entered her home.

◆ ◆ ◆

The calls from C.D. stopped abruptly. Christmas came and went without hearing from him. Gene mailed one of her handmade Christmas cards with a thank you note. This card returned after she had tried to find his home address. She had mailed the Thanksgiving note to his office address.

This telephone friend was a learning experience for Gene. It helped her sort out some social goals. She soon realized that she could not replace Jack and certainly would not want to. She would never want someone to take his place. Her fond memories seem adequate as she busily contents herself in her own independent world that includes her devoted sons and their families.

CHAPTER FIFTEEN:

Family Performances

Many times through the past forty years Gene replayed the privileged conversations she experienced with Da in his hospital room. Da was a very proud father. His standards were usually implied and rarely directly discussed. There was always the distancing between Da and his children, and yet he focused on how Gene's life would be. What would her children do as adults? How would her marriage with Jack unfold? She could see that Da was not only focusing on his other eight children, but seemed to want to know more about what Gene was thinking about her own life.

She had never had a conversation with her father before that seemed so personal. Their conversations while growing up never revealed a closeness. They never expressed how each felt about other persons. And yet, he was reaching into Gene's future life. Did he know then that he would not be around to witness her life's experiences? Did he have some views that he wanted to have patterned? She recalled that he did not want her to marry so young. He had expressed a great dislike at his having to sign for her to get a marriage license when she was only twenty. He seemed to like Jack as a person, but asking him to give his approval to marry so young made Da reach into his hidden feelings.

Da and Mom never showed any affection openly to each other when the children were around. Showing affection was not something that was done. If one of their children left for college or to go into the military, a wave was given and a response, "We'll see you." There is no doubt that both parents were functioning as they had been taught by their parents. It was only when these children married partners who did express affection that they learned to express affection. Jack had learned to kiss his mother when leaving and when arriving home. He smothered his "Geanne" by kissing her good-bye and hello for each of his veterinary calls all day long. He always showed affection and taught his sons to do the same by becoming their role model. She had to learn to show affection since it was important in her marriage.

There were times when Jack took some pressure and criticism from his father-in-law and brothers-in-law. They called him a sissy and hen-pecked. He assisted his Geanne with the care of their children. He often helped with some of the household chores. He went to the grocery. These activities were a no-no for Gene's brothers. It could be speculated that the presence of five girls waiting on these four men contributed to their macho behaviors. Jack continued to be a helpful husband and father because he wanted to do this and enjoyed the association. The opinions of Gene's family did not bother him. In fact, he often applied pressure for them to conform.

Da was very forceful in his rules. He did not permit sewing on Sunday. He wanted no ironing on Sunday. All farm machinery was to be put away at the end of each day. No farm work took place on Sunday. And yet, this man was not an overt religious man. He frowned on some community members who professed devoutness. He saw their behaviors as fakery. He also had a poor opinion of "preachers." He considered them a lazy bunch. However, his opinions were based on what he saw in this community. Many of the preachers were self-taught, and really never succeeded in getting sound thinkers to accept some of their religious shoutings.

This family never went to church together as a family. The little church was nearly a mile down the road from the farm. Da contributed financially to the church as his children were strongly advised to attend, but the influence on these young children seems to have a life-long negative impact on their religious beliefs and participation in church activities. These children attended Sunday school and enjoyed some of their good teachers. They were musically inclined and learned to sing and appreciate the hymns. There was no organ or choir in this small community church. The suggestion of some of the children to Da and Mom to go to Wapakoneta to a bigger church was abruptly put to rest.

"This is our community and you will attend this church. We would be viewed as stuck-up if we were to pass this church on the way to Wapakoneta."

When Betty, Julia or Gene related the numbers of "if you please" repeated by the preacher, both parents ignored these comments. Also, the many uses of poor English by the preacher carried no weight, so these children continued to walk to and from church. Frequently, they timed their walks in order to get a ride from a wealthy neighbor. Smithy in his shiny Peerlus auto would stop to give them a ride. The seats were covered with green plush velvet that enticed them to immediately rub their hands over these beautiful seats. Smithy seemed to enjoy this short period of association and contributed to the feeling for these children that their neighbors were important.

Sunday morning was a time Da took a bath, put on a perfectly ironed work outfit and strolled the farm. Mom usually killed a chicken, picked the feathers and cleaned the chicken perfectly before cooking it for the Sunday dinner meal. Since Da would not eat chicken as result of some strange story that happened to him as a kid, Mom prepared another meat that would

Da's mother started this beautiful peony garden.

please him. Most all meals were planned around Da's desires. Everyone sat quietly at the table until Da started to serve himself. Keeping nine children quiet while hungry was a true example of control.

Da was a neat dresser. His shirts were starched and ironed without one wrinkle. This not only applied to his dress clothes, but to his work clothes as well. When the girls had proved capable to iron his shirts, they had passed a great test. His shoes had to be shined every time he wore them. And one of the girls had as her weekly Saturday assignment to shine the shoes for the whole family. Many a time, a row of shoes lined the front porch where this process was done in order for them to dry as well as not spill polish on something in the house. This was Mom's plan.

His suits were custom tailored as he had a long torso and was slightly hippy. Mom tailored his gray work pants by taking them in at the waistline. Never did he wear a pair of the popular jeans of today. Mom purchased these gray matching shirts and pants at J.C. Penny's. Mom always patched or darned the clothing. These repairs were a work of art. Few people are that frugal today. They just throw them away and buy new ones.

Not only was Da fussy about his appearance, but his children had to look their best. Everything they wore had to match. There were occasions that they enjoyed looking like a gypsy for their daily chores, but this did not meet with approval of Da. He forbade them to wear shorts. Of course they complied. Hair was to be clean and fixed. Mom cut the hair of all the girls and boys. She had a stool on which she had everyone sit that was placed outside on top of the cistern. A cistern was a cemented collection area for collecting the rains. This provided water for washing the clothing, hair and taking of baths. It could have been a back-up in case of fire. Hair was never combed in the kitchen where Da could see it done. One strand of hair found near the table was a terrible thing. Since there were no bathrooms and no electricity, water was drawn from the cistern, heated on the large wood stove in the kitchen, and carried to a portable round tub near the heating stove. Of course, the reverse was done once the baths were finished when the dirty bath water was carried outside.

Actions taken by this family were the result of well understood rules. Rules were openly addressed one time by Da. Mom did not have to repeat them as they were clearly and plainly defined. Most of the children understood these rules were to be followed. Betty displayed her determination to do something she felt she needed to do even if it meant she not follow an already understood rule or value clearly stated before by Da.

One particular Sunday morning, Da walked into the house before he was expected only to find Betty ironing in the kitchen.

"Did you not know that ironing was not to be done in this house on Sunday?" Da firmly asked.

"I have a date and needed to iron this dress." Betty responded in a firm and loud manner that could have been viewed as sassing Da.

Da grabbed the wooden ironing board and threw it on the kitchen floor. It broke into a million splinters.

"I said, there is no ironing here on Sunday!"

"I am going to iron!" Betty responded defiantly as she stood next to him in an open and defiant manner.

Before she followed the path of the ironing board and was about to shout once again that she was going to iron, one of her sisters moved in to lead her out of the room. Betty continues to be a big ironer. She may even iron on Sunday in her own home. She never wears anything that has a wrinkle when she dresses to meet the public. In fact, the importance of wearing clothing perfectly ironed was expected of this family by both parents. Da would not wear a shirt if one wrinkle were evident on even a set of work clothes. Even to this day, the family has a thing about ironing.

A new ironing board was purchased and covered. Da stood his ground on the rule he had laid down about no ironing on Sunday. One has to wonder about behaviors and if direct conflict does not only reinforce the negative performance of all involved.

Sewing was strongly prohibited also on Sunday, and knowing that Da had the fortitude to follow up his commands, sewing was only attempted on Sunday when it could be hidden from his knowing. A family member was bribed to watch for Da coming into the house. Sewing was never attempted in the kitchen. The second floor in the girls' room served as the crime area. This room had five long windows that served as a good look out position.

All of the girls learned to sew. Mom was a masterful seamstress. She designed a dress or coat by just looking at something she had seen in a store or having it described. She paid great attention to detail and nothing was ever done halfway or sloppy. Since money was in short supply and always used to buy land, she was skilled at remaking a new dress many times from an old garment or piece of material. Gene was the fifth girl straight. She recalls having a dress that had been made over many times. It was always a new dress to her and her friends. A satin collar was put on a velvet dress with fancy buttons all of which came from other frocks. The only new materials used were for a 4-H club project. These projects were always productive as Mom watched every stitch the girls took. When it was not right, she made them rip it out until it was perfect. The attention Mom devoted toward perfection was a value still seen in this family today. It is even obvious in Gene's sons, but since she does not view herself as that detailed, she gives credit to their having learned it from Jack.

Reflections of this interesting family environment that they all experienced as one of the nine children, dominates many discussions by phone or when visiting each other. Gene often reflected on her Dad's predictions. In fact, every time she visited one of her brothers or sisters she witnessed these predictions unfold. The thirty-year spread between Ned and Karin was a long time to figure out. Da's predictions were made when Karin was eight and Ned thirty-eight.

◆ ◆ ◆

Karin was born when both parents were forty-seven. Bill, the youngest of the nine children was fifteen. He was the baby for a long time. He was so good-natured. Bill needed to be around his family for emotional support. It wasn't until it was too late that his family recognized this need. He lived in Texas and most of them didn't provide him the assurance he needed.

The goals of Bill's brothers and sisters seemed to be self-indulgent and set upon their own achievements. Their actions seemed to be fulfilling their father's predictions. Bill continued to live out his life as one overly concerned with the feelings of others. He never tried to take from others. Instead, he always gave and seemed unable to stop those who tried and did take advantage of his generous nature.

S. B., known as Junior in his younger days, succeeded as predicted. He has achieved more than did his Grandfather Place. His mannerisms reminded Da of his own dad, Dorsey. This meant that he had the respect of the community in which he lived. He desired a reasonable living and was willing to work hard to achieve this goal. Each wanted to own their own farms and to live peacefully on this farm.

S. B. was taught how to be a good farmer by a good teacher, his dad. He managed well with the capable assistance of his wife, Bernice. S.B. stayed on the family farm while his other brothers and sisters went to college, the service or other work. Having been designated as needed to farm during World War II by the draft board seemed to make S.B. feel discontentment.

He never asked for this role, but having two brothers in the service at that time prevented him from being drafted. Ned was drafted after finishing college in the School of Agriculture at Ohio State University in 1942. Bill enlisted in the air force for four years when he finished high school in 1948. By this time, he was not sent into any major battles. Gene's Jack enlisted in 1946 after finishing his college in 1945. Julia's Bob enlisted in the air force in 1944. He escaped major engagements during the war.

Pressures were applied to comply with parent's desires. S.B. was expected to get married, move into the little house on the farm. Farmers were needed to raise the necessary food during the war. This is what he did. Of course, he was a valuable asset when Da died suddenly and he managed the farming productions. He also served as a father figure for Karin since he lived within yards of the farm home. Our mother felt secure with his knowledge and dependability. Bernice, S.B.'s wife, was close to Mom and they seemed to respect each other's role. It could be said that S.B. and Bernice's destiny was controlled by the circumstances in which they found themselves, but each of us can follow the path we desire to follow even if we pursue it selfishly.

The desire to pursue one's destiny prompted S.B. and Bernice with their small three children to pull up stakes in Ohio and move to North Carolina, while seeking to buy land he could afford. He was content in his belief that Mom could rent the farm successfully. He was free to make his million and spread his wings. This departure from the pattern he was to take if he were to follow the lifestyle of his grandfather was now reflecting the real S.B. He had waited a long time to venture into the unknown business opportunities that awaited him.

Time and many hard financial decisions have proved him right in his pursuits. After thirty years as a Tar Heel, he seems content. They do visit family in Ohio and have many guests from Ohio who enjoy their available fishing opportunities. Their children are grown and content with the advantages resulting from their parent's brave achievements.

Above: S.B. fishing in front of his home
Facing page: Gene fishing, and with friends, family and cleaning fish with S.B. and Susan

Unspoken Love ♦181♦

Landscaping designed by Jack and retirement house

Chapter Sixteen:

Life After Retirement

Gene went ahead and retired in August of 1988, after Jack died in May. She had originally planned to work through the year of 1988 before she retired. Working from May to August while trying to complete the odds and ends of their new retirement home made her feel stretched as well as stressed. Coping with Jack's death caused severe stress in itself.

Gene had to have all of the hollies on the front of their property replaced when vandals drove onto her property one Friday night and flattened these young plants. It was raining quite hard when Gene walked to the mailbox to get her morning paper on Saturday morning. There were the flattened hollies lying over pools of water. Pieces of holly were strewn all over the road. Gene was sure the car that had driven onto her lawn in the wrong direction and had bent holly branches hanging out from under it.

She called the police. They were too busy to come. Security for the subdivision would not be in the office until Monday. She continued to try to find the kids who had done this. She felt that she knew who might have done it. These hollies were planted the day before by a well-known local nursery, the company who had just planted their $12,000.00 worth of trees and shrubs. As a young driver in a Volkswagen loaded with high school kids came speeding down the street loaded, he nearly hit the landscape company truck parked on the street. He slammed on his breaks. They shouted some obscenities. It was as if they decided then to take vengeance on this property. Gene wanted to go to the back street to find this Volkswagen and check it out.

Gene's neighbors came out and empathized with her. One physician neighbor left for work that morning and seemed angered at such a terrible act. Gene went back into the house and planned what she needed to do to get the hollies replanted. Later that day, Gene went outside in the rain. She grabbed the hollies, stood them up in their water-filled holes. She stomped them down until they stood upright. While stomping the last holly into its hole, she saw the small Volkswagen drive by. This kid slammed on his brakes, took another look and turned the corner to go to his house.

Did the police want to investigate this vandalism? They responded to Gene that they did not have time, but one week later, a policeman called Gene to file a report. He needed to complete his report even though he had no intention of finding the guilty teenager. He did not want to hear who Gene thought did it. Neither did the security of the subdivision devote one minute toward the resolution of this invasion of Gene's property.

Gene realized quite quickly that she would be fighting battles alone. Jack was not here to assist her. She had learned to stand on her own two feet and she could. She knew how and knew it would not be easy, but she would. She vowed right then that she would fight her own battles in the future.

When some of the contracted agreements in the building of the house were not completed satisfactorily, Gene decided to sue the builder whom they once viewed as their friend. Gene had never been in court. She won her case, but the judge had thrown out the cost of the tree replacement since the builder's attorney claimed unfair treatment. Gene learned one more time that she did have the grit and nerve to hold people accountable for their behavior. This value was so strongly embedded in Gene's growth and development when she was a child.

For two years Gene coped with the many tasks that needed to be done. She had the house repainted one year after it was built. A shoddy exterior job needed to be done correctly. This cost a lot of money for a new home.

When Gene retired from nursing in 1988, she was extremely tired. She rested and rested. They had sold a home of eighteen years. She helped her husband fight a serious life-threatening illness and saw him lose. Experiencing the death of her spouse was the third and most serious stress of her life. Retirement often gives the person a feeling that life is nearly over.

Gene did not dwell on her losses. Instead, she realized that she needed to have a purpose other than her children. She needed to force herself out of her home where she was secure. She needed to have someone appreciate her skills. She needed to have someone with whom to talk. How was she to meet these obvious needs?

◆ ◆ ◆

For starters, she bought a boxer puppy that consumed much of her free-time and continues to do so today. While living alone with a pet, Gene finds herself talking to her dog, named Trendy. She started these conversations when Trendy was only a pup. She was born in the middle of June 1989, one year after Jack's death. David, Tom, Barbara, Bryan, Eric and Allison accompanied Gene to see a new litter of boxers while visiting Tom in Raleigh. Gene had expressed her desire to have a boxer. She wanted the boxer to be two years old ideally, but she did not want to get one raised by someone else. The only alternative was to get a puppy and raise it for two years.

Trendy grows up

She selected one of the six-week-old puppies of this litter for $100 while visiting Tom and Allison in Raleigh. Soon, they were saying good-bye to Tom and Allison and driving back to Richmond. The new puppy was getting attention from everyone while David was driving. Gene had heard Barbara and David say they wanted a boxer again also. Hiedi, their boxer had died a few years earlier. Barbara concluded the day Gene selected Trendy that after one year, they would come get a puppy from a future litter of Trendy's mother.

Getting a boxer to be an adult takes some time, money and effort. First, the tail gets shortened. Next, the ears get cropped. Neutering was the next surgical procedure. Even so, there are days she lifts her leg when she is around a male dog. Usually she acts like a female. Poor thing does not have a sense of which gender she is destined to be. She has encroached upon the neighbor's flowers and patch of grass. Trendy's urine seems to kill the grass, therefore, she isn't too welcome as she seeks friends from the neighbors.

Trendy was named by Gene when the grandchildren could not come up with an acceptable name. This boxer followed a trend by being the fourth family boxer. This is how she inherited the name Trendy.

Raising a strong-headed boxer dog is not easy when you live alone. Gene soon learned that having her sons around with Jack helped in the growth and development of their other boxers. Tom kept Trendy when she was younger, and she would shape up for him. David describes her as an angel whenever they keep her. They frequently keep Trendy whenever Gene takes a trip out of state. Truly, Trendy is lonely living with an older person. She goes crazy when company comes. She always enjoys seeing Tom and Allsion as she does when seeing David, Barbara, Bryan and Eric.

Trendy developed severe anxiety in the auto on a return trip with Gene from Ohio several years ago. Now, she does not even like to get into the car for short errands. David kids his mother that it is because of her driving. But Trendy displays the same fear when David takes her in his auto. The fact that she is so comfortable at home and always in charge may contribute to her feeling that she may not get back home. Gene does give her one-half of a tranquilizer sometimes in order to take her on some errands. She tries to prevent her from staying home all of the time.

◆ ◆ ◆

After nearly two years of dealing with errands and chores such as buying groceries, getting things repaired and the oil changed such as the auto and the mowers, fertilizing the lawn and taking care of the fish in the aquarium to name a few things which Jack usually did, Gene learned she could do these because she had to do them. Jack loved to go to the grocery. Gene hated to do this. She even thought that she hyperventilated when she had to wait in lines, so she had to learn to do this errand when she was not tired or there were fewer people. He had spoiled her by doing the majority of errands. She liked to clean and cook and they often said they divided the work at home since both of them worked full-time outside of the home in very stressful working situations.

After Jack's death, Gene stayed home for two years without doing anything extra outside the home. Gene recognized the fact that she should spend time getting out of her home doing a useful task, so she accepted a part-time RN charge position at a health care center two miles from her home. She agreed to work the evening shift on every other weekend. Her experience and education made her over-qualified, but she did find this interesting and a needed service.

When there was a change in management at this facility,

Gene declined the director of nursing position. This would have been full-time and Gene had spent much time in management in similar positions. She declined this offer. She still viewed herself as a retired RN, but did accept the part-time position of staff development coordinator for the facility. Her responsibilities were to provide orientation for all departments as well as provide educational inservice programs mandated by law for all employees.

This position has provided an interest for Gene, as well as an opportunity to get some pluses for her good programs and appearance. She has worked in this position since 1991. It provides an opportunity for her to be creative in program presentations, as well as in the extensive handouts. The staff seems to realize that they have a qualified person teaching them skills needed for the care of the geriatric residents.

Gene is not a part of the management team since her position is not a management position. She misses this association as she once experienced in her other positions. Many of her peers do not know her well, because they did not work directly with her, or interact with her — hearing some of her views that were often expressed in management meetings. Gene tells herself that this negative aspect is something she will have to accept since she chooses to remain part-time and continues to work in this position. This mad money is useful in the costs of supplies used in her lawn and other unplanned expenses. She does enjoy staying near her home where she can check on Trendy and not leave her home alone for long periods of time. She too needs people and Gene is mindful of this fact.

Staying near one's home in order to be home at night does limit travel opportunities. She did travel to Arizona after Jack died to visit close friends for a two week period. These two weeks were equal to a whole year in her thinking. She also drove to Florida with a friend one year for a one-month escape in February. Tom kept

Trendy while she was gone. This trip also proved to her that her real love was to stay home where she felt more at ease and truly enjoyed living in their comfortable retirement home. Her interests in art and oil painting get neglected because of her busy life.

Gene usually drives at least once a year to Ohio to visit family on the farm and friends in nearby small communities. This trip is nearly six hundred miles one way. It is also important for her and her brothers and sisters to attend their annual alumni dinner banquet every five years. She attended the alumni banquet in 1994 in Ohio when her class was recognized. Her class gets recognition for the most in attendance from one class. They graduated in 1944. Of course, none of her classmates showed their age. When you realize most of these classmates attended the entire twelve years together there is a real apparent closeness.

Most of these families lived on farms in this area. Gene's class had eighteen graduates. Most of the other classes were small also. This school was closed when regional schools came into being. Nevertheless, even after the school was closed, the alumni association remains viable.

Of course, Gene makes trips to visit Tom near Raleigh, North Carolina. She does visit S.B. and family in the eastern part of North Carolina near the ocean. Fishing occupies much of her time when she is visiting S.B. Gene visits Allison, Tom's daughter, at Wilmington where she is in college.

Fishing desires keep Gene traveling to the Chesapeake Bay. Her close friend, Alice, has a comfortable home near a friend on the Bay. Gene fishes off the peer. This small three-day trip provides Gene with an opportunity to visit and do something she really enjoys.

Errands need to be identified as the real cause for Gene leaving her home. Golly, she does hate to do them, but it is interesting to hear about these episodes. She has made some fun out of doing the errands and this has helped her achieve them with less stress.

Gene is always alert in an effort to come up with an idea that she develops into a theme for the Staff Development bulletin board each month. She searches various stores for ideas. Ideas do come and they are original. For the month of February, it is always easy to make it beautiful as well as provide a theme that can be carried into the care of the residents.

For this particular February, Gene used tissue paper under shear paper with pale pink hearts. This gave a three-dimensional appearance for the background. Next, she attached a heart-shaped one-sided basket and lined the basket with dark red felt. This was attached to the bulletin board by staples hidden under the felt. Tucked into this basket on top of the red felt nestled a tiny white plush teddybear. Printed on the bear's chest, was "I Love You." He had little red hearts on the bottom of his paws. A copy of the Valentine she designed on her computer was placed adjacent to the bear. The theme was to relate "I Love You," with pictures depicting all stages of life. This facility is for the geriatric population. As Staff Development Coordinator, Gene tries hard to have the bulletin board theme enhance the knowledge of the staff with the focus on why they are working at this facility. The staff seems to appreciate the effort and expense Gene provides in her creations.

This bear did have a great personality and grabbed the attention of the employees as he/she peaked out of the perch where the employees clocked in and out. Gene had completed this bulletin decor by 9:30 P.M. before she taught a class to the incoming evening and night nursing staff.

Low and behold, on the following day at 2:31 to 2:35 P.M., this bear was taken by an employee as she clocked out for the day. Gene was alerted by the administrator of this terrible theft. Staff members were saddened, but that evening, Gene went and purchased a similar bear. She tucked him into the basket and tied him in place. She stapled the bear so tight that no one could easily snatch it.

Of course the return of the bear pleased the staff. How do you get someone to return "their" bear so quickly and unharmed was the question asked by many?

Gene responded with a question to these inquiries with a question: "Wasn't that something?"

Gene had related her plan of replacing the missing bear with another identical bear to the administrator. She also wanted the discussion on the missing bear to cease — enough of the negative discussion. Valentine's Day was to be a happy and loving time of the year. The employee who lifted the bear soon left her position, because the peer pressure and involvement of the other employees was more discomfort than she wanted to face. This little bear did bring out an expression of real caring in the employees which had never been seen before to this degree.

One of Gene's birdhouses.

Chapter Seventeen:

Birding

Happy New Year! They came! Yes, the bluebirds came back at 9:30 this morning. It is Sunday. Gene had slept late, so did Trendy as David's family was there last night. They brought in the New Year in a comforting way. What a great way to begin a new year. To have brought in the year with your son and his family and then to have the bluebirds arrive checking out the available houses. Who sent these birds to bring a new year with Gene?

Weather on this day was like a spring day. It was sixty-three degrees. Seeing the bluebirds for the first time each year always gives Gene courage. Nothing pleases her more than having bluebirds looking over their available houses. She questions if Jack is trying to communicate with her through these bluebirds. Could this be possible? Is he sending a message of courage to her? Why does she get courage from these tiny vividly blue birds?

Shortly after Jack died in 1988, a bluebird awakened her each morning by sitting on her bedroom window sill chirping. This is unusual behavior for a bluebird. After getting awake and preparing her breakfast in the kitchen, this tiny bird would fly to the front of the house to perch on the kitchen window sill. They would go through some kind of chatter, and then this bird would fly away until the next morning. She never determined where this bird had selected a home. This vividly blue male bird did not live then in one of Gene's birdhouses.

When several bluebirds arrived on January 1, they were looking around for a home in which to raise their family in two or three months. They hopped in and out of each house and then left until ready to move in.

Gene has noticed that whenever she has some problem to solve or one similar to something she once discussed with Jack, a bluebird is sighted in her yard. Why does she get so excited when these friendly creatures visit? She does not have the answer to this question, but after hearing her discuss her fondness and a sense of well-being when seeing them, it is obvious that she derives much satisfaction when they are within view.

Winter has not really come as yet this season even though it is January. Some snow flurries were to hit the area when a front came through that night. During the winter months, Gene makes the feed that attracts the bluebirds. They stay in the area and sometimes use the birdhouses to get in and out of the cold. They do love the raisin, cornmeal and lard mixture she prepares and puts in a wire box. This encloses the food so the squirrels will not eat it. Feeding the birds and providing warm water during the cold months does assist them as they live there all year-round.

It is now February 26 and what on earth was happening in Gene's yard? She gets such satisfaction from watching their set patterns of behavior.

When she awakened this morning and started to prepare her breakfast, she saw two tiny bluebirds, swooping down at their potential home. This Momma and Poppa had only arrived three days earlier. Now, they were defending their home while trying to build their nest. They were banging their bodies at two purple martins. These larger birds were trying but failed to enter this tiny hole at the top of the bluebird house. The martins tried to ignore these blue pests, but it was the tiny entrance that prevented these intruders from entering, so they went on their way.

For a moment, Gene had to feel sorry for these purple martins as she definitely was showing partiality. Why do these blue creatures have four handsome homes awaiting for them to bring a brood of little ones? The martins do not have a ready-made home in Gene's yard. They prefer to live in apartments placed high on a pole. They need lots of space so they can swoop and eat mosquitoes and other flying insects.

Purple martins also like to live in housing developments like the bluebirds. You can notice the multiple apartment dwellings often cited near golf courses and complexes. Gene's son, Tom, built a purple martin house when they lived next to the golf course in Salisbury. This multiple dwelling was a real work of art. Jack kidded Tom that he used pounds of glue to hold it together with multiple coats of paint. Over the years, the weather took its toll on this home. In time, this house deteriorated and received a place in the attic with the other treasures. When it became non-functional, it was very sad to accept, but everything has its time and place. It served its purpose and became one of their treasured memories. These memories served another purpose as well. Tom now has put up a multiple-dwelling, purple martin home high on a pole at his home in North Carolina. They enjoy watching the arrival and feeding patterns of these lovely birds. He plans to add another martin house in the adjacent field to his home. They have a small body of water that often attracts insects. These pesky insects are controlled by the purple martins. This is nature's plan.

Gene does not have room on her property to launch a purple martin house, so she'll stick with bluebird houses. She is confident that these small tempestuous birds have the instinct for survival and control of their territory. The territory Gene watches most is the front right side of her lawn. There stands the newest house, constructed and designed as a home in which we might want to live if we were one of these small birds. It has a front door with a knob. Everyone looking at this house falls in love with it.

◆ ◆ ◆

Assembling a bluebird house sounds a bit simple. It isn't so easy. Once it is assembled and painted, it requires that it be placed five-feet off the ground. When attached to a tree or post, it provides an avenue for squirrels or snakes to make quick access into the house. It is best to purchase a metal post. Drive it into the ground before placing the house on top of the pole. Standing on a ladder and driving the pole requires a balancing act for the senior citizen.

Speaking of age, Gene learned much about bluebirds from an elderly lady who served as a consultant for her clients. The great variety of houses for various birds along with her knowledge made her a valuable friend to anyone interested in birding. This lady was quite adamant that her views were the only ones. Soon Gene learned to listen to her. When she applied her knowledge to the real situation, she concluded that she did have knowledge worth using.

As Gene continued to buy bluebird houses and poles, this new eccentric friend inquired as to where she was putting these houses.

"You know that you should not put any house closer than one mile, certainly not four houses on the size of your property."

Yes, Gene does have four well-kept and clean bluebird houses on a little less than one acre of property. Of course, she knows better. Does she usually get bluebirds in all four houses at the same time? No, she does not. However, she does see them moving from one house to another as they raise several broods each season.

Gene looked into this house as she wondered why this was happening. This inspection revealed a complete muddied side inside this one house. This mud construction contained many bees hibernating for the winter. If they were wasps, she could not tell. Destroying this hideout was much easier at that time than waiting until they were ready to fight. Once again, this house was readied by Gene for the incoming bluebird arrivals.

When the bluebirds get serious in locating their house, one can see several pairs, one male and one female, looking at the various houses at one time. The male does the search and tries to talk the female into living in the house he chooses. In reality, she plays out the act of queen and has him wrapped around her finger — no, her heart. Once she gives the go-ahead signal, this house becomes a very busy place. Both birds busily pick and choose nesting materials found in the yard. They are especially fond of the airy fern-like materials. All of this material is carried to this tiny hole and then assembled in a circular pattern. Soon, the female takes residence and deposits tiny fertilized white eggs into this clean and ready nest. Gene has witnessed five tiny bluebirds flying out after they have grown. Five eggs are a lot to keep warm for hatching.

With the bluebirds' leasing of one of their houses to the wrens, these colorful brown birds move out from under the deck. They have lived under the deck all winter, which provides them sufficient protection through the cold months. Having these wrens take-up the other bluebird houses is a joy. The wrens sing their hearts away and the bluebirds must feel as though they have piped-in music. It's fun to see how each of these separate families live in harmony and add so much to Gene's pleasures.

The purple finches accept all of this intrusion. They have lived in Gene's yard all winter. They nest in the tall shrubs and evergreens near the house. They too raise big families and stay together for some time. Gene has seen six or more of these col-

have piped-in music. It's fun to see how each of these separate families live in harmony and add so much to Gene's pleasures.

The purple finches accept all of this intrusion. They have lived in Gene's yard all winter. They nest in the tall shrubs and evergreens near the house. They too raise big families and stay together for some time. Gene has seen six or more of these colorful birds perched on the garage spouting as she works at her kitchen sink. She keeps a feeder attached to her kitchen window. This is filled with black sunflower seeds for the various birds. To add to the excitement of this feeder, the cardinals decide to drop in. They are large and the poppa is a brilliant red. By size, they are the kings of the feeder. Gene had never seen the cardinals eat from these feeders until the two recent years. Ordinarily, the cardinals eat the berries from the hollies and other shrubs. It may be that they get a kick out of pulling rank.

When it comes to feeders, that is a very hard item to keep free of squirrels. They have tried to attach themselves to the tall skinny poles on which Gene has mounted a plastic slender tube container in which she fills with thistle seed. Yellow finches love this feed. This container has small metal perches for these tiny birds to land on, and they pull feed from the tiny slots at these locations.

These crazy, persistent squirrels jump great distances only to find they are unable to hang onto the feeder, so they land hard on the ground six feet below. They keep trying. One squirrel succeeded one day and was hanging upside down with his claws dug into the tape wrappings. Gene had wrapped the base of the feeder to the metal pole in order to make it more stable. With some adjustment to this contraption, Gene soon made it almost squirrel proof. It seems that nothing with food in it is squirrel-proof. Applying some slippery substance is considered some help as a deterrent.

Gene often recalls a sad involvement with a squirrel while living in Salisbury, their previous home. Jack had purchased a bird feeder that was advertised as squirrel-proof, but each morning the squirrels would end up hanging onto this feeder as they successfully retrieved food. Gene decided that she would warn one of the varmints. She pumped air into their small short-barreled B-B gun as she walked near the feeder. Her intent was to fire a B-B into the rear of the squirrel in order to sting him and warn him to stay away from the feeder. She fired. The squirrel fell to the ground kicking and seemingly in great distress. As she walked closer, she determined that the squirrel was hit in the neck with the one fired B-B. Blood was squirting out of the neck area. How had she missed one end for the other? There was a simple answer. She was no marksman. Of course this critter had to be put out his misery. This operating room nurse was stunned. She ended his life with a sharp shovel and buried the helpless squirrel. She never shot another squirrel in an effort to warn them. Keeping squirrels out of birdfeeders continues to be a problem Gene seems to ignore today.

The squirrels are fed by some neighbors with corn-on-the-cob. There are lots of acorns that they bury all over the place. There are also hickory nuts in abundance. Still, these nasty squirrels will dig up flowering bulbs before they grow from their planted hole. These pests are just that. They cause damage to buildings from their chewing. If they were viewed as rats, everyone would try to get them exterminated. Gene's consultant bird friend had the answer for handling the squirrels. She could sell Gene the latest thing on the market that prevented even the smartest squirrel to get food from the feeders. These are expensive items for Gene's budget in which she hasn't invested.

When the squirrels eat the buckeyes off of Gene's buckeye tree, they have touched a tender spot in her heart. Being a born buckeye, from the state of Ohio, was enhanced when Jack located a buckeye tree for their twenty-fifth anniversary from a local nursery. This was in 1971. He had the tree replanted into the yard of their retirement home. It is a living treasure and memory so dear to Gene and her sons.

◆ ◆ ◆

When one is into living life, the sweet along with the bitter is harvested. Gene recalled a very bitter situation when Jack and Gene found the dead female in one of the birdhouses the first year they moved into their new retirement home. The male fluttered at the small hole and made frightening noises to get the attention of Jack and Gene. Once they opened the door and looked inside, they found the dead mother. The cause was never determined. The other partner flies off from the home and does not return. The cleaning of this house was handled carefully. Jack was aware of the various diseases that may have caused her death.

◆ ◆ ◆

Many years later in 1996, Gene's heart was broken again. This too was another bitter harvest. A beautiful pair of bluebirds arrived at her home on February 23 to claim the same house used by a family of bluebirds last year. She had no way of knowing if these were relatives of that family.

Late in March, Gene was working in her yard when the male bluebird dropped straight down from the sky. This beautiful and lifeless bird fell two feet in front of where Gene was standing. Stunned and saddened, she picked up this lifeless bird. Resuscitation seemed out of question. How do you resuscitate a bird? CPR seemed unlikely. What about diseases? Gene didn't think it was a disease as it happened so suddenly, but what had killed this beautiful poppa bluebird?

Gene held this bird in her hands for a few minutes as she stroked its chest. When it appeared to be dead she laid the bird on top of another flue birdhouse adjacent to where she was standing. She speculated that this bird had hit a window at a fast speed and perhaps broken its neck causing it to die suddenly. His beautiful bluebird feathers were all in place. There was no bleeding, but this bird never moved from the time Gene picked it up to cuddle it.

Oh, if Jack were here, she thought. His veterinarian skills could have maybe saved the life of this precious bird. Gene recalled the time when their pet duck named Peaches was killed suddenly when a stray dog had grabbed her and broken her neck. Jack had told her at that time that fowls die suddenly with broken necks.

Gene felt for the momma bluebird. Living without her mate would be something Gene knew about. The female partner flew away and vacated the home the two of them had selected in which to raise their babies.

This little stiff bird was buried that night. She tried to console herself that another pair of bluebirds would search out a house soon. Then, she would have her lovely bluebirds to watch. As of April 23, no such luck. Not even one bluebird has been observed checking out any of the four houses in Gene's yard. The absence of any bluebirds saddened Gene into the fall and winter seasons.

◆ ◆ ◆

Gene was so intrigued with her bluebirds in 1995. She designed her usual Christmas card to relate her story to friends and relatives. A copy of that story follows:

Sharing My Joys With You at Christmastime

The bluebirds nesting at my home this past year have brought me big pleasures. Here is my story:

On January 20, 1995, several bluebirds came to my home to check out the four houses in my yard. They arrived about the time I was having my leisurely breakfast. When I saw these lovely creatures this morning, I just knew that my day was going to be okay.

A few days later, I put some more bluebird feed into their feeder. They do love the raisins, cornmeal, and lard mixture that I prepare to help them live through the winter. In addition, I have a water heater in my fountain bowl to keep it from cracking. This provides a warm water supply for all of the birds staying here for the winter.

Sometimes in March, a pair of these birds selects one of the houses they would call home. Soon they are working so hard building a comfortable nest. They make sure no other bluebirds select one of the other three houses as it would be too close to them. They are very territorial.

These houses must be up on a pole five-feet from the ground or at that height on a tree that is out in the open and no under brush. They need to glide to their home and keep it safe from predators. Bluebird houses are designed for the nest being at the bottom and the hole sized correctly for them at the top of the front side. They should have accessibility for easy cleaning once a family has departed.

Speaking of departing! In late April one Sunday morning as I sat reading the paper and sipping my coffee, and my family of bluebirds took off from near the end of my garage.

First, the papa bird perched himself on the corner of the

garage — all of this in my full view. Next, the first baby Eastern Bluebird squeezed out of the hole near the roof of their house. With papa's approval he fluttered to the top of the tree on my island some fifteen-feet away. Papa guided this tiny creature to a resting place at the top of the willow oak tree. Then he assisted four more baby bluebirds as they flew for the first time to the top of this tall tree. That made a total of five baby birds who had been fed and cared for by these two parents until this day when they entered a new world.

Can you imagine how excited this whole family must have been? Soon the momma bird checked out the house for anyone being left behind.

You see, as Trendy and I walked by their home on our way to get our Sunday paper, I concluded that they might be about to venture out of their house. One tiny bird stuck his head out at me as we passed by. These busy parents fed these hungry kids constantly. Both of these parents participated in the raising of these beautiful birds. Much could be learned by some people in the raising of their kids today.

The great impact of the above story is that January will soon be here again. I am eager to see some of my bluebird family return and go through the process of selecting a home, building a nest and raising another family of these beautiful creatures.

Just maybe you will get the "bug" and put up a bluebird house and enjoy the pleasures I have had over these many years.

Good Luck!

(As of today, February 2, 1997, no bluebirds have been sighted in Gene's yard this year. In fact, her friends and neighbors have not seen any bluebirds either.)

It was cold one morning when Trendy and Gene went outside to get the paper. There was a friendly robin bird sitting under one of the holly trees in her front yard. He or she robin was crouched down as if looking for a worm. For several years now, this robin has stayed around all winter and puts up a fuss if she goes near it. She wondered if this is the female robin that kept hitting her back bedroom window beginning at 6:00 A.M. every morning until Gene found out how to stop it. This annoying robin was driving Gene nuts at that time. Trendy jumped as if to say get away from here. Gene had to protect her security screens from Trendy's thunderous leaps. She had to replace one of the damaged screens caused by Trendy in an effort to get to these pesky birds.

After searching around from various authorities, she finally learned that she had to destroy the nest of this bird. A consultant advised Gene that the bird's reflection in the window was unsettling to this bird. She had nested next to the house in an oak tree about twelve-feet from the ground. When one nest was destroyed next to the house, she rebuilt another close by. When she finally got the message and built a nest away from the house, Gene and Trendy were freed from this annoying bird. They were now free from the flapping at the windows so early in the morning. This all started shortly after Jack's death.

Now, this one lonely robin continues to hang around Gene's home. This lonely-looking bird believes she belongs to them. She seems to get in out of the elements in a tall evergreen near Gene's garage. Even Trendy looks for this bird when they go after the morning paper. Somehow, the three of them communicate in a fashion. The message is one of support and caring.

Gene's attachment for the birds living in her yard continues. Gene lives on the memories until another bluebird decides to stop and visit with her. She works hard to see that these birds have food, water, and clean housing so they will come and go as the seasons change.

Chapter Eighteen:

Celebrating

Getting ready for Christmas each year seems to be something each of us enjoys or we wouldn't do the extras. Not only do the costs at Christmas stress us, but we all may decorate, cook and or make our Christmas cards special. Gene seems to enjoy all the various aspects in which she gets involved year after year.

For a starter, she has designed, or at least planned, the theme of the card she is going to make by Thanksgiving. Some of her friends and relatives write about their day-to-day happenings, what their kids have achieved, the expensive trips or cruises they have taken, etc. Gene finds these cards somewhat interesting. She spends time reading these lengthy letters compiled by these friends. She has even tried to envision their stories as she reads their cards. Lengthy Christmas letters will always continue to arrive as there must be a need for some people to write the news of their year and share it with their friends.

On the other side of the coin is the small group of people who send a card with their names printed and no written notes from them. Well, one year Jack and Gene informed friends and relatives that they would be dropping them from their card list unless they wrote a message. Interesting! Their Christmas card list increased and they did hear from friends about their year and how they were doing.

Gene has always enjoyed designing and making her cards. She has a creative streak that seems to drive her to try to find a different design each year. Perhaps she continues to devote this much personal attention to her cards, because many of those on her list write to tell her how much they enjoy her cards. Many write that they have saved all the cards she has sent them.

She has produced many of her designs that were made under difficult circumstances before one could have printing done fairly simply. In one particular card, which she claims is one of her favorites, she animated each of the four family members as well as their boxer dog, Tears. She drew the figures and produced copies on the Xerox. Then she used pastels to bring them to life. Tears was shown riding a rocket into outer space. These two hundred cards hand-painted in pastels were then sprayed with a sealer on the screened porch. This fixing agent prevented the colors from rubbing off onto clothing. As if this were not enough, Gene and her sons had to make the envelopes since the needed size could not be found. Her cards take on many moods. Some are very serious and with religious themes. Other cards are designed to get chuckles, explanation of flower pictures, grade cards, bird stories, sketches of houses in which they as a family had lived.

Probably the most endearing card she created was a memorial to Jack in 1988. Gene described the preparation she had made in coming up with this card. One night, she just sat down and the words flowed. She had a lovely photo that reflected her story. The printing was accomplished so easily. Even the envelopes were available from the printer at that time.

◆ ◆ ◆

Cooking is one of Gene's other special projects in getting ready for Christmas. A special fruitcake — that everyone likes — gets made early, sometimes even before Thanksgiving. She makes more cookies, candy and Christmas popcorn trees than anyone in the family. These items are a tradition for her. She created little green trees made out of popcorn and colored syrup with red hots as the lights. These are shaped quickly by hand and then dusted with powdered sugar. They are not only pretty and the favorites of all family members, but they are good to eat also. Gene had developed a unique routine by using her kitchen sink for holding the popcorn when she pours the green syrup over it. This recipe can easily produce seventy-five trees that she shapes perfectly in haste before the syrup cools off. She has made these trees since 1948. In fact, she has made them every year for the past forty-nine Christmas celebrations.

The spritz cookie is a real favorite. She uses a press for both the cookie and icing. Cookies are everywhere in her kitchen. A section of decorated tiny trees, wreaths, flowers, flakes, and so on quickly gets your attention. The multiple colors of the cookies and icing give a very festive appearance. The spritz cookie was Da's favorite cookie and Gene learned to bake them just for her dad when she was quite young.

Candy-making is a fun time as well. Fudge, divinity and peanut brittle are a few of the favorites. The peanut brittle gets raves as, "That is the best I have ever eaten." Virginia is peanut country. So a student nurse who Gene taught in her diploma program in turn taught Gene to make peanut brittle in 1964. Since this is such a popular candy, Gene developed the recipe and has taught many classes on peanut brittle-making.

Arranging these homemade goodies on attractive plates or boxes is a climax of much of the cooking. Then taking these lovely gifts to neighbors, friends and or relatives seems to highlight the theme of giving. Homemade items show real caring. They reflect that personal touch and a great deal of love and caring in the preparation. This gift is a substitute for showing love.

As Christmas gets closer the progress is assessed. Yes, the cards are mailed. The gifts have been purchased and wrapping is nearly completed. The trees inside and outside have been decorated. Clear lights are used in Virginia as they reflect the white light used by the early settlers. Occasionally a family from somewhere uses colored bulbs on the trees and other decorations. These look trashy and dowdy after you get used to the while lights and candles in each window.

The mailbox and doors are decorated with festive themes. The leaves are all vacuumed from the lawn and shrubbery. It looks like the whole outside was swept. Of course, the cleaning of the house is usually done after all of the projects, as they may cause a mess when the process is under way.

Eric, Gene's grandson, came to visit while home from college. He had grandma teach him to make noodles. Yes, homemade noodles are always on the menu for every special dinner such as holidays and birthdays. Gene continues to make the noodles because her sons, and their children love the fact that she makes them. She is the only daughter of the six who still makes her noodles. There is a big discussion always as to which family gets to take home the leftover noodles, and Gene always cooks a large amount so there are some left over to take home. Along with the noodles always goes the mashed potatoes. The noodles are served over the mashed potatoes. This whole family is big on potatoes fixed any way. Gene tries to play down the time she devotes to the various projects she finds herself engaged in while producing for her family and friends. She reaps great satisfaction as she produces her various creative projects each year. It is hard to ever think that this act of kindness will end some day. This is her way of expressing her unspoken love through her cooking.

Chapter Nineteen:

Relative Influence

This family thrives on working, playing or walking outside where they can appreciate the wonders of nature. There is no doubt this love for the outdoors originated with them as they grew up on the farm learning about nature, animals and the beauty of the landscape. They loved to work with their hands.

Today, Ned and his daughter, Sandra, have young walnut trees to care for which they planted in the recent years. These number in the hundreds. When the rain is in short supply, they water them by hand. These trees are on the land Ned owns and which is the family farmland. Sandra's land which she purchased some time past also has young walnut trees which she planted after her father started his project. Even though she lives in Wisconsin, where she teaches and her husband is a principle, she gets back to the farm to assist her parents as well as assume some management roles of her dad's farm during his episodes of illness.

◆ ◆ ◆

When Stanley and Lela's children were growing up, they assumed some chores as a result of assignment or they desired to do one over the other. The various chores were the milking of the cows which was done morning and night. Cooking and dishwashing was a chore that each girl took turns at, as no one wanted to do this every night. Cording of wood, bringing it in for the stoves and the taking out of the ashes were other chores. Gardening and lawn care were big ones during the warm months. Before the advent of having available electricity, lamps had to be filled and glass globes washed daily. Of course, the ironing was shared. Mom was particular about the washing and she did this big job and rarely relinquished this essential chore. The chickens had to be fed, eggs gathered and cleaned. Da didn't like chickens and so everyone was particular in entering and exiting the gate where chickens were kept. The "outhouse" was within the fenced area for the chickens, so this area saw a lot of traffic.

But the gardening was done with much dedication, mostly by Gene when she became old enough. There was a large lawn to mow. Mowing was started on Thursdays and finished before Saturday evenings. One flower bed between the first two driveways was the pride of the whole family. This bed of peonies was started by Da's mother when she was a young bride. There were twenty-five or more huge peony bushes over one hundred years old, iris beds, lilies, and rambling old-fashioned roses. Yuccas lined one side of this lovely area. One end near the barn was a curved row of shrubs. Some of the peony blossoms were dark reds, pink with white centers, white with pink centers, all pink, all white and some other crosses.

Gene also mowed the grass in this garden. It often required her holding the large bushes while moving under them. Mowing was done by a push lawn mower. In the spring, a load of manure was spread in this area. Since the soil there was alkaline, these plants did not need lime as it does in Virginia where the soil is acid.

For Memorial Day, or that weekend, Gene prepared many flower arrangements which she and Mom took to four cemeteries. These beautiful flowers were placed on the graves of grandparents, aunts and uncles and mom's brothers and sisters. Gene inherited this task since she enjoyed working with the flower arrangements. Mom relied upon her skills and assistance in the decorating of the various graves of the relatives. Even after the deaths of Da and Mom, Gene looked after the graves whenever she came home from Virginia. All the girls contributed in purchasing the young flowering plants each spring. Recently, Susan has taken the responsibility of selecting and planting the flowers. Kassy waters the planter on our parent's grave since she drives past the cemetaries on a frequent basis.

Susan purchased a floral arrangement one year thinking it would reduce the workload. Well, with the graves near the road, this arrangement was stolen. Gene angered by this action, purchased another floral arrangement that she had made up once she got to Ohio. She wired this arrangement around and under the planter. It did stay through the winter. It also was not as eye catching from the road.

One year when Gene went home to Ohio in the spring, she purchased some perennials thinking these would bloom at various times of the summer and fall. Well, some small chewing critters dug them up and many times ate the roots. The care of the graves and maintaining lovely flowers there was a full-time job. It required more than the yearly visits that she could only devote while living in Virginia. This is very frustrating to Gene. She had learned as a child to care for the graves by growing, arranging and placing flowers on the various graves as she accompanied her mother.

Gene's grandmother also raised lovely flowers which had a big influence on the girls in this family. Aunts and uncles kept beautiful gardens as well. One aunt, a sister of Da's mother, had a beautiful English-style garden. Gene was privileged to visit there often with her parents. This great aunt took time to name the plants and teach the care required for each plant. Gene's love of flowers was developed and nurtured as she grew into adulthood.

Aunt Helen, Uncle Virgil's wife, had a garden planned and planted by the horticulture department from Notre Dame in South Bend, Indiana. She knew the names of all of the plants. She was an earthy person and one of our favorite aunts as kids. She often made candy and brought it to this family when she visited. Aunt Helen and Uncle Virgil met as students at Ohio State University. Aunt Helen studied home economics and uncle Virgil studied agriculture. They were married by the president of Ohio State University when it was smaller. Gene drove to South Bend from Virginia after stopping in Ohio to pick-up some of the family a few years ago. They went to South Bend to celebrate Aunt Helen's one hundred year birthday. She lived a very productive life and inspired all of those around her. Uncle Virgil was Da's oldest brother.

Then there was Aunt Bina (Blanche) Da's only sister. She had style, class, was a former school teacher, and was very knowledgeable in gardening and flowers. She added much to our growth and development, but she preferred boys over girls. She did have Julia and Susan come visit and stay with her. The rest of us were not some of her favorites. We didn't mind this, as we understood her pretty well.

When Aunt Bina's son, Billy, had just graduated from high school, he was riding his motorcycle when an auto hit him and set him on fire. He lived that day until his parents could tell him goodbye at the hospital. The death of Billy was hard for all of us, but Aunt Bina and Uncle Oliver coped. She did better than Uncle Oliver, somehow. The ability to cope under severe stress seems to be a very strong asset apparent in this family.

How did they learn to cope and then pick up the pieces and go on? Religion was not always the mainstay. They seemed to pull from inner strength.

Gene recalls another aunt who had a beautiful garden and home. She and Uncle Sam did not have any children, and yet they both were great role models. Aunt Daisy was married to Mom's dad's brother. She was a music teacher and Uncle Sam a farmer. During World War II, Uncle Sam brought homemade butter to our farm and had Gene make him cream puffs. Gene was a young teenager, but loved pleasing Uncle Sam by cooking one of his favorites. He was a rather homely man, but always pleasant and even funny.

Gene visited Aunt Daisy with Mom years after Uncle Sam had died.

Frequently she was out mowing the lawn near her beautiful flower garden. Never did she complain about being lonely or feeling sad for herself. Her life seemed full and she lived on some very fond memories. My, what memories we had when her will was read. It certainly surprised all of us. She left a small amount of money to each of her great nieces and nephews on her side, as well as Uncle Sam's side. This numbered over forty or fifty of us.

Gene was the gardener on the farm when she became a teenager.

She often gets asked today as she did at their other homes as to how she developed her love for gardening. Gene always tells them she learned as a child on the farm at her home. She also had grandmothers and aunts and uncles living near their farm when she was young from whom she learned to love the growing of flowers and seeing them enhance the landscape.

Gardening and growing grass in Virginia is a terrible task. The soil is primarily clay with high acidity. You need to work peat moss in as there are almost no organic materials. Even after eighteen years of working hard to improve their yard at Salisbury, it could have still had more peat moss mixed into it. But after thirty years of working with the soil in Virginia, which at times shouldn't even be called soil, one learns to never give up. For if you give up trying to garden, you are sunk. For the newcomers to the state, it is almost an overwhelming project.

◆ ◆ ◆

While moving into their first home in Richmond, Tom became interested in creating an outside aquarium. He dug this clay mix and finally had it deep enough to shape cement which would hold the water. He tried his artistic skills a bit further when he created a real personable man. He asked Gene how to get a nose on the man. When Gene looked at his project, she realized that he was shaping a face in the sand where he would pour his cement. She advised digging deeper for the nose. As the result of Tom's creative efforts, they soon had a stern-faced man's bust with a water spout standing to the head of this attractive aquarium area. This cement man named "Stone Man" has deep penetrating eyes. Tom now has this work of art at the side of his flowing fountain, all a part of this beautifully landscaped aquarium in North Carolina.

◆ ◆ ◆

Jack and Gene became interested in playing golf after they moved to Salisbury. With both of them working heavy and challenging positions, the relished any free time in which they could play the four holes that back up to their home. Many evenings after work, they would tee four or five balls on the 16th, cut across to the 13th, 14th and back home to the 15th. Tears, their loyal boxer dog, always walked with them. In fact, she would stand ready to go onto the course the minute they came home from work. This outing was a marvelous way of releasing the pent-up pressures from the day. At the hour they went on the course, most always all players had passed the area and were on their way to the club house.

Jack took lessons and became a dedicated golfer. He played routinely on Saturday mornings with friends who helped him release his sense of humor too. They had a lot of fun and it was good for Jack to associate with friends away from work. He did win several silver trophies as result of the various tournaments held at the club. When he needed some golf supplies or wanted to look at new clubs, he visited Tommy. Tommy Wine was a really good golf pro at the adjacent subdivision in Brandermill. In fact, Tommy was one big influence when Gene and Jack selected a lot in Brandermill to build their retirement home. The pro in Salisbury was so stuck on himself and Jack did not pass out false politics. Well, quite often the pro there did not even recognize whenever they were at the club. The club at Salisbury and its membership was so status-oriented. Even after eighteen years as members, Jack and Gene never felt as though they belonged. Many of the members were surprised when they met them and learned they were the owners of the property with the beautiful garden which backed up to the fifteenth green.

Once Jack and Gene moved to Brandermill, they joined the golf club there. Since they were finishing their retirement home and working in a new yard, golf was put on hold. Certainly, the development of Jack's serious health problems that became acute within five months after moving into their new home deferred any golf activities.

Gene continued the golf membership at the club after Jack's death. They had paid the initiation fee and she thought that she may need this contact with the outside world. She started to play more golf after her retirement from nursing in 1988. She joined the nine holers and seemed to enjoy the meeting of new friends. With a few lessons and more practice, her golf improved. She developed a fairly good support group. They did help her adjust to Jack's death. However, it was extremely hard at times when she would see couples play golf as she and Jack had once done together.

This void was filled partially by Gene devoting all her time and energy to gardening at their new home. She had to look after the trees that were planted on their lot. The cost of $12,000 was a big investment. This investment would not be noticed for at least five or more years. The trees are now nine years old. They are beautiful. They provide lots of shade and leaves. The grass attracts the attention of all who pass-by the property.

Jack had purchased a new wheel horse tractor for this property. It was smaller than the one he used at Salisbury, but too big for their property now with all the new trees and shrubs. Gene traded the new tractor in for a smaller one which she could handle. This tractor has the two bags for vacuuming leaves and grass cuttings. This keeps the lawn looking like it was swept. Gene enjoys using her tractor and observing those passing by as they stretch their necks at seeing a tractor with an old lady at the wheel.

Gene has learned to change the oil and clean the tractor as needed. She has a neighbor, Norman, who has assisted with the various problems which she could not correct. Norman, started the engine after the battery was drained from grounding with water. He listens for the proper sounding of the motor and adjusts what is needed. Norman is a retired mechanical engineer and comes running the minute Gene identifies a problem.

Norman not only looks after the tractor, he has adjusted the garage doors, repaired the pole light when it was broken off, repaired the switch at the aquarium. He even brought new lights from their home which light around the fountain after dark. He grinds leaves and limbs into mulch, plays with Trendy, repairs the auto as needed and there is nothing he won't tackle.

When Gene got her new computer, both Sandra and Norman

served as instant consultants. He is willing to teach or explain what she needs to know in order to do a program or play a game. She is using her computer to write and hopefully publish topics of interest to her. How does Norman get paid for his labors? Well, Gene loves to cook and bake, so she supplies Norman and Sandra with good, fattening foods. This provides an outlet for her fondness for cooking while repaying Norman for his generous detailed repairs.

Gene uses her computer for recording garden needs and dates for planned repairs. A new heat pump was purchased in 1995 with the old one only used since 1987. This heat pump never seemed right during the whole year it was in warranty. Well, one month out of warranty in December, 1996 this new heat pump quit. This company agreed to pay for the new part, but they didn't tell Gene that they would never get the part ordered from the company. Gene continued to heat her house in December with the use of her fire place. Luckily, she had gotten a cord of wood for use in case of an ice storm which may cause the electricity to go out.

Finally, Gene pursued finding out why the repairs to the heat pump had been delayed. It was then that she learned that the part had never been ordered, and that she may well have no heat over Christmas and beyond the new year. This company had set off Gene's German temper. She demanded a new heat pump be installed by 5:00 on Christmas Eve. Further more, she demanded that the company pay for the new one which would replace the lemon she had loaded onto her the prior year.

Shortly after lunch, Gene received a call from a workman that they were bringing out a new pump. It would be installed before five that day.

The owner of the business never talked to Gene during the whole process. He passed information to a fairly incompetent employee who he thought would bluff her into waiting for a repair part for two more weeks. What this owner did not know about Gene was that she had learned as a kid to get what was due her. Through her working world, she had learned to record every time she called a repairman, what they found wrong, what they did and how long this repair lasted. Her detailed documentation served her well in proving she had reason to have a new heat pump replace the lemon she had. She had the confidence often witnessed in the Midwest women, but not often seen here in Virginia. This surprised the owner of this heating business.

Gene is still waiting for this company to schedule a workman to do a preventative maintenance visit for which she had already paid. They have never called to inquire about the new pump, or even to apologize for the stress they caused Gene. Gene was stressed trying to keep the house warm enough to prevent pipes from freezing. She added firewood to her fireplace every two hours for eleven consecutive days. She was recuperating from a new knee replacement done in September. This prevented her from getting on her knees to remove ashes.

Gene marked her latest battle of fighting for a new air conditioner that was due to her as just another problem often waged by a senior citizen living alone. Fortunately, she had learned as a young person how to sustain the courage and skills that ultimately brought her some kind of a victory. This kind of victory does take its toll on all concerned. It is a shame that anyone is put in this position at anytime in their lifespan.

Chapter Twenty:

Happenings

Gene was about to meet with a dental surgeon in May 1995. Shortly after coming home one day, she removed her partial plate — one she had worn since 1957. It always felt like she was wearing a brace. Since she was hungry, she bit into some dried apricots. Suddenly, she had a missing tooth. It was gone. Where was this tooth? She could feel the sharp edge of the root with her tongue as the root stuck above the gum. Fright set in. She must have swallowed this gold-capped tooth. This tooth was capped in 1957 when Gene had extensive dental work. She felt no pain with the remaining tooth, but the thought of having to seek her dentist was frightening.

Gene has had a great fear of dentists since she was a child. As a child, a dentist was not seen until a tooth either needed to be pulled or needed an extensive filling. Her parents were aware of the need to see a dentist, but there was no money for either immediate care or preventative care. The cost of a local anesthetic when Gene was a child was $1.00, so most all dental work was done without any local anesthetic. The family dentist would assure Gene that the pain would last only a short time. Is there any wonder she still experiences fear at the thought of visiting a dentist? She is conditioned for life even though she tries to calm herself down for her yearly preventative visits.

When Gene gained courage and presented herself to the dentist, she learned that she could take one of two proposed plans. First, have a root canal and have a peg inserted where a false tooth could be attached for support of her partial bridge, or she could have the root removed and a false tooth placed on the partial bridge. Her current bridge had three other points of attachment and losing the fourth point would not have a great impact. The root canal and false tooth attached would be $1,000 or more. It would cost much less to have the root extracted. The decision was made since Gene did not have dental insurance, and it seemed the faster and less painful way. She was given some referrals for selection of a dental surgeon.

Meeting this polite, handsome dental surgeon, relieved her mind. Her sense of humor was back and she felt quite at ease as they discussed the type of anesthesia for the upcoming dental surgery. They worked out a plan to have this extraction in his office the next week. He did not have an opening in his schedule before that time and it did not seem urgent since Gene was not in pain. Surgery did take place as planned and Gene made a fast recovery.

◆ ◆ ◆

Gene discussed with her son, David, her desire to do some publishing. She had always wanted to write a book and to get some articles published. She had set-up her den and planned to use her electric typewriter for the initial writings. David quickly convinced her that she should consider getting a computer which would make her achieve her goal in an easier manner. He also kidded his mom that she needed to be computer literate. Gene had used a computer for a few simple recordings in her last working position, but most of that information was gone after not using it for five years.

It was November, 1993 when David first suggested that Gene get a computer. Within a short time and after work one day, David met Gene to review some good buys for her needs. Within hours they had selected her computer and printer with all the connections, plus her mouse, which Gene purchased. Excited and eager to get started, David and Gene drove to Gene's home. Soon David had assembled the computer and systems. What a great help this was for Gene. She enjoyed being with David as she felt really proud to have her son take an interest in her welfare and guide her on the right road. He was well-qualified in the computer field as they surveyed the various costs and features offered by the various companies. What a great help David was as he assisted Gene.

Gene was a good typist, but had no idea as to what she needed to know to even begin operating her new computer. An initial lesson was given to her that night by David and she was in business. Of course, the questions popped up immediately. She recalled having typed a good letter which she would send to family and friends. With the push of one button, she lost the whole thing.

"David, let me tell you what I did. I don't want to waste my time like that. What do I do?"

"You will have to read your instruction books, Mom," came David's response.

Gene knew learning from the book would be hard for her. She thought she learned more easily by seeing something demonstrated. Soon, she was trying to get her answers from the book.

"Tom, I have a new computer that David helped me select and assembled for me. When can you give me a lesson?" I asked.

"Mom, you need to read your books that came with it. It would also be a good idea for you to take some classes at the local college."

Tom is a computer programmer. He realized that starting from scratch would require that Gene take some beginner classes. Soon, Gene was in some all-day classes held on Saturdays at a local college near her home. An all-day class learning about your computer makes for a big killer day, but she survived and learned some basics.

Another teacher and resource lives directly behind her home. Norman, her retired mechanical engineer neighbor was quite skilled in the operation of a computer. Luckily, Gene referred many questions to Norman. Norman also soon realized that Gene had a long way to go, but since his retirement he had time to help solve some of her questions personally. Norman and his wife Sandra would come over to Gene's home and one lesson often branched into several. In some instances when time passed before Gene really mastered the procedure, she would need prompted again. "Norman to the rescue," soon became the code. Trendy always looked forward to seeing Sandra and Norman come to visit. This dog gets so lonely while living with "Grandma" as Gene refers to herself when she and Trendy talk.

"Hello, Mom. Can I come over and go over some of the questions that you might have with your computer?" David asked as he called her one night.

"I will come over Saturday around 11:30 A.M. before lunch. I would enjoy some of your good cooking. Please do not go to any trouble. I will leave home around 10:30 A.M. and see you before lunch." stated David as he finalized his plans.

He arrived as planned and on time. He got out of his car and strolled toward Gene's front door. He presented the very image of how Gene remembered her father. She had always noticed his mannerisms and looks to be like her father's. He has big shoulders, is well-built, tall and confident in stature. His walk is similar. He has wavy hair with a wirey body. This too is like his Grandfather Place's hair. When he looks at you, his penetrating eyes seem to be reading your mind. He drives and pushes all the time trying to make every minute count.

The computer lesson began after lunch and many problems were solved. He installed a program for desktop publishing, which they have given to Gene as a gift. Gene started using this program to create various print-outs she uses in her staff development classes.

Within weeks, while Gene was using the program that David had just installed in her computer, she lost the program. She could not bring it up on the screen. Somehow, she had wiped it out, but David had taught her well. She watched him install the seven discs. He advised her to keep them in another room away from the phone for safe keeping. She retrieved the discs, installed the program again and was really proud of her progress.

"David, I lost the desktop publishing program that you installed in my computer."

"Lost it, what do you mean you lost it? You could not lose it as there are stops in the computer to prevent this from happening," said David seriously.

"Well, letters came up saying I didn't have the program, so I ran the seven discs as you taught me and the program started working. Isn't that smart of me? I am really proud of the fact that I have learned how to install new programs. Who knows what I'll do next," Gene informs him proudly.

"I don't know how you lost it, but am certainly glad you can correct the problem. You are going to be dangerous with all of your learning." David said.

Gene had gotten a Valentine's Day card a few weeks earlier from both sons. These cards told her how thankful they were for having taught them how to love. In reality, it was their dad who taught Gene so she could help teach their two sons to express love as well. These two sons, David and Tom, express and demonstrate love to their families. These two assets make for many sweet harvests.

◆ ◆ ◆

Another March 4th arrived. David turned forty-seven. Gene attended a lovely dinner party at David's home. Eric had come home for his spring break. Trendy always enjoys seeing Eric. It means that she may get some food since Eric usually leaves something for her to eat.

Eric, Gene's grandson, came to visit her while he was on spring break. She prepared a good lunch with lemon meringue pie. He puckered his lips when he ate it. He declined taking it home with him that day. Instead, he suggested that Gene keep the remainder for his dad when his parents came over for dinner the next day. Usually, all deserts go home with the kids when they come to Gene's for a meal. In fact, Gene always makes this allowance, which might mean that he double whatever she cooks.

Gene had talked about fishing when Eric called to say he would come over on Wednesday. This meant that they had to go get their fishing licenses and some fresh bait. After lunch they went to Bob's — a sportsman's shop with lots of items for all sports. It seems that they carry a lot of guns. Anyhow, Gene's license cost $1.00, since she is a senior citizen. She treated Eric to his license for $12.50, since he is a college student.

Soon they were fishing in the reservoir near Gene's home. Usually they catch bass, blue gills and perch. Gene cleans the fish since she never did teach the grandchildren to use the sharp knives needed to clean fish. Sometimes she fries them for Eric if he stays over for supper.

Gene often related to her grandchildren that if you keep the fish, you have to clean them for eating. This was a rule Gene's dad had in effect when they were kids. If they didn't want to clean the fish, they had to put the fish back while they were alive and kicking.

"You will clean the fish you catch and keep," was stated only a few times by Da.

When Gene knows that she has to clean them, she frequently puts the fish back so they can grow more. Maybe she will catch them again sometime in the future when she fishes the area. She usually hops on her bike and rides to some of her select fishing spots near her home. Neighbors look at her as she does these fun trips. One neighbor came out of his house after watching her fish for several hours.

"You fascinate me as you sit there fishing for hours," commented this retired minister.

"Yes, I not only fish, but I do a lot of thinking when I'm sitting here looking out over the water. I watch the sunset, the colors of the clouds and the various waves on the surface of the water. It is very relaxing," explained Gene.

It becomes evident as one observes Gene's lifestyle unfold that what she learned as a child has served her well in her adult life. She will never be at a loss on how to enjoy life. She is thankful that she can entertain herself. She observes so many people today who have to be entertained and rarely stay alone or content themselves.

Entertaining is not the word for what happened to Gene one day while driving. She was returning to her home one day around 4:00 P.M. when she decided to fill her gas tank. As she came down the street, she encountered a schoolbus with one blinking red light as she came up out of a valley and around a curve. On the left side of the street was the school with five parked schoolbuses. Gene's first response in seeing the bus and flashing light was that it would be turning into the school grounds. Instead, the bus stopped in front of the school on this busy road. Gene had slowed down when she entered the school zone, so she was not traveling fast as she was passing the stopped bus. She then could see both red lights indicating it was stopping and not turning. The bus driver put out the stop sign when Gene was parallel with the bus. The children had not been let off the bus when Gene passed it.

Just as Gene was beginning to pass the bus, she noticed a patrolman sitting in the school's parking lot. She also saw the driver point to her. Gene knew then that she would be hearing from the patrolman.

Where was Gene going to pull over and stop? The road was narrow and had heavy traffic. She motioned to the policeman to back-up onto the side street as he pulled-up with his flashing lights. He backed-up onto a street which was for the incoming traffic. It was divided by a median strip. Before the discussion began, Gene suggested they move their autos to the opposite side with their cars headed in the right direction.

"They're all right," he commanded.

"Don't you know that those two round, red flashing lights at the top of the bus means that it is stopping?" asked this patrolman as he made two round circles with his hands while continuing to interrogate Gene.

"Yes, I do know about the red lights and schoolbuses. I rode one for twelve years and my two sons each road them for twelve years," Gene said calmly and politely in an effort to stop the badgering she was experiencing.

"Is this your automobile? I need proof, and I want to see your driver's license."

Gene gave him her license and he was walking back to his police car, as she responded to him that this was her auto. She could let him see the title, but he rudely kept on walking back to his cruiser.

After several minutes, he strolled back to Gene's auto. He never stood where she could see his name or look at him directly. She had to twist her neck in order to engage in a conversation with this blond, robust, officer in his early twenties; good communication skills were noticeably missing.

"I am not going to give you a summons," the patrolman said.

Gene concluded that a summons meant the same as a ticket. She had never gotten a driving ticket and was not well-versed in the necessary language.

"You see, you are a senior citizen with a perfect driving record. The judge would throw out the case," continued this snarley officer.

He could not bring himself to acknowledge that the bus was hidden from Gene's view as it came up a hill and around a curve. Gene could only see the right blinking light initially on the bus and reasoned it was turning where the other buses were parked.

After Gene had gone home and regrouped, she went back to trace the paths of the bus and her auto to see why she missed recognizing that the bus was stopping and not turning. It became vividly clear to her that the curves and hills were the factors obstructing her vision. She wanted to talk with this burly police officer and relate her feelings. Furthermore, she was sure that other drivers would find this child's crossing area an unsafe site that needed to be changed. She also knew that this officer would not be receptive to her continuing the discussion on any matter. At least she was pretty sure the driver controlled the situation when children left the bus and the driver saw that they were safe.

♦ ♦ ♦

Of course, having been shaken by this encounter while driving made her recall the last time she was stopped by a patrolman. More than fifteen years ago, Gene's husband asked her to drive his auto as he needed to have the oil changed in hers. He was always particular in getting the cars taken care of on the recommended schedule.

She was cruising through the village of Midlothian near her home on her way to work in Jack's auto. She was pulled over by the patrolman with the lights flashing on his cruiser. The patrolman was polite and quite personable.

"I bet you don't know why I stopped you?" resounded this great voice which matched the subtle smile as the officer peered down at Gene.

"I know that you have identified me as an outstanding driver," Gene seriously answered. "I read in the paper that you were stopping some drivers to compliment them on their driving." Gene said.

"That sounds good," as he gave her a broad and friendly smile, "but I stopped you as your six-month inspection sticker has expired. There will be no citation if you have your husband get an inspection immediately," the officer stated.

He had listened intently as Gene explained that this auto was her husband's auto and why she was driving it on that day.

Jack got a good laugh at Gene having been stopped. Here he was worrying about Gene's auto and had forgotten about his own. They both had a good chuckle especially since no one had gotten a ticket.

◆ ◆ ◆

Taking care of an auto became a big chore for Gene after Jack's death. Gene had always washed the cars. She learned to do this as a kid when the cars had to be washed and cleaned inside every

Saturday. Her car is always clean and the grocery boys usually comment about her clean trunk as they place the groceries in her trunk.

"I'm going to nominate you for an award of having the cleanest and most orderly trunk. You should look at some of the trunks I see when I put the groceries in them," volunteered this cute teenager.

The care of the cars along with grocery-buying, and all of the other chores and errands seemed to be something Jack enjoyed. He was so thoughtful in every way to do tasks that relieved Gene of extras that she did not like to do. He truly spoiled her. Their sons do the same for their wives and families.

Widows have to get in-step with so much when their partners die suddenly. Jack always reminded their two sons of the need for an oil change, transmission checks and tire changes. Jack and Gene even bought tires for their sons at Christmas as Jack worried about their safety. He kept on top of their insurance when they had their first cars. Now, they are doing the same for their children.

◆ ◆ ◆

Gene just recalled another incident of having been stopped by a patrolman over twenty years ago. This time, she was again stopped at the outer edge of Midlothian. She commuted daily to her nursing position, which was nearly fifteen-miles from her home. On this particular morning, the patrolman informed Gene that he had been following her many miles into this small village. He also observed her speeding as he followed for miles.

"You must have mistaken me for some other auto you were following. I just turned onto this highway one mile before entering Midlothian," Gene said.

Gene had observed three other Oldsmobiles traveling around her at that time and she related that fact to the patrolman. She named the make, year and color of the other three automobiles. This had always been a practice of Gene's since she taught observation skills and had always practiced the naming cars game.

The officer checked her address. He concluded he was wrong after he had gotten back into his auto.

"Go ahead and pull out," yelled the officer.

"You have my view blocked," responded Gene smiling.

He pulled out in a furor with stones flying striking Gene's windshield.

This behavior angered Gene, but she did not chase him to tell him so. She learned from this encounter and it reinforced her thinking and encouraged her to continue to use her observation skills while driving.

◆ ◆ ◆

Knowing the make of the car, the year, color and which state somenone's license is from has been an exercise Gene created when she traveled with her children. Gene uses her mind and keeps her observation skills keen. While traveling with her children on long trips and out of state, she encouraged her children to play this game with her. They tried to select ten cars as the cars passed them. They numbered them mentally, associated the make, the color and from which state with that number. They could drop a number and add another as the various cars passed.

The game goes this way: For instance, number three could be from Texas with a black and white license and was a red Plymouth. When you get the ten cars in your mind, you can drop number five, a white Dodge from Iowa with a green and yellow license for a blue and while license plate. As you travel, you can substitute the various makes from different states and keep the observation game going. With the advent of so many small cars from foreign countries, it became more difficult to know the make and year of the cars. Good observation skills are very important in reporting any incident. Usually the details are recalled if previously practiced to recount what is in the mind and memory.

Gene's fascination with memory began with her favorite teacher at Buckland High School. She had a teacher then who taught band, basketball, math and science. In addition, he was the principle of this small village school. Who would imagine such a versatile teacher today? While teaching chemistry, algebra, and so on, he required that the students hold formulas in their heads. He also required them to do math in their heads. They could not use a pencil or paper. This was before calculators came into being and are now at the fingertips of everyone.

Gene therefore developed excellent memory skills as a young student and continued to develop them as an adult. Having a good memory has served her well in her nursing profession as well as in her personal life. We are not sure how the elephants developed their memory skills, but it might be worth researching. Have you ever seen an elephant with a pencil and paper or calculator?

When Gene was selected by this favorite teacher to be the drum major, she worked very hard to become good at it and learned to twirl her baton. Mom and Gene made her majorette outfit with wool flannel and lined it with sateen. Applying the braid and gold buttons put the final touches that made it perfect. Gene had a good figure with good-looking legs. She could strut in a very graceful way. Having good musical sense helped her feel the beat and this achievement made her parents proud even though they never expressed it to her.

◆ ◆ ◆

Ned's Big 80th Birthday Party!

Barbara, Ned's wife, sent invitations to all of Ned's immediate family and neighbors and selected friends for a surprise 80th birthday party for Ned. This was held on his birthday, May 19, 1996 at the Chalet in Wapakoneta. He did not suspect anything as his Sandra and the rest of his five children usually came to help celebrate his birthdays. Since they usually ate dinner out together, they left for this restaurant unknown to Ned. This would be the place where he would really be surprised.

No sooner than they arrived at the Chalet, than in came his four sisters and the families of his neighbors and friends. He was a bit surprised to see Gene who had driven from Virginia a few days earlier. Betty was leaving for Hawaii in a few days and so elected to not crowd in too much and therefore stayed in Pittsburgh. Neighbors and distant cousins Bryan and Liz Place were there. Beaulah or Buie as we always called her had come with mom's kid brother and his wife who were all from Lima. Uncle Lowell, mom's other brother, was there. He will be ninety in March 1997. Kassy is already planning that party. Kassy's thing is planning and giving a party for any person and/or cause. S.B. was in the middle of farming with his son, Neal, and could not make it from North Carolina at this time.

The pictures of Ned, Barbara and their children reflect that they all look good. Ned is straight in posture, has maintained an excellent weight and a really sharp mind. He has some hearing defects and seems unable to wear his hearing device. He is a product of working around noisy farm equipment without protecting his ears. Today, we know better and do practice prevention.

Everyone was advised not to bring gifts on this occasion, but Betty called Gene and stated that no one should have an 80th birthday party without gifts. They decided on a denim work jacket. Gene selected the jacket in Findlay, while visiting with Isabel in Forest prior to coming to the party. Susan wanted in on the project and she donated her share. Kassy had sent a check to Ned's family as a contribution toward the refreshments. When the check was returned to her, she too wanted in on the jacket, so Kassy paid her share. Gene had told Karin that that there was already a sufficient amount donated and that she was included as the jacket turned out to be from the sisters.

The jacket was a big hit. It fit him well and seemed sufficiently big, while allowing room for a heavy shirt. Bob Baker tried on the jacket and liked it too. You see, Bob will be seventy-nine in December. Before long, both Kassy and Bob will be eighty also. Who will be around when some of us younger ones reach their 80th?

After the party, Gene went home with Susan and Jim as planned. She had driven to their home that morning from Forest, Ohio. They spent the time together catching-up on nursing news as both of them still work as R.N.s in long-term care facilities.

On Monday, Susan and Gene set out to replant the planter on Mom and Da's grave at Fort Amanda. Ft. Amanda is a state park and the site of ravaging Indian battles. It is near the home farm now owned by Ned and Barbara. Susan had purchased a nice assortment of annuals that would survive the summer heat. Kassy will be the one watering the flowers, since she passes this place on her way to their chicken farm. Gene appreciates all of the local caring as she is too far to give the graves the attention they deserve.

After the planting, Susan drove with Gene to Kassy's where they had planned to meet for a lunch outing. Washing or ironing chores didn't keep any of the three at home on this lovely Monday. They had an excellent meal at a local Wapakoneta restaurant which offered a wide variety of buffet food. It was so good, in fact they all had eaten too much. They made several stops at the local florists as they tried to find a suitable dinner centerpiece for the party planned for the coming Wednesday. A first cousin, Fred, had invited their friends and families for a dinner party in honor of Margene, his wife, who was to celebrate her 80th. Kassy was asked to select the center arrangement. She wanted to use Gene's creative skills associated with floral centerpieces in the selection process. None of the available arrangements seemed to appeal to any of them for the purpose it would serve. This project was put on hold for the day and Kassy would seek one prior to the party on Wednesday.

They returned to Kassy's home as she insisted she had to get some cleaning done. This fun time together for these sisters was a real first. They really had a good time and experienced the fact that they could use time on a casual basis instead of always making every minute scheduled to do some work.

As planned, Gene started back to Virginia on Tuesday, May 21. She drove to David's in Richmond arriving at 7:00 P.M. She had about five stops to stretch her legs, gas-up and do the necessary nature calls.

David was in Kansas City for a meeting. Barbara had gone to a meeting, so she packed up Trendy and headed for her home some twenty miles away. When she drove into her driveway, she had driven 600 miles that day. She usually stops on the way to Ohio. But coming home is a bit different for all of us.

She unloaded her car the next day. As her polelight at her entrance was knocked-down, her retired mechanical engineer neighbor was there fixing it before Gene could get awake. The grass needed mowing. Gene wanted to be outside. The unloading of her car was done later. It could wait. She cleaned the fish filter which had driven Norman crazy trying to keep it clean. She had to give Trendy some extra attention in order to get her to make-up for having been left behind. Both Trendy and Gene were glad to be home once more.

Chapter Twenty-One:

Knee Deep in Pain

While playing golf one year ago, Gene fell while walking to her golf cart. The left foot stepped into a grass covered hole causing her to fall and twist her right knee. She skinned her hands and landed on her chest causing a black and blue bruise on her chest. Prior to this fall, she had suffered knee problems believed to be caused by arthritis. This new injury caused swelling and severe pain in her right knee.

Within a few months this knee pain prevented her from walking any distance. It was difficult for her to shop for groceries and to do her gardening. In March she sought out the best knee surgeon she could find. He had done the surgery on Bryan's shoulders and was known throughout the country, since he operated on prominent sport figures.

Once he looked at her X-ray of her of her right knee. "I can do nothing for you as the knee needs to be replaced. I will refer you to my surgeon." She was disappointed when David picked her up for lunch that day. David's office was close to this knee specialist.

Within weeks she was meeting with the knee surgeon. "Let's talk first," he said as he calmly sat down with her privately in the examining room. He didn't jump at the opportunity of having another patient on which to do surgery. This really impressed her. He explained the side effects and just what a knee replacement entailed. She went home quite impressed with this young man who graduated from Princeton and did his residency at Massachusetts General. On the following visit, prior to concluding a date for the surgery, she observed his caring and sincere approach with others in his office.

Soon the date of September 2, 1996, was set for the surgery to be done at St. Mary's hospital. Now it was time for Gene to meet with the nurse for details pertaining to getting ready for surgery.

A preoperative sheet was simple and direct. Two units of Gene's blood needed to be banked. These were banked one week before the surgery and she had done each unit one week apart. Anyone over sixty-five years of age was to have someone come with them and do the driving. Iron would have to be started at the time of banking the blood. Gene's hemoglobin tested fourteen point five at the blood bank. This was really good and so she crawled onto the table like a pro after making plans to get there.

A good friend and previous co-worker, plus an RN, drove her to the bank. This helped reduce Gene's stress as she knew she was not alone and had a knowledgeable person available if she needed her. Since the first unit of blood was banked without incident, she proceeded to bank the second. Now she was getting closer to the surgery date.

"Mom, we will come to your place and look after you when you come home from the hospital," said David.

This plan seemed great for Gene since David and Barbara volunteered to come stay with her. David would go to work from Gene's house. Trendy would do better at home, since she was to spend the days with them while Gene was in the hospital.

"Do you want me to be there when you have the surgery?"

came the question over the phone from Tom. Gene assured him she would be fine and would look forward to his coming up when she was recuperating at home. David would keep him informed of the details after the surgery. Gene and David worked out a plan to meet at the hospital at 6:00 A.M. on September 3. This was an ungodly time for Gene since she is not a morning person. She also had always seen the need to settle patients into their room prior to surgery to help reduce the stress on the day of surgery. This she believes should be done. She wants to look into this cause in the future and try to change a new process instituted by the insurance companies. Today, the insurance companies seem to be directing when a patient needs to come to the hospital. Doctors are letting this happen. The heck with how the patient feels and the increased stress imposed upon the patient. The public needs to look at this big problem.

Soon David, Barbara and Gene were waiting with twenty other patients and their families awaiting to be taken to the operating room. It was here that an acquaintance from the nursing home appeared. She was an RN in the operating room who seemed to convey confidence in the system and that Gene would be fine. Gene's family was impressed to have someone take the time to seek out Gene and her family and reassure them at this early hour.

As they were waiting in the area near the operating room, the surgeon was next to greet them. He met David and Barbara and they too were pleased with his approach. He passed the test and they too believed Gene had selected a good surgeon. This personable, well-dressed surgeon was alive and displayed vim and vigor. He presented an ideal picture of a true professional.

Next, an employee dressed in scrubs appeared to invite Gene to a small dressing room where she dressed down to the skin for the surgery. Gene's constant feeling of being too warm was of great help at this time. A thin gown somewhat covered this naked body.

Gene was wheeled into a holding area where an intravenous

was started and a review of known allergies took place. The anesthesiologist was next to discuss plans for an epidural anesthetic. He explained that she would be given something to cause her to doze during the surgery. The anesthetic would not put her to sleep. This turned out to be the case, but she did not doze off. She heard the saw when the bone was shortened to make room for the new knee. She felt the blows as the new knee was pounded in place. She had no pain, but could follow the procedure in her mind. Having worked in surgery for three years and having assisted the orthopedic surgeons brought back vivid memories. Many years had passed since Gene worked in the operating room as a scrub nurse. The sound effects were there, but there was no pain as the time passed so quickly.

The next stop was in the recovery room. She remembers her stretcher being wheeled into the slot planned out for her. Soon a nurse was telling her of the plans while in the recovery room.

"Breath deeply," she announced every few minutes.

The blood pressure was taken automatically with a device used while the surgery took place. Her right leg was wrapped from the toe to the groin with heavy dressings and covered with ace bandages. A drainage bag was attached to the drain inserted near the operative area. Heavy bleeding took place as was expected and this aspect of her care was closely observed.

What about the two units of blood Gene had banked? Well, it seems that the bleeding during the surgery did not indicate the need for the blood. In fact, the blood was never used. Gene was told that it was destroyed once she did not need it. This seemed like such a waste, but she learned that this blood was not processed for administering to anyone else. Heavy bleeding did occur in the first couple of days post-operatively. Because of her blood count and her body's ability to keep up with the loss, it was determined to not use the blood she banked before it was destroyed. Dressings were reinforced on every shift. These heavy dressings seemed to add pressure to her leg and cause more pain.

Pain! Pain! This word "pain" seemed to be terrible post-operatively for Gene. This was unusual since the epidural anesthesia was to be left in place for the first two days, but for some reason Gene's pain appeared about 5:00 P.M. the day of the surgery and could not be stopped. The epidural was pulled as it was ineffective. A morphine drip was started. This did not touch her pain as it had gotten beyond reach.

The pain Gene experienced was unreal. She had never had surgery or experienced pain before to this degree. The pain continued even with the Morphine drip until she was given a "loading" dose of something the next morning. Her pain left. Her head went numb, and she was exhausted at not having rested since before the surgery.

"Good morning," came this sweet voice from the student practical nurse. She was assigned solely to care for Gene. She announced to Gene that she wanted Gene to get up and stay up for one hour. Can you imagine that at this point Gene was slugged with a pain killer, her head was light, and this student nurse was planning to have Gene sit up for one hour? It became obvious to Gene that if she were to try to stay up for one hour with having had this new medicine, she could easily be on the floor. Gene decided to go back to bed with the assistance of another nurse, while this student was having her lunch. Gene had taught diploma student nurses for five years and so did not accept the judgment of this LPN student nurse.

Shortly after Gene went back to bed, two physical therapists were on the scene. They initiated exercises that would become a daily ritual twice a day. Bending the knee with the reinforced dressings became possible on the second day. By then, the total dressing was redone by the student nurse under the watchful eye of her instructor. With Gene having taught student nurses, it made the instructor somewhat tense. Before long, Gene and this talkative instructor struck up a free exchange on their teaching experiences. This bit of interchange soon spread and Gene was referred to as a nursing instructor.

Gene's open approach to the staff served as both good and bad. Some of the staff seemed to enjoy her company. Others resented any reference she made to the methods of care. For instance, Gene suggested that the CPM equipment not be stored on the floor between the placement on her bed every shift for her treatments. Gene was taught as a student nurse and this was reinforced in her operating room experiences that everything on the floor was dirty. She tried to soften her constructive observations by relating the prevention of cross-contamination. Her explanation to the student nurse instructor was not received well. Gene was to be the patient. They were the caregivers that really did not want any input from the patient.

The unit coordinator, equal to a head nurse position, arrived for a discussion and to introduce herself. She was a very attractive peron dressed in street clothes and wearing a stylish lab coat. Great, Gene thought, here is a progressive manager who does not have to wear a uniform for defense. Nursing is slow in rubbing elbows with other management teams in a hospital. Nurses are beginning to feel that they don't have to wear uniforms to be effective in management. Street clothing makes them more approachable and reduces a barrier. As a rule, many nurses from a diploma program feel inferior in a management role. This is all a part of their subservient teachings in their diploma programs.

The free-flowing discussion between Gene and the coordinator was a delight and a highlight Gene enjoyed. The coordinator had heard about Gene's concerns for the placement of the CPM machine on the floor and then to Gene's bed every shift. Gene suggested that it be hung on the wall and not too high as it seemed quite heavy. Realizing that Gene might pursue her concerns at a higher level, she agreed to look into the possibility of having this equipment placed where it would not be put on the floor.

Highlights of Gene's stay on this busy joint replacement unit were centered around a nearby hurricane. It had caused the electricity supply interruption. The fire alarm went off when water from the heavy rains gained entrance to the basement of the hospital. As Gene did the practice drills at the place she did some part-time work, she imagined her escape to the ground floor without using the elevators, and all this with this newly operated knee. The nurses floated around with flashlights into rooms where the emergency lights did not reach. They must have felt like Florence Nightingale did in her day.

Therapy progress was evident when many of the staff members commented on Gene's achievements as she walked with a walker down the halls. Gene's conditioning prior to this surgery was done as she worked vigorously in her yard and garden. She also had eleven years working previously in a rehabilitation facility.

Daily blood was drawn for the various tests. A blood thinner was administered daily to prevent blood clots. Blood clots and potential infections as the result of the new operative wound were possible. Antibiotics were administered in a drip for several days.

Pain continued as expected because of the direct damage to the bone when the new knee was put in place. Pain medication administered by mouth proved effective and did not slow her.

The good news came. Gene could go home on her fourth day post-operatively. Usually the patients went home on their fifth day, but since it was Saturday and her son, David, could come get her, she anxiously went home. Barbara and Trendy went on ahead to Gene's home a David collected Gene and her belongings and headed for her home.

Barbara took the new prescriptions for pain, iron and aspirin along with the needed groceries once Gene had settled in at home. Gene began to relax as soon as she was home. She does not do well away from her home, and the hospital was even worse than travel. She likes to control the situations with which she must deal. Here at home is her haven. She has always been a homebody — even as a child she would not stay away from home.

They realized she could manage well with the assistance of friends and neighbors. Also, she had therapy in her home every other day for six weeks post-op. Cleaning was one chore she didn't mind relinquishing. Some friends brought in her meals, and took her to the grocery when she had not yet been approved to drive. Her independence was preserved by everyone. Gene felt comfortable staying alone. Friends, family and co-workers called her often to offer assistance if needed. All she had to do then was to walk safely and not fall. Trendy even understood that "Grandma" needed some understanding with her walking pace.

Within weeks, Gene had progressed from the walker to the cain and then walking independently. She was driving anywhere she wanted. The errands backed up and now they needed to be handled. What a good feeling she had. The pain was gone. She was back attending to her own affairs. All she had to do was not put pressure on the knee. Bathing the dog seemed awkward at first, but she soon mastered that skill. Just taking showers after taking baths seemed second nature to her. Before long when spring comes, Gene will be out there gardening heavy and swinging golf clubs.

Chapter Twenty-Two:

Reflections by the Author

What am I thinking about this day? At this time in 1978, February 13, Jack was in the Intensive Unit following open heart surgery at the Medical College of Virginia, better known as MCV in Virginia, and I guess the nation. I graduated from there with my BSN in 1971.

As I viewed Jack immediately following his surgery with all of the tubes coming out, I focused upon the blood in the closed chest drainage bottles. There was more blood there than should have been, even though some was expected since they entered the chest cavity to do the surgery.

Soon the fellow cardiology surgeon came to talk to me. He was concerned about the excessive chest drainage. He informed me that he would watch it and hoped that he did not have to take my husband back to correct the problem. With time during the night, the chest drainage slowed down. I was looking forward to morning which was February 14. I was waiting outside the intensive unit in a small waiting area where the eleven-to-seven charge nurse passed to go on duty.

"What is your name and why are you waiting outside this unit?" she asked me in a matter-of-fact tone. "It looks like you can afford a motel," as she looked me over from top to bottom without giving me time to answer her questions.

"Dr. Lower had advised me to wait here, and yes, I could afford a motel. But, I am not going to leave this hospital," I responded in a somewhat defensive manner. "Young lady, I am a graduate nurse of this facility. Just where do you propose that I spend the night?"

Well, as she tried to soften her approach to me, she quickly gleaned that I was really angry with her as she showed absolutely no empathy.

"You can go to another floor where there is a waiting room for families with members in the intensive unit. You can come to this entrance at 5:30 A.M. and I will let you see your husband."

Our sons had gone home to be with their families as I had assured them there was nothing they could do and I would be fine. Soon I found the other families waiting in a large, visibly cold waiting area. They were all sitting on cold, plastic-covered lounges and chairs. I soon found them linen, blankets, pillows, and some snacks. No staff person ever stopped me or asked who I was or what I was doing. The other families thought I was and angel from heaven. I did give them the support that seemed to be missing from the staff. I had learned these skills in my basic nursing diploma program in 1944 to 1947 in Ohio. I had learned about this facility when I went back to school for my BSN and graduated from there in 1971.

When I appeared at the intensive care unit at 5:30 A.M. on February 14, 1978, everyone was very busy as I knew they would be. They were bathing the patients and getting them ready for the oncoming shift.

"Oh," said the charge nurse, "You are here! The patients are being bathed and I cannot let you come in at this time." She did ask my husband to write me a note since it was Valentine's Day. Jack could not speak as he still was intubated — meaning that a tube was inserted into his nostril and down his trachea that assisted him in breathing.

He wrote, "She is a nurse; she is a nurse!" This bit of information did not give me a pass to enter.

Soon it became daylight outside and I could get my orientation. I gave thanks that Jack had made it through the night without having to return to surgery for the initial excessive bleeding. He progressed fairly well and in a couple days was transferred to a private room. The staffing was inadequate on this post-operative unit. I asked for a cot and stayed in his room where I could provide the necessary nursing care.

Within days, Jack was transferred to the outpatient area, out of the main surgical building. This meant no care from the facility. He was now expected to care for himself. Of course he was not able or ready for this situation. No one could have been. Jack was a doer too, but putting on his "pantyhose" (support hose) before he stepped on the floor each morning was an impossibility for anyone having had their chest split open a few days prior to this date. The pantyhose were full-length support hose worn on both legs. One leg had a large incision down one side where the graft was taken. The full-length hose were worn on both legs to avoid the formation of blood clots and to avoid fluid retention in the lower extremities.

It became obvious that we could do all of his needed care more easily at home. The need for emergency services was the only reason I could see for keeping him there, so home we went. Our king-sized bed made it quite difficult for him to turn in bed. He had nothing to hold onto to assist him to turn in bed, so we arranged to get up and exchange sides by walking to the other side simultaneously. This little exercise during the night, along with the application of his pantyhose in the mornings, soon became funny to both of us.

Jack was improving and fairly independent when I returned to work. I just happened to be home the morning Jack went down on the kitchen floor with a heart fibrillation. This is an emergency situation. I called the surgeon who called the ambulance. We were soon on our way to the emergency room of St. Mary's hospital. With the proper medication in an intravenous drip, the pulse soon corrected to a firmer and slower rate. Back home we went again to try to get back to a normal life.

Jack had lost a lot of weight and strength. He had always fought low blood pressure. With a restricted sodium, low fat and reduced calorie diet, he soon was on the mend. This took some learning as he always seemed to enjoy working so very hard. He did agree to having a lounge chair in his office. This quiet time after his lunch became a daily occurrence which he looked forward to in the middle of his heavy and stressful work day. His secretary held his calls and he soon loved this "time out" and restful period of time. It probably extended his life by having this relaxing period in the middle of a very stressful working environment. Interactions within a poorly managed office environment can have a great influence on the amount of unnecessary stress imposed upon all employees within that area. This stress was condoned by those at a higher level.

Meanwhile, as the years flowed, February became a serious and fearful month. My sister, Julia, was murdered on February 3, 1985. My brother, Bill, returned from her funeral not feeling well. He was found dead early the next morning as he intended to rest a while in his recliner. This was within the week of Julia's death.

Jack and I were vacationing on the western side of Florida when our son David called to tell us of Julia's death. David was short of breath and said that he was passing blood rectally. Within hours he was admitted with a dangerously low hemoglobin. He was diagnosed with a bleeding gastric ulcer. With this immediate emergency, we left Florida in haste to try to reach Virginia where David was admitted. Bob, Julia's husband, had assured us that we couldn't do anything for him at this time. During our travels from Florida to Virginia, we kept in touch with our doctor who was treating David. I remember calling my friend, Alice, also an RN and associate director of nursing in another hospital in Richmond.

"Alice, would you go to St. Mary's and check on David?" I knew she knew what strings to pull for good nursing care should this be a need.

There was no question. Alice went to St. Mary's just as I had requested of her. No one will ever know how much this meant to Jack, David and me. Alice is a true friend whom I met when we first moved to Virginia in 1960 as she lived in Culpeper and replaced me as DON.

Upon arriving in Richmond, and having an opportunity to assess David's condition, we received a call from my brother, S.B. who had gone to Florida from North Carolina upon hearing of Julia's tragic death.

"Stay there with David. There is nobody here and nothing you could do by returning to Florida. Julia has been cremated and there will be a simple service here."

I hung up my clothes that I had collected to take to Florida in a downstairs closet. I remarked that I felt that I would be wearing these soon someplace on a trip. David was showing good progress with the many units of blood he had received.

I never saw Bill in Florida. They had arrived after we left in our frantic drive to Virginia to look after David. I learned after Bill's death that he had not felt well while in Florida. Of course attending the funeral of a close sister who had been murdered by her neighbor's nineteen-year-old son, stressed everyone. I've often wondered that if I had seen Bill in Florida I would have picked up some symptoms which could have avoided his death with my nursing knowledge?

Bill was a deep thinker. He always played down any heath problem he may have had. He told you what he thought you wanted to hear and not what was really happening. His thinking was advanced in many areas. He had a vivid imagination and often mixed his views with the great big stories from Texas, so truth and fiction were hard to separate at times. He suffered from manic-depressive disease which was not diagnosed until his middle years. By that time, his wife had divorced him and moved some of his five children to California. He never recovered from the separation of his children. The fact that he didn't feel comfortable discussing this with any of his brothers or sisters made it even worse. With the down-sizing of companies, he was released along with twelve or so supervisors from Texas Instrumentsp in Dallas. This personal destructive happening devastated him even more. He lived so far away from the rest of us and hid his feelings so well, we never provided the emotional support he needed until the crisis when we were notified of his hospitalization.

Jack and I were summoned to Dallas when his second wife called us from Dallas. Our personal visit with Bill in the hospital and his home at that time revealed that he needed his family more than we realized. Distance kept us from recognizing his behavior that revealed his illness.

Back to Bill's sudden death which took place in his home in Nashville in 1986. This call came informing us of Bill's sudden death while we were still numb over Julia's tragic death. Since we had warnings in Virginia of impending ice and snow heading our way, we made immediate plans to fly out of Richmond for Nashville. Yes, my clothes were all collected just as I had witnessed in a premonition. David was then showing steady improvement.

My brother, S.B., and son-in-law, Randy, drove S.B.'s new four-wheeled pick-up truck over the mountains in a very heavy snow from the east coast of North Carolina to Nashville. My sister, Betty, flew out of Pittsburgh just in time to beat the storm roaring through Ohio. My oldest brother and three sisters living in northwestern Ohio could not travel by plane as the governor had ordered everyone stay off of the roads. My brother, Ned, was in a hospital in Toledo being worked on for open-heart surgery. Bill's five children came from Virginia, Maryland, California and Tennessee. Mike, Bill's oldest son, lived near Bill. How sad it was to see his children assembled so near when he was so far away. Bill never recovered from losing his children in his first divorce. His children were still young and tried to show respect to him at the time of his death even though he was not there when they needed him in their teen years.

Bill was buried on Valentine's Day. All of us seemed to support each other even though we had been raised to not show affection or emotions. After the funeral, we all grouped in our adjoining motel rooms. We had food sent in from friends of Bill and his children. We purchased items we needed to complete a good meal. Bill's wife seemed occupied with her own immediate family. She was still stunned with the suddenness of Bill's death.

Our coping skills came into play. This card playing practice was started as we continued our renewal of relationships with Bill's kids. We had played cards at Ford's funeral in Florida and that seemed to prevent deep sadness that all of us were feeling.

Of course, we kept the family in Ohio informed of the funeral and talked with each one by phone. The phone was busy as we kept tabs on Ned's progress from his open-heart surgery on February 15 in Toledo. Then complications of a gall bladder surgery within days of his open-heart surgery seemed to be tolerated well. Soon he was back at work and running his farm. He owns the farm place and that is where he and his wife live now.

When I try to mark February as a terrible month to recall, I have to think of other months in which we experienced great sadness. Da died on June 1, 1953 when he was only fifty-five. Mom died on November 29, 1976. Jack's Dad died suddenly on November 29 also. His mother died on Memorial weekend as did

Jack. My mother lost Da, her husband, at a very young age, but she never saw one of her nine children, many grandchildren, or great grandchildren die during her living years.

In February, 1971, Jack suffered a serious posterior coronary at the age of forty-seven. Both of us had been working so hard in the yard on Sunday. Our home was built in 1970 and so much work had to be done. He had a tooth pulled the day before. It was that night, early Tuesday at 3:00 A.M. that he presented the classic symptoms of a serious heart attack when he awakened me. Within minutes our doctor was notified and we were on our way to St. Mary's emergency across the James as there was no hospital on the south side of Richmond. I recall doing eighty-miles-an-hour passing over the Huguenot Bridge. No policeman was around to lead. It was not possible for an emergency squad to find us in the country twenty-five years ago. Today you are advised to stay at home and wait for the emergency squad after calling 911. Jack remained conscious during this excruciating pain. I know that forty-percent of heart attack victims do not make it to the hospital alive. Usually they do not start in time or wait too long for the symptoms to go away.

Jack progressed well with some complications, but soon he was walking the golf course behind our home after work every day. Many months it was dark as he walked at night. He often said that he knew every rut as he walked to get in his miles required for him to regain and maintain his strength. He never complained and soon was back at his heavy work schedule. From this experience and the rush to the emergency room, I became quite apprehensive whenever he became sick.

One day I noticed that he had swollen lymph nodes all over his body. He had just finished a stint of seven months, seven days-per-week on the turkey project over in the valley. He directed that project for the governor of Virginia. There has to be some correlation between disinfectants and the turkey disease that caused this full blown case of lymphoma. This cancer of the lymph nodes required heavy chemotherapy. Jack accepted this horrible news like a trooper. He proceeded with the treatments like they were nothing. He never became nauseated. He did not ever lose the hair left on the sides of his head. You see, Jack was a handsome bald man. My family has the genes for full heads of hair and never had to explore how one with genes for baldness dealt with this fact. He took many blood transfusions as the chemo knocked his blood count. He never discussed with me the possibility of dying. He would often tell me prior to any surgery or illness that he would be fine. I do believe he felt that he would beat the odds of any health problem he encountered. It is his strength that I miss so terribly since his death in 1988.

Tomorrow is another February 14. Today I received the most beautiful Valentine from David. The verse relates that I taught him to love and how much he appreciated my having taught this skill. Truly it was his Dad who taught him to express love. Jack learned that from his mother. He was her only child and she showered much love on him. How important it is to share and express our love for one another. David's card of today has shaken me a bit. It was sincere and he took the time to select a card to let me know. Tomorrow I will call him and thank him for his thoughtfulness.

I designed Valentine's Day cards on my computer and sent them to David, Tom, grandchildren, brothers and sisters. I have learned that it is never too late to learn to tell those you love that you care about them and that you miss them. In reflection, I have had many happy Valentine's Days. I do recall the many cards and flowers from Jack. He always remembered my birthday, our anniversary and special holidays.

I want to share with you a gift I received thirty years ago from a very special nurse friend. This is from Life's tapestry, 1964, by Nancy Schneider, A Brownie Creation by Rust Craft.

> God gives us joy
>   that we may give;
> He gives us joy
>   that we may share;
> Sometimes He gives us
>   heavy loads to lift
> That we may learn
>   to bear.
> For life is gladder
>   when we give,
> And love is sweeter
>   when we share,
> And heavy loads
>   rest lightly too
> When we have learned
>   to bear.

Have Stanley and Lela's children "turned-out" as Da prediced forty-four years ago? They have achieved well. Their children have demonstrated many of the values taught to them by their parents. These values were so ingrained in these nine children.

They have displayed deep determination, hard dealings among each other, continuing the pride of the family farm and keeping family ties close.

It is apparent that these descendants do care about each other. They keep in touch even though they have distanced their homes. True, they scattered from Ohio. This roaming spirit was predicted and came to pass. Flexibility in coping with change is obvious too.

These descendants are living in or have lived in Texas, Tennessee, Florida, North Carolina, Virginia, Pennsylvania,

Marilyn, Illinois, Kentucky, Minnesota, Indiana, Wisconsin, Washington D. C., Missouri, California, Michigan and Arizona. They have displayed that they can join others anywhere. Having flexibility and coping are some of the greatest assets one can possess as one fulfills life's goals.

The independent personalities Da saw in his adult children have served to propel them far just as he predicted and expected.

Fort Amanda Vigils

Just getting to Fort Amanda situated in northwestern Ohio at least once a year was a goal Gene set for herself after the death of her father in 1953. Living out-of-state for the past thirty-eight years required some real planning on her part. She renews her vows to her parents at this time. It has always seemed essential for her to reflect upon the good times while there in this quiet area. Her thoughts spread to her paternal grandparents as well, since they are buried next to her parents.

The well-kept graves with their distinguished markers hold hundreds of treasured archives for Gene and her brothers and sisters. As children they learned more history and shared some tragic events when a relative or neighbor was buried in this designated reverent area.

Fort Amanda was preserved after a tragic battle of some local Indians and the settlers of that area. Walking paths led to the stately monument along the Auglaize River. Picnic areas grew with covered halls for recreation events should rain become a problem. Most of all, it was known as a lover's paradise for the young at heart.

Gene and Jack strolled these private paths when they were feeling the strong love pangs. It was always considered safe during their young dating years. Stories are told of how every young couple so madly in love agreed together to always be in love with each other and would continue after their marriage.

Fort Amanda serves several purposes for Gene. She not only renews her vows to her parents, but also gets great pleasure in reliving the physical love she shared with Jack as they walked the many private paths when she visits yearly in person. While during the year, Gene often visits Fort Amanda in her thoughts. She finds her thoughts lean toward discussing problems as well as recognizing what is good with her life with both her parents and Jack, her deceased husband.

Gene had never desired to be buried at Fort Amanda. She lived too far away for her children to consider this. She believes that her children's thoughts and plans as to where they would be living would be a great factor in deciding a burial place or cremation for Gene. She has no feelings regarding her remains after her death. She believes, as do many of her brothers and sisters, that once you die, you are dead and that is it. They believe that Heaven and Hell are here on earth as you live your life. Their seemingly lack of real religious beliefs are the result of being deep scientific thinkers, as well as their early association with poor religious role models at the church near their farm. They are realists and believe they are responsible for their own behaviors and these behaviors, considered by some to be sins, once done are not forgiven or forgotten.

When Julia and Bill died one week a part in 1985, the community near the farm was sure they would both be buried at Fort Amanda. They just knew that this was to be. Julia had discussed a desire to be buried at Fort Amanda and had expressed a view that she would be on the same lot as her parents.

Julia had resided in Florida for many years and so her husband decided upon cremation. His plan did not call for Julia being buried in Fort Amanda. As the family all knows, he never sought the opinions of this strong-willed family. He did what he had to do at that time and so the family had to accept these actions.

Bill had remarried in Nashville to his third wife and she too decided that Bill would be buried in Nashville. She had never seen Fort Amanda. None of us had ever heard Bill's burial desires. He was just too young to think about such plans. He was not one of the children who went with their parents to a funeral or took flowers for special occasions when he was young. He also lived most of his life out of state so Fort Amanda did not seem to have the same attraction for him.

Nevertheless, the members of the community related that they just couldn't believe that Julia and Bill had died since they were never buried at Fort Amanda. This is the thinking of the older generation in the community. Everyone was always buried at Fort Amanda. You see, most of the neighbors and community members had never lived anywhere else and so being buried at Fort Amanda was a fact and not a decision to be made.

Gene, and with Eric.

Addendum

Computer Written Letters

With the passing of three years, Gene learned a lot of computer skills by reading and demonstrations from her son, grandson Eric, Norman, college classes and lots of practice. She soon learned to have fun and play golf and bridge on her computer. With a Christmas gift from David and Barbara of software on desktop publishing, Gene was headed toward starting her goal of writing. She subscribed to writer's magazines and purchased books she needed as identified by a close young friend, Elizabeth.

Gene began writing letters on her computer before she knew how to save what she was writing. She thinks some of her good letters disappeared when she pressed the wrong key. She started with these letters for the purpose of keeping her family and friends informed of her progress in learning to live alone. Of course, Trendy, her boxer dog occupies much of her time. Her dog also shows caring and returns love. These letters give a good read on Gene's activities. They reflect many values and achievements which she thinks might be worth sharing with other readers.

Hello Again to Friends and Family,

Good morning! My first letter on my new computer brought some fast responses. Others ignored my fun-time letters, but I need to catch up on some of my latest endeavors for some of you. Somehow, I lost the first written letter from my computer, so the following letter will serve as number one.

In the past weeks, I attended a potluck dinner for a group of widows organized by one of my golfing buddies. She had sixteen of us as an opener. We organized to meet for an upcoming Christmas party. I have had mixed feelings about what this group does mean to me. It seemed to be a big hit for some of the others there.

Then I played golf in a group of retired senior men golfers. They needed some of us from the nine-hole women's golf group as most of the wives do not play golf. This outing was a special fundraiser. We enjoyed a special dinner after the chilly, but fun, outing. My partner invited me to go fishing on the Chesapeake Bay on the 19th. It would cost nearly $100 and leave Richmond at 5:00 A.M. that morning. We were to fish for rockfish. Well, I passed as this guy who liked to talk about himself and his wife. Did I want to hear this kind of story while fishing?

Now for the interesting part: The security man finally called to tell me he would fix my outside light. After my trying to get this non-working light repaired for the past eight weeks, this was a surprise. During our conversation he asked if I would like to meet one of his other clients. After hearing the statistics, I agreed his client could have my telephone number to call me.

When this man called me this past Friday afternoon, we learned that we had a lot in common. Both have dogs. He is a professional. His mother came from Lima, Ohio. Each of us have a lovely home. We each have two children. Our spouses died five and six years ago. Each of us are not too eager to become involved with anyone else after each were happily married forty-two years.

Since each of us lead fairly busy lives and both still work part-time, we agreed that it would be after December, 16 before we had time to meet. Don't you want to hear more?

Tom and Allison were here this weekend. Of course, we went shoe shopping just as we always do. They are fun to have around.

David's kids are coming for Thanksgiving, so I will try to get the house cleaned and some windows washed.

I just had stone put on the driveway. It cost a lot to get it graded too.

My grass shows that I have really been working outside. Just put the third organic fertilizer on the lawn in order to get ready for winter. Leaves seem to be under control after five or more removals with the use of my wheel horse tractor for vacuuming the lawn.

I really enjoyed the recent visit from Kassy and Bob. You need to try to visit me too. I am noted for putting food in your mouth when you try to talk and will try to improve on that score. I still have two boxes of candy bars from my trick or treats. Couldn't load any on Tom. I will wait until Eric comes home from college next week. He and David will take them off my hands.

It is time to close this rattling on and get ready to go do some teaching. I would rather be outside, but my mad money earnings do keep me from tight budgeting.

Best to all of you at Thanksgiving. Not sure if I am going to create a Christmas card this year. We'll see.

Fondly, Georgene, Gene, or Geanne and Trendy

January 5, 1995

Hello to Family and Friends in 1995,

There is so much to tell you about the Holidays we enjoyed and to thank you so much for making it so pleasurable for Trendy and me.

With Allison flying in Christmas Day from Charlotte, Trendy and I met her at the Richmond airport while Tom was driving from Raleigh. We went directly to David's as that is where we had our big meal and unwrapped gifts from the family. The dinner was so good and the gifts useful as well as needed by some of us.

I am looking for more of the money-sorting machines like the one I had given to Tom and David. Tom likes to leave his change laying around. David likes to count his. This battery driven toy soon was wanted by everyone. Tom gave his to Alison, his stepdaughter. He wants one for Allison, his daughter and himself. I guess he knows of others who need them too. They are fun and I gave mine to Seth, Tom's stepson, since kids come first at Christmas. Now I don't have one either.

Yesterday, I went to the Price Club to try to locate more money machines. These one-time-for-sale machines were long gone since I had bought them in October, 1994, but we will all search for them at a good price and try to buy the missing ones.

Tom and Allison spent Christmas night with me and had a chance to catch up on rest by sleeping in. They had both been on the run with having attended their other family parties. They drove back with some Christmas cooking seemingly objecting to taking it for fear of gaining weight. I thought Tom's other new family members who didn't try to come here needed to be remembered and enjoyed some very good Christmas cooking.

My Christmas cooking and New Year's cooking got out of hand a little bit for me. Of course, the spritz cookies were made in all shapes and colors. These were Da's favorite cookie. I know that I have made these cookies and popcorn trees for every Christmas since 1949. Then there are the good fruit cakes. This recipe is Burdella Fisher's prize creation. She gave this recipe to me in 1957. These too, I have made every year since. It seems to be a hit and more people say that this fruitcake is the best they have ever eaten. Of course the fudge, divinity and peanut brittle get made. I did a lot of candy-making while growing up. I really made some messes in Mom's kitchen, but I followed the rule that if you made the mess, you cleaned it up. Cleaning the mess was the hardest part, but at least Mom let me cook anything I wanted to cook. She never complained about the mess I made or the supplies I used. The cost of cooking supplies today is a great expense for someone on a retirement income, but I do get great pleasure out of my Christmas cooking. It is just one more way to show my love and caring. My feet ached and I really washed the skin off my hands as I cooked long hours. After all these years, I am beginning to catch on as to why some people don't cook like I do at Christmas, but they are missing all of this loving attention.

My heat pump went defunct on Christmas Eve. The on-call repairman advised me that I should go on emergency heat until Tuesday morning. When Tuesday came, it took some know-how and several days of work. Can hardly wait to get the electric bill for use of emergency heat. We joke that David will take care of that since he has been an engineer at Virginia Power for the past twenty-five years. He usually responds to comments such as these that he will make sure that they charge a lot so his salary can go up.

With Christmas over, the decorations must come down. I dismantled the snow and flower arrangement that I had tied on the mailbox. Walkers were so fascinated with this that they had to really study it every time they passed my home. In reality, it ended up looking like something you might find in a cemetery, which made me vow to not use it again. No one stole this old and artificial arrangement as I hear they are doing in some cemeteries around the country. How terrible. Maybe the new Republican congress will change all of these terrible people and return our world to what we once knew. I doubt that this will happen!

Errands! Errands are driving me mad. Just when I thought I had them caught up, I had to start again yesterday to take care of the more urgent ones. First, we deposited stray checks in the bank and checked my balance at the bank. Next, to the veterinarian for shampoo and to deliver their Christmas. They closed too early this past year and Trendy missed them on Friday before Christmas. Then, on to the Price club without successfully finding the money-sorting machines. We got oil for the wheel horse tractor and hand lawn mower. These important pieces of equipment are having their oil drained. I will vacuum the leaves that blew in from the neighbors with the last gusts.

On to the Southern States store where I get Trendy's dog food and some birdseed. While at the grocery for fresh milk and fruit, I purchased lard, raisins, and cornmeal for the bluebird feeder. Next, to the post office for stamps as it was on the way home. Since my mail was stolen from my mailbox near the road with many personal checks paying bills, I now take my outgoing mail to the post office.

Then I picked-up a pair of winter white slacks from the cleaners next door to the post office. They could not find them. This will require another errand trip in the future.

Yes, I did pick up a developed roll of film while at the grocery. They were recent Christmas pictures. They turned out quite well and the first taken with my new camera. My old camera got too close to the sprinkler one day when I forgot to bring it into the house after using it. I do keep taking pictures as they will be something to remind me of the days gone on before when I am old, or is it older?

As the result of my making the mixture of lard, cornmeal, flour and raisins, the birds and squirrels are going "nuts" literally this morning. It is fifteen degrees, fairly snappy for Virginia this morning. They are fluttering around like it was a spring day.

Of course you are wondering what has happened to my pesky talkative man. Well, he did not call after Christmas. Maybe after a twenty-minute dissertation of his activities, he stopped to recognize that maybe I had a good Christmas as well. This self-serving dental pilot had been flying his Cherokee around and helping to move his attorney son to the mountains in Virginia.

Some people are so lucky to find an ear for listening to their accomplishments. I have never had to listen to a bragging man. I am not eager to begin. As long as my environment does not get invaded any further, I can listen for forty-five minutes every two or three weeks. It seems that his full-time dental practice keeps him fairly busy. Being a dentist, he has learned probably to do a one-way conversation. Dentists usually talk to you when you can't respond, but now you know the direction this so-called friendship is going, and going, and going.

By now most of you have realized that I have captivated your time with my computer playtime. I find it great fun to just type as I think. Making copies with my printer allows sending copies to all of you so easy.

I should sign off and get ready to visit the podiatrist. She is trying some new orthotics as a relief to my aching feet and heels. Besides, I have "deformed" feet that look like a big "Z." I have had a broken bone on the outer side of my left foot. Each foot has large spurs on the heels. She does not think that weight is a problem. Isn't she a psychologist too? Arthritis seems to be an obvious problem as reflected in the X-rays and the real cause of my discomfort. Let me hear some cures you oldies have experienced. No, I can not sit down and let some one wait on me. Sounds good, but where do you find this kind of caretaker?

Sorry I did not get to Ohio for Bob Mercer's memorial. I talked to him just before he died. I called him in Florida when I heard his condition was quite serious. He was friendly and fairly resigned to his outcome. He seemed to appreciate my call and my expression of concern while he was living. Take care of the living and the rest will fall in line is my philosophy.

The new calendars have been hung in all rooms in my home. I use them as part of the decor. Kassy and Bob are cruising around Panama as I write this letter. If any of you know the current address of Buie Dingledine, please send it to me as my Christmas card to her was returned. Keep calling and writing. Actually, some of you do a very good job at both.

Best to you, love, Georgene, Geanne or Gene and Trendy

May 30, 1995

Dear Family and Friends,

Don't get too excited! This will not be one of those long and ranting episodes. I just owe a few letters to some of you, so will try to get some information out to you regarding my happenings in the past weeks and my future social events as planned.

Getting through Memorial weekend is always hard. It was on May 26, 1988 that my life changed suddenly when Jack died during an angioplasty procedure. Fortunately, I had learned many independent skills by that time and so life does go on. It was a rainy and ugly weekend here in Virginia. I needed the time to work on clothes. I altered both old and new clothing and have a few outfits in mind for upcoming events.

Kassy's letter with clippings a few weeks ago was greatly appreciated. Susan is the loyal and regular writer with the news happenings around the home place. I am amazed at the social events that occur and all of you seem to keep attending these affairs. I'll have to forgo the family reunions other than our planned immediate family one. I have not been to Ohio since last May when my high school class celebrated its 50th anniversary at the alumni banquet. I understand the alumni was a great success due to the good planning by the committee that Karin and Terry served.

I recently had dental surgery after breaking off one of my gold crowned teeth. The sad part was that I swallowed the tooth, gold and all, and never really searched for it. My Geiger counter didn't work too well. This now means adding one more tooth to my partial bridge. It hurts a bit when I have to pay for this since my insurance policy does not include dental insurance, and I have the best policy the Virginia retiree policies permit.

Last week I experienced a sight that I bet none of you have ever seen. I have waited all these years to see this beautiful action. Well, as I sat leisurely reading the Sunday paper and sipping my coffee, my family of bluebirds took off from their house at the end of my garage. First, the papa bluebird perched himself on the corner of my garage — all of this in my full view. Then, the first baby Eastern bluebird squeezed out of the tiny hole near the roof of their house. With popa's approval he fluttered to the top of the tree on my island. Popa bird guided this tiny creature to a resting place as he assisted the four others. Yes, I said four. That makes a total of five baby bluebirds that I witnessed flutter to a new world. Can you imagine how excited they must have been and with the parents in full control? Soon the momma bird checked the house for any left behind. You see, as I went for my paper that morning accompanied by Trendy, I concluded that these baby birds were about to venture to the outside world. One stuck his head out at me as we passed, and these poor parents fed those hungry kids constantly. Both of the parents participated in the raising of these beautiful birds.

Much could be learned by some people today in their kid-raising.

Then I worried about how these tiny birds would spend the night out in their new world. I have not seen them as yet, but as in the past, they come back and raise another family and so the story goes on. Bird-watching has always fascinated me. In order to have the birds to watch you have to have fresh water and feed. I just cleaned two bird baths a few minutes ago as I fed the fish in the outside aquarium.

I always clean the birdhouses after each departure. They sometimes spend nights in these vacant houses when it is so very cold, but it seems that they only live in the houses when they are raising their young. I'm not sure where they stay during the winter, but I feel sure they stay in the area. This is something that I will have to research.

I cleaned my four-feet-deep by eight-feet-in-diameter circle outside aquarium in the island. After netting twenty brightly-colored goldfish and lifting the tiny frogs out to their bigger relatives, I cleaned from the bottom upward. Working around big pots of waterlilies and the centered fountain requires a careful touch, but this job was completed in nearly a days effort on my part. Now, the fish glide under the blooming lilies. My filter is cleaned daily and it is quite an ongoing task. This always brings me joy in my accomplishments. With these chores already taken care of this day, I'll get on with this letter.

My bragging continues! My yard and flowers attract all who pass my home. Some have reached down to feel the grass and maybe doubted that it was for real. The garden club women, and some of my golfing associates as well, just rave every time I see them at the club. You see, this was one month ago the garden club toured my yard. I'm still getting my needed praise. Truly, the trees we had planted eight years ago, as well as the landscaping, are simply beautiful for this area. These are not the gardeners found in the Midwest.

My two friends from the Chesapeake Bay were my house guests last week as we played our annual member-guest golf tournament. We played a practice game on Wednesday and that took the energy we needed on Thursday for this lovely event. I cooked some good cheese cake, potato salad, and grilled the meat and veggies on my new electric grill.

I'm planning on visiting at the Bay the weekend of June 10th where I'll spend hours fishing off the peer. I love this activity and they are such good hostesses. David may go along as he has wanted to see this retreat. My catch is not always too great, but the fun and solitude I experience are not measurable.

Tomorrow afternoon Trendy and I will go to David's for supper. Trendy will stay with them for several days as I make a trip to Charlotte, North Carolina. Allison's high school graduation ceremony is on Friday at 9:00 A.M. I'll travel on Thursday and join Tom and Gray when they arrive early Friday morning after their driving from Raleigh. I'm looking forward to this occasion. Allison plans to continue her education at a college at Wilmington, N.C.

Yes, my book is still in the making. I have not had the time to write, but my mind is full of thoughts to put down whenever I get through this busy Spring season.

I attended a farewell dinner for our Assistant Administrator last Friday night. She leaves the position at The Health Care Center at Brandermill Woods on the 31st. I continue to work part-time as their staff development director. This mad money helps me to defray costs of gardening and golfing madness, but if I did quit all three endeavors, I could stay home and work on my book. Will give this more serious thought "tomorrow."

I am scheduled to play in our member-member golf tournament on June 8th and 15th. I do need time to practice and rest for this affair. Isn't this maddening? I can't find time to rest so I can practice and will play well. I had heard how we do slow down when we get older. At the ripe age of sixty-nine, I have slowed plenty. Just what to give up has always been the question. I always conclude to this quandary that having adequate money seems to be the basis for everything we plan or do.

Here I have done it again, but doesn't this agenda sound a bit like Kassy's and Betty's busy lives? Who wins the prize? How does age figure into this equation? Give me the answer when I join you on the July 4th weekend in Ohio at Salt Fork for our second family reunion.

Don't expect to see a skinny Gene. It took a long time to accrue this adipose and so will take time to shed. Guess I like myself as I am or I would do something about this weight. Maybe I accept it rather than like it. Each person has his own ideas of what is important to him.

Right now, for the sake of all of us, it is important to sign off. Take care and write. Come visit when you can. I have lots of room for guests.

Love, Georgene, Gene or Geanne and Trendy

August 1, 1995 (Betty's birthday????)

Hello to you again,

As the result of my falling on the golf course last week and taking a chunk out of my left hand by the thumb, I am responding to your letters again with my computer. I stepped into a hole with my left foot. Grass covered the hole. I was walking briskly to my golf cart. Carts cannot be driven off the golf paths at this club, and so it requires that you sometimes walk a long way to get to your ball. Of course, it slows the play of the game. I was lucky to learn that all my bones worked and none seemed to be broken. I did skin my right knee as it twisted in the fall. The fall bruised my chest and hurt my pride and ego. My golfing buddies were supportive until I could regroup and continue on with the golf game. Many of them recalled having known about this unmarked hole, so getting it filled is an important goal.

Everyone is suffering from the heat and trying to stay inside as much as possible. I now have a beautiful blooming lotus. It has been attracting many friends and the walkers as they pass my home in the cool hours. Sometimes, I pretend that I am not at home just to watch the spectators view my whole yard in amazement. The fact that so many notice and admire my horticultural skills, keeps me working that much harder.

Thanks to so many of you for responding to my hastily typed documentary on our second family reunion. It prompted me to edit it and so have included more of the participants and corrected some of the errors. For instance, I had Betty and Kassy switched in their roles as grandmothers. This sounds pretty good now. I might send it to the *Readers Digest.* Just imagine how many reunion accounts they must receive.

Let me hear from you before the reunion in 1998. Letters from Susan, Kassy and Ellen recently addressed their busy social lives. Kassy and Bob taking their small grandchildren to the Auglaize County Fair sounds like an amazing fete. Susan called the past Sunday prior to their enjoyment of eating out. It seems that Jim is doing fine recuperating from his surgery. He has time on his hands. However, if Jim traded places with Kassy and Bob and took small children to the fair, his free time would feel really good.

Allison is settled into her new single apartment in Wilmington, North Carolina and is about to start her first year of college. Eric leaves this coming Saturday for Virginia Tech. David's just got back after a week at Myrtle Beach. Tom celebrated his 45th birthday on July 31st at Myrtle Beach. I attended a senior outing, nearly one-thousand people, mostly women, at Winchester last Wednesday. This musical program was presented by the Shenandoah Music Conservatory. Camelot was done very well and worth the three-hour program. This trip made me give up my independence for the day. The bus driver did the driving without my help. I'm always glad to get home in the evening after participating in a large group activity.

It is time to turn this off and get going on my errands which include the post office and the grocery. It is too hot to take Trendy, so she will continue her lazy days of watching me do all of the work.

Love, Georgene, Geanne or Gene and Trendy

November 13, 1995

Dear Friends and Family,

Getting my personal letters written seems to be one of my hardest chores here of late. Since I have just finished business letters related to my work, I'll switch to "home time" and prevail upon my computer and my skills to compose something which may be meaningful to most of you.

Thanks for the news from Kassy and Susan. Sorry to hear of Faye Dingledine Whetstone's death. I still do not have Buie's address. Can one of you send it to me so I can correspond to her regarding her daughter's death?

Glad that Susan and Jim sold their home and are enjoying learning to know and how to use the new one. I'm sure their successful sale of all of those antiques has helped to reduce the pressure of that big investment.

Tom called last night and finalized the Thanksgiving plans for me. He and David's families will have Thanksgiving dinner with me on the 25th. Barbara is having her family on the 23rd. I declined eating two dinners. Tom's Seth is celebrating his 18th birthday on the 23rd in North Carolina. Not sure of this date and if Allison will be here as she is planning to spend her college break in Pittsburgh. Her mother and step-father moved to Pittsburgh since he is an employee of U.S. Air. Allison flies free as a benefit to family members. She may arrange to stop here in Richmond on her return to Wilmington at the end of the break.

Eric will be home from college at the end of this week. He is to return on the 26th. He now has his car at college so will arrange to come home as his schedule permits.

Barbara and David are to fly to Las Vegas this week for a meeting and vacation. I have not taught them as yet how to play craps. I learned to play with a $5.00 chip by staying on "Do Not Pass." You do not throw the dice when it comes your turn. I learned this pattern of craps before we attended Las Vegas years ago. I broke even and had an opportunity to observe many lose thousands of dollars. At that time, Jack was sure I was going to gamble away our plane tickets. My friend Lyla from North Dakota stayed with me and watched out for my safety. When the "big wheels" came out and looked me over, she encouraged me to move to another table. Just what was this lady dressed in her gold and glitter doing so long at a table and not losing any money? These fun memories will stay with me forever. I am now offering my nursing skills to you in case you need a travel companion. My expenses would be at your expense, of course.

I am still suffering with sore knees. Finally, I saw my doctor last week as well as my podiatrist. My physician wanted to take water off my knee, but I declined since he thought a medicine he prescribed might do the trick. After three days on Daypro, I reacted with a rash that seemed like the one I experienced whenever I came in contact with penicillin. Of course, I stopped taking this expensive medicine which cost $42 for thirty pills. My knee pain responded positively to the three-day treatment.

My improved knees permitted me to work in my yard for two days with my tractor and leaf blower. I am trying to save the fall grass seed from all of the rains. We have had three to four inches of rain every Friday for weeks. Now I hear we might get some snow or sleet tonight. Won't that be a change? I do hear that you Northern people are getting snow. Isn't all of this a bit early this year?

More on my knees. The podiatrist advised that I continue with the orthotics which she had stopped for awhile. I am to keep ice on both knees for twenty minutes three times a day. I have exercises to do to strengthen the flexing leg muscles. Trendy thinks that I am playing with her when I hold my legs out straight and count to ten. She tries to position her tummy for me to scratch. Try these exercises along with me and see if you have a good response. It is something for you to do as a preventive measure and then maybe we will be shaped up to go on longer shopping sprees

Isabel's son, Dane, is recovering with his new lung transplant at the University of Virginia as he lives in Charlottesville. He had his surgery one month ago today. He is showing improvement after this long stay in the intensive care unit. Isabel will be coming to Virginia to spend two weeks with Dane during his recovery once he is ready to go home. She may spend a few days with me before flying out of Richmond on her way back to Ohio.

It is time to start baking some fruitcakes, and I need to start some household chores. Trendy is here on the bed in the den wondering if I'm going to stay home with her today. She is not sure since I'm still in my warm-up suit that goes over my P.J.s. I do have to return some books to the library and pick-up a new book at the book store. I am now getting serious in learning how to get a book published. This new book should give me some more insight on the necessary steps.

Please consider this letter as my personal note to you. Now it is your turn to write.

Love, Georgene, Geanne and Gene, and Trendy

May 30, 1996

Dear Family and Friends,

My recent trip to Ohio helped spice up my life. I had to get clothes, auto and self ready for the trip. Didn't really prepare for the heat spell I encountered. The sweltering few days just about put me under. My body system was use to sixty-five degrees. I learned that I missed some one-hundred-degree readings in Virginia.

The sun is shining here after days of rain. The rain just about got to everyone here, and I know what it has done to you Midwesterners. Fortunately, I had mowed my lawn on Wednesday after arriving home on Tuesday.

Yes, I drove back in one day as I had done nothing but rest while I visited with you. With five walks periodically, I drove to David's after leaving Susan's at 7:30 A.M. and arrived there at 7:00 P.M. Pretty good timing for a five-hundred-fifty-mile trip. There I picked up Trendy. She wasn't sure she wanted to come home with me. She still has a fear of riding in a car.

Upon arriving at my home the reality of work faced me. It was to the grocery, mow the lawn, unpack and get my clothes in order, have the pole light post repaired, to the strawberry farm, get ready for Memorial weekend. Memorial weekend is always sad since Jack's death on May 26, 1988.

Barbara and David invited me over for a delicious steak cookout on Sunday night. It remained cold and wet for the entire weekend. This seemed the way it was over the entire nation.

I have finally opened my mail, answered the messages on my recorder, and taught a few classes at The Health Care Center.

Ned's surprise 80th birthday party was very nice and something we should do more often while people are living. He was surprised. Everyone looked good and the honored guest seems to look younger each year. We sisters wish him much pleasure in the wearing of his new denim jacket. Thanks again Barbara for inviting me. You see, I am just like the rest of the family. Have a party, invite me, and I'll surely come. Don't forget to give me an 80th birthday party in ten years.

As mentioned, I visited the strawberry farm. I took strawberry shortcake to David's and gave some to the neighbors for their feeding the fish while I was gone. The berries also served as payment for repairing my pole light knocked-down while I was gone. I had plenty left over for me to eat until I couldn't face another strawberry. Maybe by next year, I will have forgotten about this year.

Enclosed are some pictures I had taken of you as I visited in various places. Blame the photographer if you are not pleased. It is never the subject that causes bad pictures. I still have another roll to finish and will get it developed once it is full, so maybe the last ones will be the best.

Thanks for your hospitality and making me feel welcome. All of your efforts were appreciated and certainly the driving force for me to visit at this time.

Don't forget, an invitation is always out for you to visit me here in historic Virginia.

All for now, love, Geanne, Gene or Georgene and Trendy

October 2, 1996

Dear Friends and/or Family,

In an effort to update you on my progress, I'll resort to relating some details of what is happening around here with the use of my computer. Your individual efforts expressed in your many cards, calls and flowers reflected your caring for me.

Progressing to the fourth week of my right knee replacement has been interesting and certainly a new learning experience, and yet, I know that I have many more new situations to face as I progress further.

To start with, my children and families helped me through the initial post-op phase. Checking me out of the joint replacement unit after four post-operative days of my complaining of severe pain, seemed a welcome step for all of us. Trendy joined us at home after spending time with Barbara and David. She walked very carefully around my walker and as I progressed back to the cane.

My neighbor's and friend's good cooking was a real pleasant treat after the kids trusted me to stay alone. Having the house cleaned, groceries brought to the house, newspaper brought to my door was truly individualized care. The mail from my box was brought to my front door early each morning by a neighbor. This was very thoughtful and appreciated so much by me. The fish were fed, filter changed and talked to daily by another neighbor.

The physical therapist arrived between 9 and 10 A.M. to begin putting me through the paces every other day for three weeks. In addition, I practice these exercises times three daily. The swelling is going down and the new knee is taking on a natural look. Of course, the old left knee is no prize to look at but it still works.

The lawn has been aerated, fertilized and seeded and enjoying a soft rain of the past twenty-four hours. Getting this accomplished took the efforts of many. We have had beautiful fall weather and permitted me to be outside at a very slow pace.

My plans are to see my surgeon on October 11th and return to work a few hours per week by October 21st. I should be driving by then and return to my very important independence. Take care and thanks so much for your support.

Love, Geanne, Gene, or Georgene and Trendy

November 16, 1996

Dear Family,

Susan informed me of a cousin's death. He popped in my mind this past week and verifies once more my ESP skills. Do you remember Karin learning of my skills when she was very young? I was told it was due to my being born with a veil over my head. The one good thing it does for me is that I get a message to slow down just before I meet a patrolman — this is the truth.

Another check is on its way to Kassy for flower expenditures.

My agenda is not too social, but I have gotten the following things done in the recent weeks. I think it is quite remarkable, and I'm tired just thinking about it. It went like this.

My auto had a transmission leak. It was repaired for $90. They also fixed my car door for which I had been waiting for a part for over two years. You guessed it, they don't make them anymore. The manager said he could have some screws through the arm to hold it firm. All of this work took some five hours to wait. I used this time to review my recent book writings. I had the yard aerated, then I put the grass seed and organic fertilizer down. I do the October and November plan for this area. Twice weekly, I have spent three hours or more blowing leaves and vacuuming them with the my tractor.

I had a cord of wood delivered for the time when electricity might go out due to ice or something. I purchased the plastic for covering it today. David will help spread it when he comes over to paint. He is doing my windows and other trim. He had to replace some exterior pieces above the windows which were not covered well and could not be seen while standing on the ground. I couldn't afford to hire this done and he wanted to do the repairs and paint as needed. He just painted his house which would have cost him $4,000.

The plumber came yesterday to repair two toilet flushers that had been running too long. He brought his helper this time. Two years ago he brought his wife along. I was never sure if he needed protection from me or if I needed protection from him. He was quite friendly this time and thought I should go dancing like him and his wife do. He suggested that I talk my boyfriend into going. That was his way of finding out if I had such a thing. Don't believe one is in the cards for me at this late date.

I returned to work on October 21st for a few hours I thought. The man I had taught to help reduce my workload one year ago quit while I was out with my knee. Now I have oriented his replacement and cut back my working hours, but twenty hours-per-week was too much after being off seven weeks.

I have all the plants from outside replanted and old ones in new pots brought inside for the winter. It almost looks like a greenhouse with the many planters I was given recently, and I had decided to reduce this work load.

To the vet I went to get shampoo, new flea and tick medicine that goes on the back of the neck between Trendy's shoulders. I also picked-up gentocin solution for Trendy's itching feet and ears. This followed her yearly shots. I think she even got a polio vaccine this time. Somehow, I must get her entered into my budget. I do give her a bath weekly and save some money.

Then the plastic bird feeders fell apart. I now have a cheap glue gun and have repaired the feeders, cleaned them and have them back up for the winter. Of course, I got their new bag of feed from Southern States along with Trendy's food.

The fish needed attention in addition to their daily feeding. I put an electric water warmer in the fountain dish to keep warm water for the birds and to prevent it from freezing. At one time, David and Tom dismantled the fountain and carried it into the garage for the winter. Now it does not freeze. Therefore, carrying the fountain in for the winter is no longer necessary.

My tractor was cutting higher on one side, so Norman, my handy neighbor, spent four hours in my garage repairing it. He took it apart and welded the parts at his place. This mechanical engineer is cheap and convenient. He is retired and only fifty-nine. His wife has stopped coming along with him. I imagine she will start coming again now that I have my knee replacement. In addition to my bragging on the projects while he does them, I cook some food for them. I prepared for them a delicious pot of beef stew with cabbage wedges on the top, fruit salad, hot rolls and pumpkin pie. Trendy is always eager to help me take food over to them. She gets the attention she wants. Trendy has learned to go to their back door when I let her out. She barks for them to come to their door and speak to her.

I wash the car weekly and vacuum it. The grocery boys comment that I should get the award for the cleanest trunk. Speaking of a trunk, I have made two visits to the grocery since I can drive again. On the first trip, I spent $205 and last week $155. That is a lot of bags to carry into the house and groceries to put away. Jack always did this chore. He liked to go to the grocery. I doubt that I will ever enjoy this task. Since I budget $350 a month for grocery supplies which includes all of the cleaning stuff and food for the dog, I have over-spent and it is only the middle of the month. My back-up supply had gotten low and I'm trying to restock now that I can drive.

Socially, I go to therapy for my knee twice a week through next week and then once a week for another week. My surgeon asked me to have someone push down on the top of my knee to make sure the back of the knee touches the floor or bed. I still haven't found the guy to help me with this problem. The therapists do a good job of it during the therapy sessions.

Yes, I voted. David reminded me that my man won. Some polls revealed that Clinton was disliked by the men because he was so handsome. This does make some sense as to why he gets many of the women votes.

I cleaned my closets and now have cold weather clothing available. I am reorganizing my den closet and chests. I am moving all of my sentimental items along with more albums to the front closet. I will put them into hand bags in case I need to save them in a hurry. I got to thinking about this when my toaster acted up and wouldn't shut off. I also watched a TV special which alerted people that toasters do catch on fire and are the cause of many house fires. They said that the plastic materials that they are made of does burn.

I caught-up on mending, altering of clothing and shortening of new slacks. I would love to have a new sewing machine. I would make some more flags. My friend needed her machine back and so I stopped my flag-making projects. My machine is a $69 Spiegel purchased in 1948 prior to David's birth in March. Any donations around to meet this need? I'm sure that you are using yours too.

My activity today was a sobering one. A previous working colleague, a clinical specialist in psychiatry, age 54 may have taken her life and was found several days later. She was a fun person always thinking of others. She worked with staff on my units when they had problems, while I worked at a local hospital.

I will conduct an inservice program for all of our employees at work on Thursday. This will also be a training session for the gal who will do them in the future.

I am tired of recalling my activities. Still there are more. Now, I must focus on Thanksgiving and Christmas. I need to remember to keep it simple. Doesn't that sound trite? Take care, write and come visit.

Love, Geanne, Gene, or Georgene and Trendy

M. Georgene Roth

Biography of Miriam Georgene Place Roth

Presented in February 25, 1992
by Eric Roth, age 17
Grandson of the Author

My grandmother (on my father's side of the family) was born on April 10, 1926. Miriam Georgene Place Roth was one of nine children (three boys and six girls) who grew up on a farm in Auglaize County, close to Wapakoneta, Ohio. Her father raised hogs to buy land, which he used to grow a variety of crops. Living on a farm, the majority of their needs were met by their own farm products, and thus it was necessary to buy only a few things, such as flour and sugar, and necessities like shoes and fabric. My grandmother's mother was an excellent manager of the household, and one of the things she invested her time in was sewing. Mrs. Place made all the clothes for the whole household from fabric which was bought from the store or from clothing given to them. Since my grandmother had other older sisters, she inherited most of her clothes, which were usually remade many times. About the only new item of apparel she ever got were shoes. Her father was very strict about that; shoes were to be kept polished and neat.

Recreation-wise they did activities for fun such as cards, pinochle tournaments, skating and sledding in the winter, and swimming. In the early spring, when the running springs had filled the nearby stone quarry with water, my grandmother and her brothers and sisters liked to dive off the fifty-foot bluff into the water. In addition to these past times, they liked to compare the tractors which their family owned and argue over what kinds of tractors were the best — this scenario was similar to the way teenage boys of today love to discuss cars. Other hobbies she enjoyed were gardening and making doll clothes for the neighborhood children.

The children also enjoyed sporting activities. Many of her brothers and sisters were members of their high school varsity basketball teams. Grandma herself was the drum major in the marching band. Her mother had made her outfit and she taught herself how to twirl the baton. Besides the marching band, she belonged to the 4-H club eight years. With the activities she joined, she went to and from school fairly often, usually by hitching a ride with the neighbors.

Another thing my grandmother recalled when I talked with her was when they got electricity and indoor plumbing on the farm. She was about twelve-years-old at the time when the Tennessee Valley Power was linked to her home. Before electricity, there was a windmill which kept a battery charged. This battery was used to power the radio. One night, she recalled she couldn't use the radio, because her father wanted to hear President Roosevelt's speech which was to be broadcast later that night. Her father was fond of Roosevelt because he organized work programs to lift the nation out of the Depression.

In addition to electricity, plumbing was connected shortly after her father put in bathrooms. Water no longer had to be brought in from the well. This was especially convenient in cold weather when the pump at the well would be frozen over and they would be put through the hassle of heating water on the stove to thaw the pump early in the mornings.

School was also an important part of life in the Place family.

Mr. Place stressed the importance in succeeding in school, and my grandmother and her siblings did exceptionally well; two or three of her brothers and sisters were valedictorians of their classes. Grandma herself was one of the few classmates to complete college. Later, the children each paid off their loans once they finished college.

After graduating from high school, Grandma went into nursing at the cost of only $300 — that included books, food and housing, and some other expenses. While in her three-year diploma program, she married Dr. Roth. (She had been dating him for five years before their eventual marriage.) She married Albert John (Jack) Roth on her twentieth birthday in 1946 with her father's permission.

All the while, my grandfather had been in college at Ohio State University studying to become a veterinarian. He graduated in 1945 and started a practice in a small farming community north of Lima, Ohio. It was in the fall of 1946 that he enlisted into the army before he was drafted and fulfilled his ROTC commitment. He received a lieutenant commission at the time of going into the army. He was shortly promoted to the rank of captain. During his two-year stint, he and my grandmother traveled to many of the Midwestern states. Captain Roth was stationed in Missouri and transferred to Minnesota when my dad was due to be born. My grandmother stayed in Ohio with family until my dad was born on March 4, 1948 while Grandpa found a place for them to live in Minneapolis.

When my father was eighteen-days-old, they traveled by auto to Minneapolis. Captain Roth drove their personal auto for the army as he made out-of-state trips in his various assignments. This left my grandma and my dad home alone during the week. She could only wash clothes one day a week in the apartment they lived in, and the rent was terribly high while living conditions were not the best. To top it all off, she had no method of transportation other than walking, because Dr. Roth needed their only car for his heavy traveling. Finally, when she couldn't stand living in that apartment anymore, she put a catchy ad in the paper that she had written in the form of a poem. This ad stated that they were looking for a place to live. A nursing supervisor, who caught on from the poem that my grandmother was a nurse, invited Captain and Mrs. Roth to use their home for less rent than they were previously paying. The owners were going to their northern cabin and they needed somebody to take care of their home.

When Dr. Roth was discharged from the army in 1948, he and my grandmother moved to Forest, Ohio where they lived for five years. In 1950, Tom, my uncle, was born, and when he was three and my father was five, the Roths moved on to Springfield, Ohio. There my grandmother started back into nursing, working two evenings a week. Once her children were in school, she worked more hours per week. She switched to working as a scrub nurse in the operating room.

In 1959, the family moved to Frankfort, Kentucky, where Dr. Roth became assistant state veterinarian — a nice position. Unfortunately, one year later, things were ruined when the Commissioner asked him to ignore certain practices which should not have been going on. Dr. Roth resigned from his job and took a position he had been offered in Virginia. There in Culpeper, Virginia, my grandmother became the Obstetrical Supervisor and then was promoted to the Director of Nursing in this newly opened, acute care hospital.

Two years later in 1962, my grandmother and grandfather left Culpeper and moved to Richmond. At the time, my father was fourteen years old and Tom was twelve. Dr. Roth was in charge of regulatory control in the agriculture department. He kept sick animals from entering Virginia and prevented them from being sent away from Virginia. My grandmother, left the director of nursing position to become an instructor of student nurses at Richmond Memorial Hospital School of Nursing.

Later in 1967, she went to school at VCU, Virginia Commonwealth University, to work toward getting her BSN degree. Her senior year, she transferred into the nursing program at The Medical College of Virginia, a part of VCU. She wanted to graduate from an accredited college program so she could proceed with her master's program.

The year before in 1971, the family moved to another part of Chesterfield County south of Richmond where they had a home built in the Salisbury subdivision. Soon after, she went back to school to work towards her Masters degree, then Dr. Roth had a serious heart attack. She needed to work to help pay for David and Tom's college education at this time.

They lived soundly in Salisbury for seventeen years until in 1987 when they moved to Brandermill subdivision. They had the same builder build their retirement home. But shortly after Dr. Roth retired, he died in the hospital while having an operation performed in which a balloon was used to widen the heart arteries.

Currently, my grandmother lives with her dog Trendy and enjoys her nursing position at the Health Care Center at Brandermill Woods where she teaches the staff. Working one to two days a week at her own schedule, still provides her free time for such favorite activities as golfing, painting in oils, gardening, and publishing articles on Alzheimer's disease.

Today, if you were to ask her about old times, you could not help but notice the way her face lights up as she recalls fond memories, especially those of childhood — that period which started for her on April 10, 1926. Such was the time when a new Ford automobile cost $310 and gas 23 cents a gallon; items such as bread and milk were 9 cents and 56 cents a half gallon.

April 10th was also the birthday of other famous people.

Among them are Omar Sharif, Claire Boothe Luce, and William Booth. All of these distinguished people, I feel, are lucky to share the same birthdate as my special grandmother.

Eric Roth

Third Place Family Reunion

1998

The third reunion of the descendants of Stanley and Lela Place was held on July 31st through August 1st at Salt Fork Lodge at Cambridge, Ohio. A total number of 90 members plus senior honoree, Uncle Lowell Graessle, belong to this family. An estimated 60 people came and went during various events of the two-day affair. Uncle Lowell is Mom's brother and he serves well as an historian as well as to dignify the group at his alert age of 91.

Realizing that this reunion effort was started in 1990 by David Roth when he made an effort to go to Ohio and re-establish direct contact with the senior family members is remarkable. Out of this effort, three reunions, one every three years, seems well established. A voluntary chairman from the grandchildren's group gives this endeavor the stability needed to pull off such an event. Much is yet to be achieved well into the future under this very capable leadership.

Ellen Baker and husband John Doolittle planned and executed this year's reunion. Progressive correspondence with specific details kept coming to each member, keeping everyone well informed of their role and the anticipated plans. These details are essential in order to select the location, make reservations,

plus the program planning which was excellent again this year.

Once everyone was checked into the lodge, groups met in various rooms to renew relationships. Kassy and Bob served many good refreshments and this was quite a hit. Elizabeth Ryan and Shelly Place, both seven years old, renewed their friendships as the adults moved about. Friday night partying centered around card playing — bridge, euchre, and poker. A movie produced by Dan Kattman was a big hit. A new game "Life Stories" was introduced by Karin as Tarry used his camcorder to record histories of various story telling which will be ongoing in the future.

On Saturday morning at 7:30 A.M., a White Elephant silent sale began as was previously advertised. This effort to which Betty and Kassy had devoted much time and effort along with the other family couples reaped a sum of $462.69. This was to defray expenses incurred for this reunion.

Each sibling was assigned a portion of the program for the dinner on Saturday night which unfolded as follows: invocation by Susan; history of the original homesteading of the farm by Ned and daughter, Sandra; information of the Place Notes previously compiled by Uncle Virgil Place (Da's brother); family tree handout explained by Kassy; video and oral histories by Karin and Tarry; Daughters of American Revolution (DAR) by Betty, also presentation of Place family bible to Sandra for safe keeping; S. B. introduced his granddaughter, Amanda Place, as she performed a dance skit of a hobo she originated; Gene's explanation of the Place flag and information on her book-writing and the upcoming publication of Unspoken Love; Place cookbook efforts explained by Kay Place Douglas; birthday cake cutting and wishing of Happy Birthday to Betty for her 79th on this date, August 1st; video watched and introduced by Milton of his daughter, Annaliesa Place playing a classical rendition on her violin. (She is a very accomplished violinist at the age of 19 and started her lessons at the age of 3. She will enter Peabody this fall to continue her studies. She did not perform in person due to a previous commitment in California.)

Voluntary verbal suggestions for future money-making endeavors for the purpose of covering the rental areas for meeting rooms were discussed. Many good ideas will be considered by the upcoming chairman, Jo Ann Mercer Mizek, Julia's daughter. She will also plan with the input of all of the group for the next reunion in 2000 which will be two years from now.

Many individual groups gathered following the family dinner on Saturday night and this provided another avenue for becoming further acquainted. Sunday breakfast in the dining room provided an opportunity to say good-byes and head home to the various destinations. Of course there was no hugging or kissing. The unspoken love was in full view. Driving home offered great opportunities for recapping this historic event. It seemed to be the consensus that these reunions would go on under the very capable direction of the middle-aged grandchildren. How fortunate this family is to have this very capable leadership. As mentioned repeatedly, our parents would be so proud of their family and the values they instilled in their children in operation to this date. Sandra Kattman said it very well in her post-1995 reunion notes when she identified another factor. She pointed out that the partners selected by this family added additional strengths to this already capable family. This is an invaluable fortune and an inherited wealth that is the legacy our parents gave to this family, the Place family — at present totalling 90 members.

Tally of 50 Years

The photo taken in 1949 (see page 294) features the entire family, including three-year-old Karin. A recent photo taken in 1998 is missing the parents and two of their children. The toll of roughly fifty years is apparent. However, this family continues to function and is really a very closely knit group. They all keep in touch during the year. Recently, when the seven children joined each other along with their children and their children's children at their 3rd annual family reunion started in 1992, caring was vivid and needed. This attractive, vivacious and hardworking family has so much going for them. Their father predicted high achievements for his children when he was gravely ill. He would not have been disappointed as his predictions unfolded. His children learned good problem solving skills. They accepted the challenge of seeking good educations. Further, they have seen that their children achieved well in this endeavor. They sought out into new places of employment and living. These descendants live or have lived in Texas, California, Florida, North Carolina, Louisiana, Kentucky, Michigan, Minnesota, Wisconsin, Indiana, Marilyn, Pennsylvania, Wisconsin, Arizona, Tennessee, Missouri., Alabama, Puerto Rico and Virginia to name a few. As result of seeking the unknown, they have gained a vast variety of experiences and new friends.

Working is essential to this whole group. Ned continues to look after his cattle and farms at the age of 82. Kassy, known as Mary Kathryn, does endless good deeds for friends and family alike. Only recently, she and husband, Bob, built a beautiful new retirement home at the age of 80. This new home shows their class and style which has been apparent all of their lives. Their social agenda would make the average person groan. They have a party for every reason. These parties are fun and feature wide varieties of food prepared by Kassy. Bob and Kassy are superb host and hostess. They could give lessons to the very best.

Keeping score is not easy on the next candidate. Betty moves so rapidly physically and mentally, that one has a huge race trying to keep up with her. High achievement describes her just as it did both Ned and Kassy. She wins the honors at her golfing club as the best golfer in her class. She has held top offices in the DAR and continues to devote endless hours in the achievement of their goals. Educationally, she is a CPA and has been honored as an outstanding instructor. She gets behind the goals of the family reunions and brings and arranges the photos of ancestors for all of the younger clan to see and learn to appreciate. Betty attends the special ceremonies such as weddings and graduations of nieces and nephews as she flies to the various destinations. Energy should have been her middle name. Her husband, Bill, often smiles and comments, "Isn't she something?"

Susan holds her own by having practiced as a registered nurse until her retirement at the age of 75. She and Jim built a one-story home within walking distance of their larger home. She is into quilting, afghans, and various glass and antique collections. Her big love is playing euchre. She appreciates music and has a good voice. Surprisingly, she did not study in this area. Having no children, she keeps track of her many relatives.

Julia moved to Florida with Bob when they tried to escape the cold climate of Ohio. This area sadly was where Julia was murdered in 1985 by a neighbor boy of 19 which ended her happy-go-lucky life. She did learn to know and love her two small grandchildren, Grant and Jill, and tried to visit them as often as she could. Jo, her only child, continues to live in Ohio with husband Larry. Julia was a good golfer, loved sports, enjoyed making her own tailored clothing. Having lupus did cause her to lose some of her beauty. Her flirtatious mannerisms and sense of humor took her far.

Gene's life has been clearly covered. She feels quite proud of her family, and so she has shared many details with you, the reader, in her book, Unspoken Love, in 1998.

Converting to Tar Heel country seems to have been a smart move for S.B., Bernice and their family. This is home now and they have gained the respect as good homesteaders and managers in their community. S.B. has applied good farming practices as he has purchased land and become independent financially. They entertain you royally and S.B. is the best fishing guide ever. He is very detailed and keeps you safe when out on his lake across from his home. He enjoys fishing off of Cape Hateras and is recognized as a super friend to those who get to know him. He tries to put on a gruff face, but soon one can penetrate this exterior. Over the fifty years, he has achieved financially and apparently self satisfaction with his life.

Losing Bill at the early age of 54 in 1985 is still a bitter pill to swallow for this family. Any loss is extremely difficult of this proud and close knit family. Bill's five children have continued to keep in touch. They continue to keep close ties with Bill's brothers and sisters. Bill did achieve in various areas of the Air Force, as supervisor at Texas Instrument and with his mild mannerisms made many lasting friends. He had a very creative mind and did not get to achieve as he would have liked due to some health problems for which he never accepted. Manic depressive disease hampers one's sense of security. Failure to recognize this condition during his three unsuccessful marriages caused him great stress. He did not keep close contact with his children once his first marriage failed. His failure to stand up for himself put him into a special category. He often let others take advantage of his good nature. Frequently, he showered gifts on others in an attempt to win their approval and gain their support. He never caused conflict and was quite uncomfortable when it entered his life. We all miss him so much. Bill was fifteen when Karin was born in 1945. He had been the baby.

Karin was the ninth child born to these parents at their age of 47. She was not necessarily planned, but added tremendous joys to their lives. Unfortunately, Karin was only-eight years-old when Da died. It was S.B. who became her substitute father since he lived in the small house on the farm. He and Bernice took Karin with them as she was near the ages of their children, Karin's nieces and nephews. Karin was active in her school activities as a cheer leader, played the glockenspiel and valedictorian. No doubt she developed a sense of responsibility for Mom while growing up. She did marry a classmate, Tarry, and continues to live in the community in which she grew up. She has not had the roaming spirit so apparent in many of her older brothers and sisters. In fact, many of Karin's classmates and friends were unaware of the large family from which Karin came. Her older brothers and sisters had moved from this community when she was quite young. Karin does not brag or toot her horn. She always attends family gatherings and contributes greatly. She tries to understand just what makes the older family members tick. She never experienced growing up with so many around her and what it was like using each other's space.

Now, fifty years since the family picture was taken, this family still displays a sense of belonging and caring. Of course they don't display a hug or kiss. At best, they will give you a handshake. After fifty years, they are proud, close, caring and sensitive to the feelings of the others even though they still can't show their Unspoken Love.

Left: Stanley Place Family — Front row: Mary K., Stanley, Lela, Ned. Second row: Stanley Jr., Karin Back row: Georgene, Julia, Bill, Susan, Betty

The third Place family reunion, August 1998

Front row, le... ...4r: Lowell Graessle (Uncle), Mary Place Baker, Susan Place Kinstle, Betty Place Pigozzi, Karen Place Whetstone
Left to right: Ned W. Place, Georgene Place Roth, Stanley B. Place, Jr.

1998 Place Family Reunion